PENGUIN C

THE BOOK OF MARGERY KEMPE

MARGERY KEMPE, born *c.* 1373 of well-to-do middle-class parentage in King's Lynn in Norfolk, was married at twenty, had a vision of Christ in her madness following her first childbirth, and, after early failures as a businesswoman, saw visions and felt herself called to a spiritual life. At about the age of forty, when she had borne fourteen children, she persuaded her husband to join her in a mutual vow of chastity, and then embarked on an eventful life of pilgrimage in England, Europe and the Holy Land, visiting both great and humble religious figures of her day, ceaselessly seeking the counsel of mystics and recluses. Always a controversial figure, her devotion characteristically expressed itself in loud weeping and cries, which often divided priests, congregations and fellow pilgrims into friends or enemies, and she was several times in danger of being burnt at the stake as a heretic. Towards the end of her life she dictated in an account of her travels and visions her spiritual autobiography, and the discovery of a unique manuscript in 1934 has restored to English literature the earliest autobiography in English.

B. A. WINDEATT is Professor of English in the University of Cambridge, and a Fellow of Emmanuel College.

The Book of Margery Kempe

Translated by B. A. WINDEATT

PENGUIN BOOKS

PENGUIN BOOKS

Published by the Penguin Group
Penguin Books Ltd, 80 Strand, London WC2R ORL, England
Penguin Group (USA) Inc., 375 Hudson Street, New York, New York 10014, USA
Penguin Books Australia Ltd, 250 Camberwell Road, Camberwell, Victoria 3124, Australia
Penguin Books Canada Ltd, 10 Alcorn Avenue, Toronto, Ontario, Canada M4V 3B2
Penguin Books India (P) Ltd, 11 Community Centre, Panchsheel Park, New Delhi – 110 017, India
Penguin Group (NZ), cnr Airborne and Rosedale Roads, Albany, Auckland 1310, New Zealand
Penguin Books (South Africa) (Pty) Ltd, 24 Sturdee Avenue, Rosebank 2196, South Africa

Penguin Books Ltd, Registered Offices: 80 Strand, London WC2R ORL, England

www.penguin.com

First published 1985
Reprinted with a revised bibliography 1994
Reprinted with revised Further Reading 2004
033

Printed in England by Clays Ltd, St Ives plc
Filmset in Monophoto Photina

ISBN-13: 978–0–140–43251–0
ISBN-10: 0–140–43251–5

www.greenpenguin.co.uk

ALWAYS LEARNING   **PEARSON**

Botte for I am a woman, schulde I therfore leve
that I schulde nought telle yowe the goodenes of
God?

Dame Julian of Norwich, *Revelations of Divine Love*
(The Shorter Version)

For trusteth wel, it is an impossible
That any clerk wol speke good of wyves,
But if it be of hooly seintes lyves . . .
By God! if wommen hadde writen stories,
As clerkes han withinne hire oratories,
They wolde han writen of men moore wikkednesse
Than al the mark of Adam may redresse . . .

Chaucer, *The Wife of Bath's Prologue*

Contents

Introduction

The Text of Margery Kempe's *Book*

The Book of Margery Kempe, the earliest surviving autobiographical writing in English, was lost for centuries until, in 1934, a fifteenth-century manuscript came to light, which had long been in the possession of an old Catholic family, the Butler-Bowdons.[1] In the late Middle Ages, however, the manuscript had been in the possession of the Carthusians of Mount Grace Priory, near Northallerton in Yorkshire, where it had been annotated by readers interested in mystical experience.[2] Yet although her *Book* had disappeared, the name of Margery Kempe had survived, because of the printing (*c.* 1501) by Wynkyn de Worde of a seven-page quarto pamphlet of extracts from the more devotional parts of the book, *A shorte treatyse of contemplacyon taught by our lorde Ihesu cryste, or taken out of the boke of Margerie kempe of Lynn*. (A single copy of this pamphlet survives, in Cambridge University Library.) When Henry Pepwell came to reprint these extracts in a selection of mystical pieces in 1521, he described the authoress Margery Kempe as 'a devoute ancres' (i.e. anchoress, or recluse). When the *Book* was rediscovered this century it might thus have been expected to contain the writings of a religious recluse, perhaps another Julian of Norwich. In fact, the *Book* is as different from Dame Julian's *Revelations* as Margery Kempe is from Julian herself. Of Margery's devotion no reader can be in doubt, but the turbulent life that she looks back on in dictating her book is far removed from the peace and the withdrawal from the world which are the experience of the recluse.

Margery could neither read nor write, as is indicated on a number of occasions in her *Book*. The story of how it came eventually to be written down is set out in the Proem and in chapter 89; her first attempt to dictate it (perhaps to the son who figures in Book II) results in a completely illegible text, and it is only with effort and time that she manages to get it rewritten by a priest and then adds the last ten chapters. In a work dictated to a priest many years after the events it describes, by a self-confessedly illiterate woman late in life, the texture of the written English and the overall organization of material may not be so entirely Margery's responsibility as it would have been had she been capable of putting pen to paper herself. Yet many modern readers, noticing the links between the vigour of the *Book*'s style and the vigour of Margery's character, will sense that in her *Book* we hear recorded, however tidied, much of the accent of an authentic voice, the voice of a medieval Englishwoman of unforgettable character, undeniable courage and unparalleled experience.

Margery's Life and *Book*

Margery Kempe was born in the prosperous medieval port of King's Lynn in Norfolk (then called Bishop's Lynn) in about the year 1373 – she tells us that she was about sixty in a late chapter of her book datable to 1433 (Book II, chapter 5). She was the daughter of John Brunham, a burgess who held a number of honourable positions in the Lynn of his day. Some cutting remarks at her husband's expense reveal Margery's pride in her father and family, while extant archives record John Brunham as being five times Mayor of Lynn (in 1370, 1377, 1378, 1385 and 1391). He was one of the town's two members of parliament (in 1364–5, 1368, 1376, 1379–80, 1382–3 and 1384), an alderman of the influential Trinity Guild in the town, and coroner, justice of the peace and chamberlain at various times. At the age of twenty (i.e. in about 1393), Margery tells us she was married to John Kempe, whose family also appears in the Lynn records, although Margery's husband never seems to have cut a figure in Lynn comparable to that of her father, and she touches in her *Book* on her husband's concern with his debts.

Passing in silence over her childhood – which she never mentions other than in recalling how on several occasions she confessed the sins of her whole life from childhood to the present – Margery opens her *Book* with the madness and spiritual crisis that followed the birth of her first child. She is rescued from this by a vision of Christ, but does not take to heart the spiritual lesson of her illness, and only the collapse of her subsequent business ventures bows her pride. Intimations of paradise soon follow, and sexual relations with her husband now disgust her, but he insists on his rights. At this time some of what are to prove Margery's most persistent traits first appear – her frequent sobbing and weeping, and her continual thinking and talking of heaven. At this stage, too, she records how our Lord enters into conversation with her during her meditations – conversations that are to continue throughout the *Book* – and how in her contemplation she imagines herself present at the birth of both the Virgin and of Christ, and bustles about giving a helping hand with practical housewifery (chapters 6–7).

After these early episodes of her post-conversion experience, the *Book* records Margery's victory over her husband in her struggle to live a life of chastity, a victory which is formalized with a vow. In this our Lord lends her considerable assistance, sometimes terrifying her husband at his moments of desire, and later giving Margery the idea of a wily financial bargain when her husband threatens to resume his conjugal rights at the roadside, as they travel through the countryside on pilgrimage during a sultry June day (chapter 11). This memorable scene can be dated to what was approximately Margery's fortieth year when, after twenty years of marriage, she had borne her husband fourteen children, as she reveals later in the *Book*. Apart from the son who figures briefly in Book II, none of these children is ever mentioned by Margery, apart from briefly and generally in several prayers.

Margery now enters on a life of pilgrimage, and of travel to meet and converse with the spiritually minded. On these travels she meets with frequent criticism, detraction and even threats. At Canterbury she is chased by a crowd threatening to burn her as a Lollard (chapter 13), the first occurrence of an accusation that is to recur and bring many trials, despite Margery's evident orthodoxy in her devotion to the sacrament, frequent confession, fasting, pilgrimages and holy images, all of which were questioned in Lollard writings.[3] Throughout, she speaks her mind and gives more than as good as she gets, with many a swift answer and many an apt retort to those ostensibly much better educated and more experienced than herself.

Margery visits and recalls her conversations with historically identifiable people, from the great and grand, like Archbishop Arundel and Bishop Repyngdon of Lincoln, to the less known female recluse in Norwich whom Margery refers to as 'Dame Jelyan', that same Julian of Norwich whose writings of her own revelations have secured her recognition nowadays as the greatest woman writer in English before the novelists.[4] She also has a series of encounters with spiritually inclined men of quite humble lives and local fame, whose support for Margery is not fleeting, and sustains her across years of difficulty: the nameless Dominican anchorite at Lynn, the saintly Richard of Caister at Norwich, the Carmelites Alan of Lynn and William Southfield, her confessor Robert Spryngolde, and another unnamed priest who reads mystical texts to her. Such local figures are the outward supports to Margery in a world perceived by her as largely critical and hostile, where she is inwardly sustained by confabulations with our Lord – spiritual speakings to her soul that reaffirm her intentions and her longings, and enable her to assume something of a prophetic role, albeit at the homely level set by her personal horizons.

Margery's foreign pilgrimages certainly took her far beyond the horizons of Lynn – to the Holy Land, Assisi and Rome, and Santiago de Compostela – yet few travellers can have had less to say about the experience of travelling as such than Margery.[5] She is not concerned with being a travel writer. We hear only of her immediate difficulties (especially the antipathy her fellow pilgrims have towards her) and of the visions and meditations experienced during her visits to the holy places.

To read in some of the surviving memoirs of late medieval travellers to the Holy Land[6] of all the fuss, the commotion, the claustrophobic crowding and lack of privacy or security on the pilgrim galleys sailing from Venice to Jaffa, to read of the tense and hurried tour under Moslem supervision of the Palestinian sites, quickly followed again by the trying return voyage to Venice, and then to remember that Margery Kempe describes almost nothing of what struck contemporary travellers as so memorably difficult and so nervously absorbing, is to register how utterly Margery's memory excludes almost everything but what she sees as the spiritually significant side of life.

She does, however, dwell upon her difficulties as a foreign pilgrim in Italy (chapters 30–42), but this is because of the way that her vocation as pilgrim is hampered by the difficulty of being a lone woman abroad, with little or no money, and no command of foreign languages. Predictably enough, the conspicuous behaviour of this woman dressed all in white, her weeping and crying out, attract criticism which, because she sees it as persecution endured for Christ's sake, becomes by its very repetitiousness not so much a threat as a cumulative confirmation of the rightness of her own path. And alongside all her detractors, Margery finds friends and supporters among the clergy, the pious laity, and the humblest folk.

It is not long after her return to Norfolk from Italy and the Holy Land that Margery is off once more, this time sailing from Bristol for Santiago de Compostela in Galicia. But characteristically, Margery gives us no descriptive detail of her voyage and her stay at the great shrine of St James other than the barest recollection of how many days the round trip took. Rather more space is spent upon her difficulties at Bristol before sailing, difficulties which as ever seem inseparable from the character she is, difficulties which as ever tend to vindication in Margery's own eyes.

On returning home, her travels through England are complicated by a series of arrests and examinations as a heretic (chapters 46–54). At Leicester the Mayor shows great animus against her as a suspected Lollard. While in custody, she thinks the Steward of Leicester is about to rape her. Her examination before the Abbot of Leicester, however, only reveals the orthodoxy of belief that she shows throughout her *Book*, and she is eventually able to leave. She proceeds to York, where she is again summoned to explain herself, this time before the Archbishop, who finds her orthodox, but orders her out of his diocese. When about to cross the Humber on her way south, she is again arrested as a Lollard and once again brought before the Archbishop, who soon lets her go, on condition that she proceeds to London to gain an authorizing letter from the new Archbishop of Canterbury.

The scene of Margery's *Book* now settles in Lynn and its environs, and is much occupied with the mixture of hostility and support that she receives on account of her weeping and crying. As ever, Margery recalls the cares of this world alongside her visions and her conversations with our Lord, which come more and more to dominate the latter chapters of the first book. In a series of Passion meditations Margery imagines herself present at the events of the first Easter from the betrayal of Christ through to the Resurrection (chapters 79–81), and not only present but actively involved as the busy and solicitous helper and handmaid of the Virgin. In these later chapters Margery's spiritual recollections leave behind the more chronologically presented narrative of external events in earlier chapters. After some further chapters of conversation with our Lord (84–88), Margery left off her *Book* as dictated to her first scribe.

When the whole *Book* was re-written up to this point some years later, Margery took the opportunity to add ten further chapters (a second, if unequal, 'Book'), covering the most memorable events that befell her after the *Book* was first written. These chapters largely concern her remarkable and exhausting late travels, first accompanying her German daughter-in-law home by sea to Danzig in Prussia, and then her pilgrimages to Wilsnack and Aachen on her way home across Europe. Perhaps because Margery – by now older and infirm – could no longer take such travels as much in her stride as she had done when younger, she sketches much more here of the feeling of travelling, its moments of vulnerability, of terror and of *longueur*. Yet one theme which remains continuous with the earliest chapters is, of course, the constant and wearing difficulties presented by the attitude of other people, and the opportunities for self-vindication that these inevitably provided for Margery.

No rounded conclusion is offered – simply Margery's return home after her travels to Lynn, where she receives an understandably grumpy welcome from her confessor, whom she soon mollifies, with God's help. If we hanker for some kind of final vignette on which our own imaginations can linger as we take leave of Margery, we have to construct such a scene rather against the grain of Margery's method, imagining her in old age, as she briefly says, reconciled in her home town to her circle of sympathizers. In fact, Margery's dictation of her recollections ends here characteristically and authentically without any formally contrived or artistic sense of climax. She has simply ceased to speak.

Margery's *Book* and its Background

'Bless us! How could a woman occupy one or two hours with the love of our Lord? I shan't eat a thing till I find out what you can say of our Lord God in the space of an hour' (Richard of Caister in chapter 17)

As a woman who could not read or write, Margery finds visits to converse with sympathetic people especially important, and from many of these people she will have received the wisdom they themselves had gathered from reading contemporary spiritual writers. Because Margery herself could not read we should not under-estimate her access to the content of spiritual books. Indeed, in her consultation with Caister, she tells him how the Trinity sometimes spoke to her soul 'so excellently that she never heard any book, neither Hilton's book, nor Bride's book, nor *Stimulus Amoris*, nor *Incendium Amoris*, nor any other book that she ever heard read, that spoke so exaltedly of the love of God . . .' (chapter 17). And much later in her *Book*, when she tells how a young priest who came to Lynn was prepared to read to her, she again mentions the very same books: 'He read to her many a good book of high contemplation, and other books, such as the Bible with doctors' commentaries on it, St Bride's book, Hilton's book,

Bonaventura's *Stimulus Amoris, Incendium Amoris*, and others similar' (chapter 58). Margery also tells how at her very first meeting with this priest and his mother the priest reads aloud from the Bible and moves her deeply, and how in later times she made him look up things for her in the scriptures and in the doctors.

Throughout her *Book* Margery shows her retentive memory working to recall or allude to various passages of scripture, and the repeated reference to these four books conveys something of Margery's connections with contemporary devotion through the texts she heard read. By 'Hilton's book' Margery presumably means Walter Hilton's *The Scale of Perfection*,[7] a work of spiritual counsel distinguished not only by the great dignity and grace of Hilton's English style but also by his deep humanity and understanding of the difficulties of contemplative life. By referring to *Incendium Amoris* Margery shows she has heard something of perhaps the most characteristic and celebrated single work of the earlier fourteenth-century English mystic, Richard Rolle of Hampole (d. 1349).[8] The *Incendium Amoris* (*The Fire of Love*), written in Latin, offers a practical guide to the spiritual life, shot through with Rolle's autobiographical vividness and written very much from within the continuing experience of a fervent mystic. In hearing something of these very different masterpieces by two of the great fourteenth-century English mystics, Margery gained access to the mainstream of current mystical writing in England, while she also enjoyed lengthy conversations with Dame Julian of Norwich, as she recalls (chapter 18). Of the medieval English mystics it is thus only with the works of the author of *The Cloud of Unknowing* that Margery – unsurprisingly – shows no familiarity, for she is unlikely to have relished that astringent exposition of the *via negativa*, with its withering characterization of literal-minded contemplatives.[9] Margery's spiritual school is very different – a passage from one of her devotions (chapter 28) reveals Margery's familiarity with one of Richard Rolle's *Meditations on the Passion*,[10] where Christ's wounded body is likened to a dovecote, and underlines Margery's attachment to the tradition of meditation on the events of Christ's life. Margery's religious sensibility is saturated in this kind of tender devotion to the manhood of Christ, found among the works of St Anselm and embodied in the most influential *Meditationes Vitae Christi*.[11]

The *Stimulus Amoris* (which Margery mentions being read to her on several occasions) is also related to this tradition of meditation on the events of Christ's life which so markedly colours Margery's visions. The *Stimulus Amoris*, which was often wrongly attributed to St Bonaventura, is a composite devotional poem, comprising a series of meditations on the Passion followed by a treatise on the spiritual life and contemplation, and ending with some devout meditations. The second chapter, to which Margery particularly refers, deals with 'compassion for Christ's Passion'. Available in an English version, *The Prick of Love*,[12] attributed in some manuscripts to Walter Hilton, the *Stimulus Amoris* is but one of the many instances of the availability in later medieval England of English translations of works of contemplative interest. The extent of Margery's association during her life with the inhabitants of what she calls 'Dewchlond' – i.e. the German-speaking lands together with the Low Countries – has often been noted, and a number of the works of the great medieval Dutch and German mystics were known in England, as well as those from further afield.[13] Margery's friend, the Carmelite Alan of Lynn, is known to have prepared indexes of both the *Stimulus Amoris* and the *Revelations* of St Bridget of Sweden, the other book that Margery mentions as being read to her by the priest.

St Bridget and 'St Bride's book', as Margery calls it, are mentioned in Margery's *Book* in ways that suggest how potent a model the Englishwoman found for herself in the life and revelations of the visionary Swedish saint. When (in chapter 20) Margery sees a marvel during mass, our Lord rather gratifyingly tells her, 'My daughter Bridget never saw me in this way . . . just as I spoke to St Bridget, just so I speak to you, daughter, and I tell you truly that every word that is written in Bridget's book is true, and through you shall be recognized as truth indeed.'

St Bridget of Sweden (1303–73) was of noble birth, and

connected with the royal house. She was married at thirteen, but persuaded her husband to remain chaste for two years. Eventually Bridget bore eight children, but was drawn increasingly to a strict religious life. She went to Santiago on pilgrimage with her husband in 1341, and on his death in 1343 devoted herself to the life of a visionary, pilgrim, and foundress of a new order of nuns. She dictated her revelations to her spiritual director. In 1349 Bridget left for Rome, where she stayed for the rest of her life, making a pilgrimage to the Holy Land in 1371 at Christ's command. The cult of St Bridget in England in Margery's day was extensive; the influence of her life and of her visions and devotions was great,[14] and in this the Bridgettine house of Syon Abbey, visited by Margery in her *Book*, was most important.

For Margery Kempe the model provided by St Bridget must have been particularly powerful. St Bridget's social status was, of course, more exalted than Margery's relatively modest bourgeois life: she was of the highest birth, in middle age she struggled at the divine command to learn Latin, she was instructed to found a new order, to involve herself in great affairs, to denounce abuses. Yet the pattern of her life as a married mystic, the transition from wife to Bride of Christ, the sustainedly visionary experience of her life – all such things will have appealed to Margery in vindicating the potential of the female mystic.

But St Bridget, while an important example and influence, was by no means the only female visionary brought to Margery's attention by those who read to her, advised her, or discussed their own reading with her, as the events of chapters 62 and 68 suggest. In chapter 62 the priest who is himself writing down Margery's *Book* tells how his confidence in her was badly shaken by the general impatience shown at her weeping and crying, until he was led to read the *Vita* of the *béguine* Mary of Oignies, whose saintly life was similarly characterized by the gift of uncontrollable tears. Both the *Stimulus Amoris* and Rolle's *Incendium Amoris* are also cited here in support of manifestations of mystical fervour, as is St Elizabeth of Hungary, while a little later one of Margery's learned friends repeats the selfsame incident as that read by Margery's scribe from the life of Mary of Oignies to support Margery's tears, suggesting how accessible to those in England interested in the spiritual life were the examples of continental female piety.

Mary of Oignies (d. 1213), born of wealthy parents at Nivelles in Brabant, was married off at fourteen, despite her wish for the religious life.[15] She persuaded her husband to live chastely, however, and they devoted themselves to nursing lepers at Williambroux. She led a life of great austerity and holiness, and her fame drew so many visitors that she eventually retreated to live as a hermit in a cell next to the monastery at Oignies, where she died. She had visions and ecstasies, was especially devoted to the Passion of Christ and the sacrament, and had the gift of prophecy.[16]

Many features of Mary's experience are echoed in the life of Margery Kempe. Mary of Oignies privately mortifies her flesh beneath her clothes, and persuades her husband to live chaste. She weeps copiously at the thought of the Passion. She cannot behold a crucifix, or speak, or hear others speak, of the Passion without falling down in a swoon. If she tries to restrain her tears they only increase. She is asked by a priest to stop her weeping and sobbing in church. When confessing trivial sins she is so overcome with contrition that she has to cry out like a woman in labour. She does not eat meat. She has the fellowship of blessed spirits who delight her ears with a marvellously sweet and merry melody. She wears a coat and mantle of white wool. She is told by the Holy Ghost that she will pass straight to paradise and spend no time in purgatory. Like Margery, she has a miraculous vision of the sacrament as it is held between the priest's hands at mass. Like Margery, she has at Candlemas a vision of the Presentation in the Temple. Like Margery, she is so 'drunk with charity' that she is sometimes unaware of the passing of time. And just as Margery tells a tale of a blossoming tree to illustrate the shortcomings of the clergy, so Mary of Oignies calls a newly ordained priest who sings his first mass in her presence 'a new tree now flowered, of which our Lord has ordained to me the first fruits . . .'

Even in this summary account of the holy life of Mary of Oignies
the reader of *The Book of Margery Kempe* will find many echoes of
Margery's experience.

The *Life* of Mary of Oignies in a Middle English version survives
in a Bodleian Library manuscript[17] together with English translations of the lives of several other holy women, one of the works of
Suso, and some material on the life of the great Italian mystic St
Catherine of Siena (d. 1380) – a collection which in itself suggests
the kind of reading that some of Margery's advisers would draw
upon. St Catherine's writings were known and translated in later
medieval England[18] and, like Margery, the Italian visionary saw
herself as a bride in a mystical marriage to the deity. The experiences and writings of other female mystics of the Middle Ages
will often seem paralleled and echoed in Margery's own book, and
the example of such mystics as St Mechthild of Hackeborn[19] and
Blessed Elisabeth of Schönau was known in England. The *Mirror
of Simple Souls* of Marguerite Porete (burnt as a heretic in 1310)
was translated from French into an English version,[20] and was
also translated into Latin by that Mount Grace mystic, Richard
Methley, whose own ecstasies were compared with Margery
Kempe's by the annotators of the manuscript of her *Book* at Mount
Grace Priory.

It is also intriguing to recall the association between Margery's
experience and the experience of such other female mystics as
Blessed Angela of Foligno and Blessed Dorothea of Montau, not
because evidence survives that their lives were known in England,
but because Margery on her pilgrimages actually visited the areas
where these mystics had lived. Thus, though there is no evidence
that Margery had direct knowledge of the life of Angela of Foligno,
at Assisi she visited the site of some of Angela's experiences and
could well have heard tell of the example of this remarkable local
figure.

Blessed Angela of Foligno (*c.* 1249–1309) lived a worldly life as
a well-to-do wife and mother up to the age of forty, but suddenly
underwent a conversion, although initially she was ashamed to
confess all her sins. Her family having all died, she was able to

devote herself to a life of poverty and penitence. She wept ceaselessly, cried aloud when she heard the name of God, and fell into a fever upon seeing a picture of Christ's Passion. It was difficult for her not to talk of God. She thought of herself as drinking the blood from Christ's side, and wanted, for love of Christ, to suffer the vilest death and humiliation. She was subject to fits of screaming which astonished everybody, and people said she was troubled by devils. She was so ashamed that she wondered whether this was indeed true. She had ecstasies and visions, and was ardently devoted to the crucified Christ. Her Franciscan confessor acted as her secretary and wrote down what she dictated.[21]

Margery's visit to Danzig late in life makes especially interesting the parallels between her experience and that of the Prussian visionary and ecstatic, Dorothea of Montau, who spent her married life in Danzig and whose cult would have been strong there at the time of Margery's visit.

Blessed Dorothea of Montau (1347–94), who describes herself as illiterate, was married at sixteen to an older man and bore him nine children, all but one of whom died young. From 1378 she experienced ecstasies. She was badly treated by her husband, although a mutual vow of chastity eventually followed, and Dorothea was allowed weekly communion. She went on pilgrimage to Aachen with her husband, and to Rome on her own. She could find no one in Danzig who understood her inner life and pilgrimage offered her the opportunity to seek out spiritual counsellors. After her husband's death in 1390 Dorothea became a recluse at Marienwerder Cathedral, under the direction of the pious John of Marienwerder, who wrote accounts of her visions and her life. A decisive influence on Dorothea's life was the example of St Bridget, whose relics were carried through Danzig on their return from Rome to Sweden in 1374. And, like Margery Kempe, this middle-class married woman who struggled to lead a religious life tells how she experienced a kind of spiritual drunkenness, and was also noted for her frequent and sustained holy tears.[22]

Both Angela's weeping and shrieking, and her intensity of feeling, and the life of the married Dorothea and her gift of tears, offer parallels with the experience of Margery Kempe, whose own life was made so persistently difficult by her gift of loud and frequent tears. It is essential to retrieve some sense of the spiritual value and desirability that was accorded to the gift of such tears in those days. Their spiritual value was confirmed to Margery – in a discussion of her understandably recurrent concern with discerning authentic tokens of the Holy Ghost – by no less an authority on the contemplative life than Julian of Norwich ('When God visits a creature with tears of contrition, devotion or compassion, he may and ought to believe that the Holy Ghost is in his soul,' chapter 18). It is this sense of the value of holy tears that lies behind Margery's exchange with the Archbishop of York, to whose rough question 'Why do you weep so, woman?' she replies firmly, 'Sir, you shall wish some day that you had wept as sorely as I.'

Reading Margery's Life

'And therefore she would not for all this world say otherwise than as she felt . . .' (chapter 61).

In these dictated recollections of a woman who could not read or write it is human speech itself which continually catches and sharpens the attention and offers a clue to reading Margery's life. Margery's *Book* was not, after all, set down to answer the expectations of later readers of autobiography.[23] Margery would probably not have believed that human experience was worth recording for its own sake. The Proem makes clear that this life is being recalled because of God's wonderful dealings with Margery, to God's glory rather than Margery's. The perceiving of pattern in one's life, which has determined the art of more modern autobiographers, is thus undertaken by Margery from a rather different vantage-point. Indeed, by later standards of autobiography, the presentation of pattern and progression may seem disconcertingly absent or elusive. There is little concern with chronology and with noting the passing of time, little sense of ageing and of the changing phases of life. The presentation of the subject's relationships with her chief friends is mostly rather interrupted. Touches of local colour and realistic detail come vividly and spasmodically before the reader's eyes, yet observation of the outward world – often significantly hazy and offhand anyway – was very far from what Margery would have seen to be her purpose, as a woman gifted with revelations. In spite of this we cannot claim Margery's *Book* to be the autobiography of a great mystic – the quality of her mystical experience prevents this – but it remains one of the most immediate 'Lives' of the period.

For Margery, the form of her writing was predominantly directed by the strong continuity of purpose that she saw in her own life. By comparison with the recollected revelations of the great mystics, Margery's *Book* is almost too autobiographical, too concerned with the mundane difficulties and obstacles that confronted Margery in life. Her record of those visionary experiences which were to her own mind most extraordinary – particularly her conversations with our Lord – are often among the least individual and lively parts of her work in both style and content, while other parts of her text may seem individual at the expense of authentic spiritual understanding.

Margery may be observed consistently handling the figurative language of traditional spiritual literature – particularly the nuptial imagery of mystical union with God – with an endearingly earthbound awkwardness. In following the conventional imagery of the mystical marriage-bed, the wedding, the body of the spouse, Margery's realizing imagination produces an unnerving directness and concreteness, as when God informs her: 'You may boldly, when you are in bed, take me to you as your wedded husband . . . You can boldly take me in the arms of your soul and kiss my mouth, my head and my feet as sweetly as you want' (chapter 36). It is characteristic of Margery that she will take over the mystical tradition of applying metaphors of sense perception to the mystic's experience of God and apply them with such concrete force as to risk losing the spiritual in the vigour of the real (although she is noticeably careful – perhaps because of challenges to her orthodoxy – to mention how God speaks 'to her mind', 'in her soul', and so forth). Yet Margery's limitations as a would-be mystic are balanced by her strengths as a strikingly individual and vivid talker and rememberer, as is shown by the way she recalls how she experienced some tokens of the Holy Ghost in chapter 36: the rushing wind and the dove of the Holy Spirit are apprehended by Margery Kempe as the sound of a pair of bellows and the song of a robin redbreast 'that often sang very merrily in her right ear'.

In the end we must accept the *Book* as it is, a unique survival which it is pointless to think less of – by measuring it against other works and genres – when the writing seems to have so much in it of the life it seeks to present. It would be misleading to take the *Book* as if it were the transcript of conversations in which a medieval Englishwoman remembers her life. The writing has clearly been much more edited and shaped than this – edited by the bookish concerns of the scribe, and shaped and focused by that spiritualizing lens through which Margery looks back at her experience.

Yet there remain indications that we are dealing with an incompletely edited transcript – the lack of shaping in the material presented and the limitations of the spiritual life that is portrayed. There is no sense of a perceived development and interpretation which might mark a more contrivedly presented autobiography. There is also striking openness, as when Margery includes the early story of her sexual temptation in chapter 4, with its anti-climactic conclusion when she falls prey to her own will and is then rebuffed by the man who had tempted her. There seems a comparable honesty in her account of such an incident as that in which her fellow travellers desperately try to avoid her when crossing from Calais home to England ('What the cause was, she never knew' – II, chapter 8). For although Margery understandably remembers her successes along with her failures, she seems immune to embarrassment, and is perhaps without the kind of self-consciousness which would have led her to re-write her experiences in a way that blurred over the awkward corners and sharp edges of her own personality, and only left the rough surfaces and bloodymindedness of other people's characters.[24]

The continuity of the *Book* lies in Margery's own will and, as something of a prophet in her time, the local structure of her writing is often determined by the recollection of a sequence of events which proved her foresight. As an illiterate person, the role of human speech seems central to Margery's remembering of past events, and happily central to her dictated account of that past. Her sensitivity to the spoken word is displayed in her feeling that she is being crucified by the cruel words of others. Challenged to justify herself, continually placed in the position of being tested, Margery must also speak out clearly for herself. So it is natural that she should compose and shape written 'scenes' through the interchange of remembered speech and the climax of some successful riposte. The degree to which Margery represents scenes from years before in direct-speech exchanges may make some modern readers suspect some subsequent 'improvement' in the writing of her history. There is certainly a likelihood of this, although the powers of the unbookish mind to remember scenes in terms of spoken exchanges can often still be remarked. If we imagine ourselves with Margery's 'unlettered' awareness, her ability 'to answer every clerk' is clearly a reflection of the favour shown her and of her extraordinary vocation. In this light it is understandable that Margery would long preserve in memory her exchanges with the monk whose sins she reveals to him (chapter 12), or her trouncing of her detractors at Canterbury (chapter 13). In both cases she takes on the established and advantaged; it would be natural for her to husband in her memory the spoken 'text' of these triumphs. Clear in her mind that she should not rush into writing – indeed she almost left it too late – she was, possibly from her earliest experience, committing to the record of a kind of inner memory-book the challenges and exchanges which would one day, she felt, be outwardly set down in her *Book*, and in the meantime would serve to sustain her conviction in her often lonely and isolated spiritual pilgrimage.

It is in direct speech that Margery seems to recall some of the most pointed and independent moments of her long-past experience. (Indeed, the frustrations of not being able to speak, or to understand speech, on her foreign travels are so extreme for Margery as to be the subject of miraculous relief.) To the mild but cautious Bishop of Lincoln Margery records her grand answer that she will indeed visit the Archbishop, but not for the reason he suggests (chapter 15); she recalls the words with which she boldly rebukes Archbishop Arundel for the misconduct of his household (chapter 16). The accuracy of Margery's memory, where this can be cross-checked with recorded events, is impressively good, while her recollection of what was said to her at their meeting by Dame Julian of Norwich is also impressive with a different kind of accuracy, in that what Margery records Julian as saying rings true in content, and even in style, with Julian's own writing. Since it seems unlikely that Margery would know anything of Julian's written work, her memory of this conversation is at once a precious witness to the wholeness of vision, life and counsel in Dame Julian, and a witness to the quality of Margery's own power to recollect what was said to her both on this and, by implication, on other occasions.

When Margery returns to England after her travels her trials and difficulties with authority are naturally occasions that Margery recalls in terms of the testing questions put to her and her answers to them. She is always good at catching the edge in other people's voices, and although it was not her purpose to provide character-sketches of the people she encounters, her modern readers will feel they know something, none the less, of a person like Archbishop Bowet, because Margery's account allows him to speak in his own, splendidly testy, words.

In fact, there are far too many memorable moments in the *Book* to recall here, where the vividness of the speech brings alive the presence of those around Margery, or highlights her own relation to them. There are the comments of neighbours ('Why do you talk so of the joy that is in heaven? . . . You haven't been there any more than we have,' chapter 3). There is the apparently reasonable comfort offered by a priest for her shriekings ('Woman, Jesus is long since dead,' chapter 60), which enables Margery to rise to the magnificent retort: 'Sir, his death is as fresh to me as if he had died this same day, and so, I think, it ought to be to you and to all Christian people.'

Indeed, it is the kindly-meant advice of menfolk as Margery is taken under arrest towards Beverley ('Woman, give up this life that you lead, and go and spin, and card wool, as other women do, and do not suffer so much shame and so much unhappiness ...') which leads Margery to spurn such counsel in terms that reveal her idea of her vocation: 'I do not suffer as much sorrow as I would do for our Lord's love, for I only suffer cutting words, and our merciful Lord Christ Jesus ... suffered hard strokes, bitter scourgings, and shameful death at the last ...' (chapter 53). As her extraordinarily heightened and suggestible imagination shows, Margery is able throughout her *Book* to step into the life of Christ and out again. Those constantly recollected scenes of his life, reinforced in her mind's eye by her visits to the Holy Places, form a kind of extra life concurrent with her own and which she sees suffused, superimposed, simultaneous, with the world of ordinary streets and rooms, humble mothers and their children. As a woman both entangled in the world and beckoned out of it, at one time nursing her senile and incontinent husband, at another called to contemplation, the extraordinary strains and variousness of Margery's life as she remembers it give her text the unevenness of living, and mean that her *Book*'s very weaknesses prove its strengths, as a work of human memory and the life of the self.

*

In rendering Margery Kempe's *Book* from Middle English the present translation aims to give a readable text for the modern reader, while remaining as close as possible to the form of the original. In the translation, the syntactical pattern of Margery's text has been kept as far as possible: her sentences are often long and rather loosely connected, and some of her most recurrent forms of connection and transition are simply effected by 'and' and 'then', which are mostly retained here. But some of Margery's characteristic diction – such terms as 'boisterous' or 'dalliance' – have had to be changed in the present text, because of their altered associations for the modern reader. The translation is based upon the unique manuscript, now British Library Additional MS 61823, as edited by Sanford Brown Meech and Hope Emily Allen (Early English Text Society, O.S. 212, 1940), with the kind permission of the Early English Text Society.

Suggested Chronology of the Life of Margery Kempe

1417   Margery visits York, and London (chapters 50–55).

1421   23 January. The great fire at Lynn (chapter 67).

c. 1431   Margery's son and husband die (II, chapter 2).

1433   2 April? Margery embarks at Ipswich (II, chapter 3).

1433   10–13 April? Margery in Norway (II, chapter 3).

1433   April–May. Margery's sojourn in Danzig (II, chapter 4).

1433   10–24 July. Exhibition of the four holy relics at Aachen (II, chapter 7).

1434   29 July? Margery arrives at Syon Abbey (II, chapter 10).

1436   23 July. Priest begins to revise Margery's Book I (Proem).

1438   28 April. Priest begins to write Book II (II, chapter 1).

1438   13 April. Admission of one Margery Kempe to the Guild of the Trinity at Lynn; further mentioned, 22 May 1439.

THE BOOK OF
MARGERY KEMPE

*

The Proem

Here begins a short treatise and a comforting one for sinful wretches, in which they may have great solace and comfort for themselves, and understand the high and unspeakable mercy of our sovereign Saviour Jesus Christ – whose name be worshipped and magnified without end – who now in our days deigns to exercise his nobility and his goodness to us unworthy ones. All the works of our Saviour are for our example and instruction, and what grace that he works in any creature is our profit, if lack of charity be not our hindrance.

And therefore, by the leave of our merciful Lord Christ Jesus, to the magnifying of his holy name, Jesus, this little treatise shall treat in part of his wonderful works, how mercifully, how benignly, and how charitably he moved and stirred a sinful wretch to his love, who for many years wished and intended through the prompting of the Holy Ghost to follow our Saviour, making great promises of fasts, together with many other deeds of penance. And she was always turned back in time of temptation – like the reed which bows with every wind and is never still unless no wind blows – until the time that our merciful Lord Christ Jesus, having pity and compassion on his handiwork and his creature, turned health into sickness, prosperity into adversity, respectability into reproof, and love into hatred.

Thus with all these things turning upside down, this creature,[1] who for many years had gone astray and always been unstable, was perfectly drawn and stirred to enter the way of high perfection, of which perfect way Christ our Saviour in his own person was the example. Steadfastly he trod it and duly he went it once before.

Then this creature – of whom this treatise, through the mercy of Jesus, shall show in part the life – was touched by the hand of our Lord with great bodily sickness, through which she lost her reason for a long time, until our Lord by grace restored her again, as shall be shown more openly later. Her worldly goods, which were plentiful and abundant at that date, were a little while afterwards quite barren and bare. Then was pomp and pride cast down and laid aside. Those who before had respected her, afterwards most sharply rebuked her; her kin and those who had been friends were now her greatest enemies.

Then she, considering this astonishing change, and seeking succour beneath the wings of her spiritual mother, Holy Church, went and humbled herself to her confessor, accusing herself of her misdeeds, and afterwards did great bodily penance. And within a short time our merciful Lord visited this creature with abundant tears of contrition day by day, insomuch that some men said she could weep when she wanted to, and slandered the work of God.

She was so used to being slandered and reproved, to being chided and rebuked by the world for grace and virtue with which she was endued through the strength of the Holy Ghost, that it was to her a kind of solace and comfort when she suffered any distress for the love of God and for the grace that God wrought in her. For ever the more slander and reproof that she suffered, the more she increased in grace and in devotion of holy meditation, of high contemplation, and of wonderful speeches and conversation which our Lord spoke and conveyed to her soul, teaching her how she would be despised for his love, and how she should have patience, setting all her trust, all her love and all her affection on him alone.

She knew and understood many secret things which would happen afterwards, by inspiration of the Holy Ghost. And often, while she was kept with such holy speeches and conversation, she would so weep and sob that many men were greatly astonished, for they little knew how at home our Lord was in her soul.[2] Nor could she herself ever tell of the grace that she felt, it was so heavenly, so high above her reason and her bodily wits; and her body so feeble at the time of the presence of grace that she could never express it with her words as she felt it in her soul.

Then this creature had great dread of the delusions and deceptions of her spiritual enemies. She went by the bidding of the Holy Ghost to many worthy clerks, both archbishops and bishops, doctors of divinity, and bachelors as well. She also spoke with many anchorites, and told them of her manner of life and such grace as the Holy Ghost of his goodness wrought in her mind and in her soul, as far as her wit would serve her to express it. And those to whom she confided her secrets said she was much bound to love our Lord for the grace that he showed to her, and counselled her to follow her promptings and her stirrings, and trustingly believe they were of the Holy Ghost and of no evil spirit.

Some of these worthy clerics took it, on peril of their souls and as they would answer to God, that this creature was inspired with the Holy Ghost, and bade her that she should have a book written of her feelings and her revelations. Some offered to write her feelings with their own hands, and she would in no way consent, for she was commanded in her soul that she should not write so soon. And so it was twenty years and more from the time that this creature first had feelings and revelations before she had any written. Afterwards, when it pleased our Lord, he commanded and charged her that she should have written down her feelings and revelations, and her form of living, so that his goodness might be known to all the world.

Then the creature had no writer who would fulfil her desire, nor give credence to her feelings, until the time that a man living in Germany [3] – who was an Englishman by birth, and afterwards married in Germany and had there both a wife and a child – having good knowledge of this creature and of her desire, and moved, I trust, through the Holy Ghost, came to England with his wife and his goods, and dwelt with the said creature until he had written as much as she would tell him in the time that they were together. And afterwards he died.

Then there was a priest that this creature had great affection for, and so she talked with him about this matter and brought him the book to read. The book was so ill-written that he could make little sense of it, for it was neither good English nor German, nor were the letters shaped or formed as other letters are. Therefore the priest fully believed that nobody would ever be able to read it, unless it were by special grace. Nevertheless, he promised her that, if he could read it, he would willingly copy it out and write it better.

Then there was such evil talk about this creature and her weeping, that the priest out of cowardice dared not speak with her but seldom, nor would write as he had promised the said creature. And so he avoided and deferred the writing of this book for nearly four years or more, notwithstanding that this creature often entreated him about it. At last he said to her that he could not read it, and for this reason he would not do it. He would not, he said, put himself in peril over it. Then he advised her to go to a good man who had been great friends with him that first wrote the book, supposing that he would best know how to read the book, for he had sometimes read letters written by the other man, sent from overseas while he was in Germany.

And so she went to that man, asking him to write this book and never to reveal it as long as she lived, granting him a great sum of money for his labour. And this good man wrote about a leaf, and yet it was little to the purpose, for he could not get on well with it, the book was so badly set down, and written quite without reason.

Then the priest was troubled in his conscience, for he had promised her to write this book, if he could succeed in reading it, and he was not doing his part as well as he might have done, and so he asked this creature to get the book back again, if she fittingly could. Then she got the book back and brought it to the priest very cheerfully, praying him to work with a good will, and she would pray to God for him, and gain him grace to read it and to write it as well.

The priest, trusting in her prayers, began to read this book, and it was much easier, as he thought, than it was before. And so he read over every word of it in this creature's presence, she sometimes helping where there was any difficulty.

This book is not written in order, every thing after another as it was done, but just as the matter came to this creature's mind when it was to be written down, for it was so long before it was written that she had forgotten the time and the order when things occurred. And therefore she had nothing written but what she well knew to be indeed the truth.

When the priest first began to write this book his eyes failed, so that he could not see to form his letters and could not see to mend his pen. All other things he could see well enough. He set a pair of spectacles on his nose, and then it was much worse than it was before. He complained to the creature about his troubles. She said his enemy was envious of his good deed and would hinder him if he might, and she bade him do as well as God would give him grace and not give up. When he came back to his book again, he could see as well, he thought, as he ever did before both by daylight and by candlelight. And for this reason, when he had written a quire he added a leaf to it, and then he wrote this proem to give a fuller account than does the following one, which was written before this. *Anno domini* 1436.

The Preface

A short treatise of a creature set in great pomp and pride of the world, who later was drawn to our Lord by great poverty, sickness, shame, and great reproofs in many divers countries and places, of which tribulations some shall be shown hereafter, not in the order in which they befell, but as the creature could remember them when they were written.

For it was twenty years and more from the time when this creature had forsaken the world and busily cleaved to our Lord before this book was written, notwithstanding that this creature had much advice to have her tribulations and her feelings written down, and a White Friar[1] freely offered to write for her if she wished. And she was warned in her spirit that she should not write so soon. And many years later she was bidden in her spirit to write.

And then it was written first by a man who could neither write English nor German well, so that it could not be read except by special grace alone, for there was so much obloquy and slander of this creature that few men would believe her.

And so at last a priest was greatly moved to write this treatise, and he could not read it for four years together. And afterwards, at the request of this creature, and compelled by his own conscience, he tried again to read it, and it was much easier than it was before. And so he began to write in the year of our Lord 1436, on the next day after Mary Magdalene,[2] after the information of this creature.

BOOK I

*

Chapter 1

When this creature was twenty years of age,[1] or somewhat more, she was married to a worshipful burgess [of Lynn][2] and was with child within a short time, as nature would have it. And after she had conceived, she was troubled with severe attacks of sickness until the child was born. And then, what with the labour-pains she had in childbirth and the sickness that had gone before, she despaired of her life, believing she might not live. Then she sent for her confessor, for she had a thing on her conscience which she had never revealed before that time in all her life.[3] For she was continually hindered by her enemy – the devil – always saying to her while she was in good health that she didn't need to confess but to do penance by herself alone, and all should be forgiven, for God is merciful enough. And therefore this creature often did great penance in fasting on bread and water, and performed other acts of charity with devout prayers, but she would not reveal that one thing in confession.

And when she was at any time sick or troubled, the devil said in her mind that she should be damned, for she was not shriven[4] of that fault. Therefore, after her child was born, and not believing she would live, she sent for her confessor, as said before, fully wishing to be shriven of her whole lifetime, as near as she could. And when she came to the point of saying that thing which she had so long concealed, her confessor was a little too hasty and began sharply to reprove her before she had fully said what she meant, and so she would say no more in spite of anything he might do. And soon after, because of the dread she had of damnation on the one hand, and his sharp reproving of her on the other, this creature went out of her mind and was amazingly disturbed and tormented with spirits for half a year, eight weeks and odd days.[5]

And in this time she saw, as she thought, devils opening their mouths all alight with burning flames of fire, as if they would have swallowed her in, sometimes pawing at her, sometimes threatening her, sometimes pulling her and hauling her about both night and day during the said time. And also the devils called out to her with great threats, and bade her that she should forsake her Christian faith and belief, and deny her God, his mother, and all the saints in heaven, her good works and all good virtues, her father, her mother, and all her friends. And so she did. She slandered her husband, her friends, and her own self. She spoke many sharp and reproving words; she recognized no virtue nor goodness; she desired all wickedness; just as the spirits tempted her to say and do, so she said and did. She would have killed herself many a time as they stirred her to, and would have been damned with them in hell, and in witness of this she bit her own hand so violently that the mark could be seen for the rest of her life. And also she pitilessly tore the skin on her body near her heart with her nails, for she had no other implement, and she would have done something worse, except that she was tied up and forcibly restrained both day and night so that she could not do as she wanted.

And when she had long been troubled by these and many other temptations, so that people thought she should never have escaped from them alive, then one time as she lay by herself and her keepers were not with her, our merciful Lord Christ Jesus – ever to be trusted, worshipped be his name, never forsaking his servant in time of need – appeared to his creature who had forsaken him, in the likeness of a man, the most seemly, most beauteous, and most amiable that ever might be seen with man's eye, clad in a mantle of purple silk, sitting upon her bedside, looking upon her with so blessed a countenance that she was strengthened in all her spirits, and he said to her these words: 'Daughter, why have you forsaken me, and I never forsook you?'

And as soon as he had said these words, she saw truly how the air opened as bright as any lightning, and he ascended up into the air, not hastily and quickly, but beautifully and gradually, so that she could clearly behold him in the air until it closed up again.

And presently the creature grew as calm in her wits and her

reason as she ever was before, and asked her husband, as soon as he came to her, if she could have the keys of the buttery to get her food and drink as she had done before. Her maids and her keepers advised him that he should not deliver up any keys to her, for they said she would only give away such goods as there were, because she did not know what she was saying, as they believed.

Nevertheless, her husband, who always had tenderness and compassion for her, ordered that they should give her the keys. And she took food and drink as her bodily strength would allow her, and she once again recognized her friends and her household, and everybody else who came to her in order to see how our Lord Jesus Christ had worked his grace in her – blessed may he be, who is ever near in tribulation. When people think he is far away from them he is very near through his grace. Afterwards this creature performed all her responsibilities wisely and soberly enough, except that she did not truly know our Lord's power to draw us to him.

Chapter 2

And when this creature had thus through grace come again to her right mind, she thought she was bound to God and that she would be his servant. Nevertheless, she would not leave her pride or her showy manner of dressing, which she had previously been used to, either for her husband, or for any other person's advice. And yet she knew full well that people made many adverse comments about her, because she wore gold pipes on her head,[1] and her hoods with the tippets were fashionably slashed. Her cloaks were also modishly slashed and underlaid with various colours between the slashes, so that she would be all the more stared at, and all the more esteemed.

And when her husband used to try and speak to her, to urge

her to leave her proud ways, she answered sharply and shortly, and said that she was come of worthy kindred – he should never have married her – for her father was sometime mayor of the town of N., and afterwards he was alderman of the High Guild of the Trinity in N. And therefore she would keep up the honour of her kindred, whatever anyone said.

She was enormously envious of her neighbours if they were dressed as well as she was. Her whole desire was to be respected by people. She would not learn her lesson from a single chastening experience,[2] nor be content with the worldly goods that God had sent her – as her husband was – but always craved more and more.

And then, out of pure covetousness, and in order to maintain her pride, she took up brewing, and was one of the greatest brewers in the town of N. for three or four years until she lost a great deal of money, for she had never had any experience in that business. For however good her servants were and however knowledgeable in brewing, things would never go successfully for them. For when the ale had as fine a head of froth on it as anyone might see, suddenly the froth would go flat, and all the ale was lost in one brewing after another, so that her servants were ashamed and would not stay with her. Then this creature thought how God had punished her before – and she could not take heed – and now again by the loss of her goods; and then she left off and did no more brewing.

And then she asked her husband's pardon because she would not follow his advice previously, and she said that her pride and sin were the cause of all her punishing, and that she would willingly put right all her wrongdoing. But yet she did not entirely give up the world, for she now thought up a new enterprise for herself. She had a horse-mill. She got herself two good horses and a man to grind people's corn, and thus she was confident of making her living. This business venture did not last long, for shortly afterwards, on the eve of Corpus Christi, the following marvel happened. The man was in good health, and his two horses were strong and in good condition and had drawn well in the mill previously, but now, when he took one of those horses and put him in the mill as he had done before, this horse would not pull in the mill in spite of anything the man might do. The man was sorry, and tried everything he could think of to make his horse pull. Sometimes he led him by the head, sometimes he beat him, and sometimes he made a fuss of him, but nothing did any good, for the horse would rather go backwards than forwards. Then this man set a pair of sharp spurs on his heels and rode on the horse's back to make him pull, but it was no better. When this man saw it was no use, he put the horse back in his stable, and gave him food, and the horse ate well and freshly. And afterwards he took the other horse and put him in the mill. And just as his fellow had done so did he, for he would not pull for anything the man might do. And then this man gave up his job and would not stay any longer with the said creature.

Then it was noised about in the town of N. that neither man nor beast would serve the said creature, and some said she was accursed; some said God openly took vengeance on her; some said one thing and some said another. And some wise men, whose minds were more grounded in the love of our Lord, said it was the high mercy of our Lord Jesus Christ that called her from the pride and vanity of this wretched world.

And then this creature, seeing all these adversities coming on every side, thought they were the scourges of our Lord that would chastise her for her sin. Then she asked God for mercy, and forsook her pride, her covetousness, and the desire that she had for worldly dignity, and did great bodily penance, and began to enter the way of everlasting life as shall be told hereafter.

Chapter 3

One night, as this creature lay in bed with her husband, she heard a melodious sound so sweet and delectable that she thought she had been in paradise.[1] And immediately she jumped out of bed and said, 'Alas that ever I sinned! It is full merry in heaven.' This melody was so sweet that it surpassed all the melody that might be heard in this world, without any comparison, and it caused this creature when she afterwards heard any mirth or melody to shed very plentiful and abundant tears of high devotion, with great sobbings and sighings for the bliss of heaven, not fearing the shames and contempt of this wretched world.[2] And ever after her being drawn towards God in this way, she kept in mind the joy and the melody that there was in heaven, so much so that she could not very well restrain herself from speaking of it. For when she was in company with any people she would often say, 'It is full merry in heaven!'

And those who knew of her behaviour previously and now heard her talk so much of the bliss of heaven said to her, 'Why do you talk so of the joy that is in heaven? You don't know it, and you haven't been there any more than we have.' And they were angry with her because she would not hear or talk of worldly things as they did, and as she did previously.

And after this time she never had any desire to have sexual intercourse with her husband, for paying the debt of matrimony[3] was so abominable to her that she would rather, she thought, have eaten and drunk the ooze and muck in the gutter than consent to intercourse, except out of obedience.

And so she said to her husband, 'I may not deny you my body, but all the love and affection of my heart is withdrawn from all earthly creatures and set on God alone.' But he would have his will with her, and she obeyed with much weeping and sorrowing because she could not live in chastity. And often this creature advised her husband to live chaste and said that they had often (she well knew) displeased God by their inordinate love, and the great delight that each of them had in using the other's body, and now it would be a good thing if by mutual consent they punished and chastised themselves by abstaining from the lust of their bodies. Her husband said it was good to do so, but he might not yet – he would do so when God willed. And so he used her as he had done before, he would not desist. And all the time she prayed to God that she might live chaste, and three or four years afterwards, when it pleased our Lord, her husband made a vow of chastity, as shall be written afterwards, by Jesus's leave.

And also, after this creature heard this heavenly melody, she did great bodily penance.[4] She was sometimes shriven two or three times on the same day,[5] especially of that sin which she had so long concealed and covered up, as is written at the beginning of this book. She gave herself up to much fasting and keeping of vigils; she rose at two or three of the clock and went to church, and was there at her prayers until midday and also the whole afternoon. And then she was slandered and reproved by many people because she led so strict a life. She got herself a hair-cloth from a kiln – the sort that malt is dried on – and put it inside her gown as discreetly and secretly as she could, so that her husband should not notice it. And nor did he, although she lay beside him every night in bed and wore the hair-shirt every day, and bore him children during that time.

Then she had three years of great difficulty with temptations,[6] which she bore as meekly as she could, thanking our Lord for all his gifts, and she was as merry when she was reproved, scorned or ridiculed for our Lord's love, and much more merry than she was before amongst the dignities of this world. For she knew very well that she had sinned greatly against God and that she deserved far more shame and sorrow than any man could cause her, and contempt in this world was the right way heavenwards, for Christ himself chose that way. All his apostles, martyrs, confessors and virgins, and all those who ever came to heaven, passed by the way of tribulation, and she desired nothing as much as heaven. Then she was glad in her conscience when she believed that she was entering upon the way which would lead her to the place that she most desired.

And this creature had contrition and great compunction, with plentiful tears and much loud and violent sobbing, for her sins and for her unkindness towards her maker. She reflected on her unkindness since her childhood, as our Lord would put it into her mind, very many times. And then when she contemplated her own wickedness, she could only sorrow and weep and ever pray for mercy and forgiveness. Her weeping was so plentiful and so continual that many people thought that she could weep and leave off when she wanted, and therefore many people said she was a false hypocrite, and wept when in company for advantage and profit. And then very many people who loved her before while she was in the world abandoned her and would not know her, and all the while she thanked God for everything, desiring nothing but mercy and forgiveness of sin.

Chapter 4

For the first two years when this creature was thus drawn to our Lord she had great quiet of spirit from any temptations. She could well endure fasting – it did not trouble her. She hated the joys of the world. She felt no rebellion in her flesh. She was so strong – as she thought – that she feared no devil in hell, for she performed such great bodily penance. She thought that she loved God more than he loved her. She was smitten with the deadly wound of vainglory and felt it not, for she desired many times that the crucifix should loosen his hands from the cross and embrace her in token of love. Our merciful Lord Christ Jesus, seeing this creature's presumption, sent her – as is written before – three years of great temptations, of one of the hardest of which I intend to write, as an example to those who come after that they should not trust in themselves nor have joy in themselves as this creature had – for undoubtedly our spiritual enemy does not sleep but busily probes our temperament and attitudes, and wherever he finds us most frail, there, by our Lord's sufferance, he lays his snare, which no one may escape by his own power.

And so he laid before this creature the snare of lechery, when she thought that all physical desire had been wholly quenched in her. And so she was tempted for a long time with the sin of lechery, in spite of anything she might do. Yet she was often shriven, she wore her hair-shirt, and did great bodily penance and wept many a bitter tear, and often prayed to our Lord that he should preserve her and keep her so that she should not fall into temptation, for she thought she would rather have been dead than consent to that. And in all this time she had no desire to have intercourse with her husband, and it was very painful and horrible to her.

In the second year of her temptations it so happened that a man whom she liked said to her on St Margaret's Eve[1] before evensong that, for anything, he would sleep with her and enjoy the lust of his body, and that she should not withstand him, for if he might not have his desire that time, he said, he would have it another time instead – she should not choose. And he did it to test what she would do, but she imagined that he meant it in earnest and said very little in reply. So they parted then and both went to hear evensong, for her church was dedicated to St Margaret.[2] This woman was so troubled with the man's words that she could not listen to evensong, nor say her paternoster, nor think any other good thought, but was more troubled than she ever was before.

The devil put it into her mind that God had forsaken her, or else she would not be so tempted. She believed the devil's persuasions, and began to consent because she could not think any good thought. Therefore she believed that God had forsaken her. And when evensong was over, she went to the said man, in order that he should have his will of her, as she believed he desired, but he put forward such a pretence that she could not understand his intent, and so they parted for that night. This creature was so troubled and vexed all that night that she did not know what she could do.

She lay beside her husband, and to have intercourse with him was so abominable to her that she could not bear it, and yet it was permissible for her and at a rightful time if she had wished it. But all the time she was tormented to sin with the other man because he had spoken to her. At last – through the importunings of temptation and a lack of discretion – she was overcome and consented in her mind, and went to the man to know if he would then consent to have her. And he said he would not for all the wealth in this world; he would rather be chopped up as small as meat for the pot.

She went away all ashamed and confused in herself, seeing his steadfastness and her own instability. Then she thought about the grace that God had given her before, of how she had two years of great quiet in her soul, of repentance for her sins with many bitter tears of compunction, and a perfect will never again to turn to sin but rather, she thought, to be dead. And now she saw how she had consented in her will to sin. Then she half fell into despair. She thought herself in hell, such was the sorrow that she had. She thought she was worthy of no mercy because her consenting to sin was so wilfully done, nor ever worthy to serve God, because she was so false to him.

Nevertheless she was shriven many times and often, and did whatever penance her confessor would enjoin her to do, and was governed according to the rules of the Church. That grace God gave this creature – blessed may he be – but he did not withdraw her temptation, but rather increased it, as she thought.

And therefore she thought that he had forsaken her, and dared not trust to his mercy, but was troubled with horrible temptations to lechery and despair nearly all the following year, except that our Lord in his mercy, as she said to herself, gave her every day for the most part two hours of compunction for her sins, with many bitter tears. And afterwards she was troubled with temptations to despair as she was before, and was as far from feelings of grace as those who never felt any. And that she could not bear, and so she continued to despair. Except for the time that she felt grace, her trials were so amazing that she could not cope very well with them, but always mourned and sorrowed as though God had forsaken her.

Chapter 5

Then on a Friday before Christmas Day,[1] as this creature was kneeling in a chapel of St John, within a church of St Margaret in N., weeping a very great deal and asking mercy and forgiveness for her sins and her trespasses, our merciful Lord Christ Jesus – blessed may he be – ravished her spirit and said to her, 'Daughter, why are you weeping so sorely? I have come to you, Jesus Christ, who died on the cross suffering bitter pains and passion for you. I, the same God, forgive you your sins to the uttermost point.[2] And you shall never come into hell nor into purgatory, but when you pass out of this world, within the twinkling of an eye, you shall have the bliss of heaven, for I am the same God who has brought your sins to your mind and caused you to be shriven of them. And I grant you contrition until your life's end.

'Therefore, I command you, boldly call me Jesus, your love, for I am your love and shall be your love without end.[3] And, daughter, you have a hair-shirt on your back. I want you to leave off wearing it, and I shall give you a hair-shirt in your heart which shall please me much more than all the hair shirts in the world. But also, my beloved daughter, you must give up that which you love best in this world, and that is the eating of meat. And instead of meat you shall eat my flesh and my blood, that is the true body of Christ in the sacrament of the altar. This is my will, daughter, that you receive my body every Sunday,[4] and I shall cause so much grace to flow into you that everyone shall marvel at it.

'You shall be eaten and gnawed by the people of the world just as any rat gnaws the stockfish.[5] Don't be afraid, daughter, for you shall be victorious over all your enemies. I shall give you grace enough to answer every cleric in the love of God. I swear to you by my majesty that I shall never forsake you whether in happiness or in sorrow. I shall help you and protect you, so that no devil in hell shall ever part you from me, nor angel in heaven, nor man on earth – for devils in hell may not, nor angels in heaven will not, nor man on earth shall not.

'And daughter, I want you to give up your praying of many beads, and think such thoughts as I shall put into your mind. I shall give you leave to pray until six o'clock to say what you wish. Then you shall lie still and speak to me in thought, and I shall give you high meditation and true contemplation. And I command you to go to the anchorite at the Preaching Friars[6] and tell him my confidences and counsels which I reveal to you, and do as he advises, for my spirit shall speak in him to you.'

Then this creature went off to see the anchorite as she was commanded, and revealed to him the revelations that had been shown to her. Then the anchorite, with great reverence and weeping, thanking God, said, 'Daughter, you are sucking even at Christ's breast,[7] and you have received a pledge of paradise. I charge you to receive such thoughts – when God will give them – as meekly and devoutly as you can, and then come and tell me what they are, and I shall, by the leave of our Lord Jesus Christ, tell you whether they are from the Holy Ghost or else from your enemy the devil.'

Chapter 6

Another day, this creature gave herself up to meditation as she had been commanded before, and she lay still, not knowing what she might best think of. Then she said to our Lord Jesus Christ, 'Jesus, what shall I think about?'

Our Lord Jesus answered in her mind, 'Daughter, think of my mother, for she is the cause of all the grace that you have.'

And then at once she saw St Anne, great with child, and then she prayed St Anne to let her be her maid and her servant. And presently our Lady was born, and then she busied herself to take the child to herself and look after her until she was twelve years of age, with good food and drink, with fair white clothing and white kerchiefs. And then she said to the blessed child, 'My lady, you shall be the mother of God.'

The blessed child answered and said, 'I wish I were worthy to be the handmaiden of her that should conceive the son of God.'

The creature said, 'I pray you, my lady, if that grace befall you, do not discontinue with my service.'

The blessed child went away for a certain time – the creature remaining still in contemplation – and afterwards came back again and said, 'Daughter, now I have become the mother of God.'

And then the creature fell down on her knees with great reverence and great weeping and said, 'I am not worthy, my lady, to do you service.'

'Yes, daughter,' she said, 'follow me – I am well pleased with your service.'

Then she went forth with our Lady and with Joseph, bearing with her a flask of wine sweetened with honey and spices. Then they went forth to Elizabeth, St John the Baptist's mother, and when they met together Mary and Elizabeth reverenced each other, and so they dwelled together with great grace and gladness for twelve weeks. And then St John was born, and our Lady took him up from the ground with all reverence and gave him to his mother, saying of him that he would be a holy man, and blessed him.

Afterwards they took leave of each other with compassionate tears. And then the creature fell down on her knees to St Elizabeth, and begged her that she would pray for her to our Lady so that she might still serve and please her.

'Daughter,' said Elizabeth, 'it seems to me that you do your duty very well.'

And then the creature went forth with our Lady to Bethlehem and procured lodgings for her every night with great reverence, and our Lady was received with good cheer. She also begged for our Lady pieces of fair white cloth and kerchiefs to swaddle her son in when he was born; and when Jesus was born she arranged bedding for our Lady to lie on with her blessed son. And later she begged food for our Lady and her blessed child. Afterwards she swaddled him, weeping bitter tears of compassion, mindful of the painful death that he would suffer for the love of sinful men, saying to him, 'Lord, I shall treat you gently; I will not bind you tightly. I pray you not to be displeased with me.'

Chapter 7

And afterwards on the twelfth day, when three kings came with their gifts and worshipped our Lord Jesus Christ in his mother's lap, this creature, our Lady's handmaiden, beholding the whole process in contemplation, wept marvellously sorely. And when she saw that they wished to take their leave to go home again to their country, she could not bear that they should go from the presence of our Lord, and in her wonder that they wished to leave she cried so grievously that it was amazing.

And soon after, an angel came and commanded our Lady and Joseph to go from the country of Bethlehem into Egypt. Then this creature went forth with our Lady, finding her lodging day by day with great reverence, with many sweet thoughts and high meditations, and also high contemplations, sometimes continuing weeping for two hours and often longer without ceasing when in mind of our Lord's passion, sometimes for her own sin, sometimes for the sin of the people, sometimes for the souls in purgatory, sometimes for those that are in poverty or in any distress, for she wanted to comfort them all.

Sometimes she wept very abundantly and violently out of desire for the bliss of heaven, and because she was being kept from it for so long. Then this creature longed very much to be delivered out of this wretched world. Our Lord Jesus Christ said to her mind that she should remain and languish in love, 'For I have ordained you to kneel before the Trinity to pray for the whole world, for many hundred thousand souls shall be saved by your prayers.

And therefore, daughter, ask what you wish, and I shall grant you what you ask.'

This creature said, 'Lord, I ask for mercy and preservation from everlasting damnation for me and for all the world. Chastise us here as you wish and in purgatory, and of your high mercy keep us from damnation.'

Chapter 8

Another time, while this creature lay [1] in her prayer, the Mother of Mercy appeared to her and said, 'Ah, daughter – blessed may you be – your seat is made ready in heaven before my son's knee, and whom you wish to have with you.'

Then her blessed son asked, 'Daughter, whom will you have as companion with you?'

'My beloved lord, I ask for my spiritual father, Master R.' [2]

'Why do you ask for him more than your own father or your husband?'

'Because I can never pay him back for his goodness to me, and the gracious trouble that he has taken in hearing my confession.'

'I grant you your wish for him, and yet your father shall be saved, and your husband too, and all your children.'

Then this creature said, 'Lord, since you have forgiven me my sin, I make you my executor of all the good works that you work in me. In praying, in thinking, in weeping, in going on pilgrimage, in fasting, or in speaking any good word, it is fully my will that you give half to Master R. to the increase of his merit, as if he did these things himself. And the other half, Lord, spread on your friends and your enemies, and on my friends and my enemies, for I will have only yourself for my reward.'

'Daughter, I shall be a true executor to you and fulfil all of your will, and because of your great charity that you have to comfort all your fellow Christians, you shall have double reward in heaven.'

Chapter 9

Another time, as this creature prayed to God that she might live in chastity by her husband's permission, Christ said to her mind, 'You must fast on Friday both from meat and drink, and you shall have your wish before Whit Sunday, for I shall suddenly slay [all sexual desire in][1] your husband.'

Then on the Wednesday of Easter week,[2] when her husband wanted to have intercourse with her, as he was used to before, and when he was coming near to her, she said, 'Jesus, help me,' and he had no power to touch her at that time in that way, nor ever after that with carnal knowledge.

It so happened one Friday before Whitsun Eve, as this creature was in the church of St Margaret at N. hearing mass, she heard a great and dreadful noise. She was greatly dismayed, very much fearing public opinion, which said God should take vengeance upon her. She knelt there, holding her head down, and with her book in her hand, praying to our Lord Christ Jesus for grace and for mercy. Suddenly – from the highest part of the church vault, from under the base of the rafter – there fell down on her head and on her back a stone which weighed three pounds, and a short end of a beam weighing six pounds, so that she thought her back was broken in pieces, and she was afraid that she would be dead in a little while. Soon after she cried, 'Jesus, mercy,' and immediately her pain was gone.

A good man called John of Wereham,[3] seeing this marvel and supposing that she had been severely injured, came and pulled her by the sleeve and said, 'How are you feeling, ma'am?'

This creature – entirely well and in one piece – thanked him for his kindness, all the time marvelling and greatly amazed that she now felt no pain and had felt so much a little before. Nor did she feel any pain for twelve weeks afterwards. Then the spirit of God said to her soul, 'Take this for a great miracle, and if people will not believe this, I shall work a great many more.'

A worshipful doctor of divinity called Master Aleyn, a White

Friar,[4] hearing of this miraculous event, inquired of this creature about the whole manner of this occurrence. He – desiring the working of God to be glorified – got the same stone that fell upon her back and weighed it, and then he got the beam-end that fell upon her head, which one of the keepers of the church had put on the fire to burn.

And this worshipful doctor said it was a great miracle, and our Lord was highly to be glorified for preserving this creature against the malice of her enemy, and he told it to many people and many people greatly glorified God in this creature. And also many people would not believe it, but preferred to believe it was more a token of wrath and vengeance than of mercy or favour.

Chapter 10

Soon after, this creature was moved in her soul to go and visit certain places for spiritual health, in as much as she was cured; and she could not without the consent of her husband. She asked her husband to grant her leave and he, fully believing it was the will of God, soon consented, and they went together to such places as she was inclined.

And then our Lord Christ Jesus said to her, 'My servants greatly desire to see you.'

Then she was welcomed and made much of in various places, and because of this she had a great fear of vainglory and was much afraid. Our merciful Lord Christ Jesus – worshipped be his name – said to her, 'Don't be afraid, daughter – I shall take vainglory from you. For they that honour you honour me; they that despise you despise me, and I shall chastise them for it. I am in you, and you in me.[1] And they that hear you, they hear the voice of God. Daughter, there is no man so sinful alive on earth that, if he will give up his sin and do as you advise, then such grace as you promise him I will confirm for love of you.' Then her husband and she went on to York and to other different places.

Chapter 11

It happened one Friday, Midsummer Eve,[1] in very hot weather – as this creature was coming from York carrying a bottle of beer in her hand, and her husband a cake tucked inside his clothes against his chest – that her husband asked his wife this question: 'Margery, if there came a man with a sword who would strike off my head unless I made love with you as I used to do before, tell me on your conscience – for you say you will not lie – whether you would allow my head to be cut off, or else allow me to make love with you again, as I did at one time?'

'Alas, sir,' she said, 'why are you raising this matter, when we have been chaste for these past eight weeks?'

'Because I want to know the truth of your heart.'

And then she said with great sorrow, 'Truly, I would rather see you being killed, than that we should turn back to our uncleanness.'

And he replied, 'You are no good wife.'

And then she asked her husband what was the reason that he had not made love to her for the last eight weeks, since she lay with him every night in his bed. And he said that he was made so afraid when he would have touched her, that he dared do no more.

'Now, good sir, mend your ways and ask God's mercy, for I told you nearly three years ago that you[r desire for sex] would suddenly be slain – and this is now the third year, and I hope yet that I shall have my wish. Good sir, I pray you to grant what I shall ask, and I shall pray for you to be saved through the mercy of our Lord Jesus Christ, and you shall have more reward in heaven than if you wore a hair-shirt or wore a coat of mail as a penance. I pray you, allow me to make a vow of chastity at whichever bishop's hand that God wills.'

'No,' he said, 'I won't allow you to do that, because now I can make love to you without mortal sin, and then I wouldn't be able to.'

Then she replied, 'If it be the will of the Holy Ghost to fulfil what I have said, I pray God that you may consent to this; and if it be not the will of the Holy Ghost, I pray God that you never consent.'

Then they went on towards Bridlington and the weather was extremely hot, this creature all the time having great sorrow and great fear for her chastity. And as they came by a cross her husband sat down under the cross, calling his wife to him and saying these words to her: 'Margery, grant me my desire, and I shall grant you your desire. My first desire is that we shall still lie together in one bed as we have done before; the second, that you shall pay my debts before you go to Jerusalem; and the third, that you shall eat and drink with me on Fridays as you used to do.'

'No, sir,' she said, 'I will never agree to break my Friday fast as long as I live.'

'Well,' he said, 'then I'm going to have sex with you again.'

She begged him to allow her to say her prayers, and he kindly allowed it. Then she knelt down beside a cross in the field and prayed in this way, with a great abundance of tears: 'Lord God, you know all things. You know what sorrow I have had to be chaste for you in my body all these three years, and now I might have my will and I dare not, for love of you. For if I were to break that custom of fasting from meat and drink on Fridays which you commanded me, I should now have my desire. But, blessed Lord, you know I will not go against your will, and great is my sorrow now unless I find comfort in you. Now, blessed Jesus, make your will known to my unworthy self, so that I may afterwards follow and fulfil it with all my might.'

And then our Lord Jesus Christ with great sweetness spoke to this creature, commanding her to go again to her husband and pray him to grant her what she desired: 'And he shall have what he desires. For, my beloved daughter, this was the reason why I ordered you to fast, so that you should the sooner obtain your desire, and now it is granted to you. I no longer wish you to fast, and therefore I command you in the name of Jesus to eat and drink as your husband does.'

Then this creature thanked our Lord Jesus Christ for his grace and his goodness, and afterwards got up and went to her husband, saying to him, 'Sir, if you please, you shall grant me my desire, and you shall have your desire. Grant me that you will not come into my bed, and I grant you that I will pay your debts before I go to Jerusalem.[2] And make my body free to God, so that you never make any claim on me requesting any conjugal debt after this day as long as you live – and I shall eat and drink on Fridays at your bidding.'

Then her husband replied to her, 'May your body be as freely available to God as it has been to me.'

This creature thanked God greatly, rejoicing that she had her desire, praying her husband that they should say three paternosters in worship of the Trinity for the great grace that had been granted them. And so they did, kneeling under a cross, and afterwards they ate and drank together in great gladness of spirit. This was on a Friday, on Midsummer's Eve.

Then they went on to Bridlington and also to many other places, and spoke with God's servants, both anchorites and recluses, and many other of our Lord's lovers, with many worthy clerics, doctors and bachelors of divinity as well, in many different places. And to various people amongst them this creature revealed her feelings and her contemplations, as she was commanded to do, to find out if there were any deception in her feelings.

Chapter 12

This creature was sent by our Lord to divers places of religion, and amongst them she came to a place of monks, where she was very welcome for the love of our Lord, except that there was a monk, who held great office in that place, who despised her and set no value on her at all. Nevertheless she was seated at mealtime with the abbot, and frequently during the meal she uttered many good words as God would put them into her mind – the same monk who had so despised her being present with many others to hear what she would say. And through her conversation his feelings began to incline strongly towards her, and he greatly savoured her words. And so afterwards this monk came to her – she being in church and he also at the time – and said, 'I hear it said that God speaks to you.[1] I pray you to tell me whether I shall be saved or not, and in what sins I have most displeased God, for I will not believe in you unless you can tell me what my sins are.'

This creature said to the monk, 'Go to your mass, and if I may weep for you, I hope to have grace for you.'

He followed her advice and went to his mass. She wept amazingly for his sins. When mass was ended, this creature said to our Lord Christ Jesus, 'Blessed Lord, what answer shall I give to this man?'

'My beloved daughter, say in the name of Jesus that he has sinned in lechery, in despair, and in the keeping of worldly goods.'

'Ah, gracious Lord, this is hard for me to say. He will cause me much shame if I tell him any lie.'

'Don't be afraid, but speak boldly in my name – in the name of Jesus – for they are not lies.'

And then she said again to our Lord Jesus Christ, 'Good Lord, shall he be saved?'

'Yes,' said our Lord Jesus, 'if he will give up his sin and follow your advice. Charge him to give up his sin – and be shriven of it – and also the office that he has outside.'

Then the monk came back: 'Margery, tell me my sins.'

She said, 'I beg you, sir, do not ask after them, for I undertake that your soul shall be saved, if you will follow my advice.'

'Truly, I will not believe you unless you tell me my sins.'

'Sir, I understand that you have sinned in lechery, in despair, and in the keeping of worldly goods.'

Then the monk stood still, somewhat abashed, and afterwards he said, 'Say whether I have sinned with wives or with single women?'

'Sir, with wives.'

Then he said, 'Shall I be saved?'

'Yes, sir, if you will follow my advice. Sorrow for your sin, and I will help you to sorrow. Be shriven of it and give it up with your whole will. Leave the office that you hold outside,[2] and God shall give you grace for love of me.'

The monk took her by the hand and led her into a beautiful room, gave her a great dinner, and afterwards gave her gold to pray for him. And so she took her leave at that time.

Another time, when the creature came again to the same place, the said monk had given up his office at her advice, and was turned from his sin, and made sub-prior of the place, a man of good conduct and disposition – God be thanked – and he gave this creature a great welcome and highly blessed God that he ever saw her.

Chapter 13

On one occasion, when this creature was at Canterbury in the church amongst the monks, she was greatly despised and reproved because she wept so much – both by the monks and priests, and by secular men, nearly all day, both morning and afternoon – and so much so that her husband went away from her as if he had not known her, and left her alone among them, choose how she might, for no further comfort did she have from him that day.

So an old monk, who had been treasurer to the Queen when he was in secular clothes, a powerful man and greatly feared by many people,[1] took her by the hand saying to her, 'What can you say of God?'

'Sir,' she said, 'I will both speak of him and hear of him,' repeating to the monk a story from scripture.

The monk said, 'I wish you were enclosed in a house of stone,[2] so that no one should speak with you.'

'Ah, sir,' she said, 'you should support God's servants, and you are the first that hold against them – our Lord amend you.'

Then a young monk said to this creature, 'Either you have the Holy Ghost or else you have a devil within you, for what you are speaking here to us is Holy Writ, and that you do not have of yourself.'

Then this creature said, 'I pray you, sir, give me leave to tell you a tale.'

Then people said to the monk, 'Let her say what she wants.'

And then she said, 'There was once a man who had sinned greatly against God and, when he was shriven, his confessor enjoined him as part of his penance that he should for one year hire men to chide him and reprove him for his sins, and he should give them silver for their labour. And one day he came amongst many great men, such as are here now – God save you all – and stood among them as I now stand amongst you, they despising him as you do me, the man all the while laughing and smiling and having good sport at their words. The chief among them said to the man, "Why are you laughing, you wretch, when you are being greatly despised?"

"Ah, sir, I have great cause to laugh, because I have for many days been taking silver from my purse and hiring men to chide me for remission of my sin, and today I can keep my silver in my purse, I thank you all."

'Right so I say to you, worshipful sirs. While I was at home in my own part of the country – day by day with great weeping and mourning – I sorrowed because I did not have any of the shame, scorn and contempt that I deserved. I thank you all highly, sirs, for what, morning and afternoon, I have received today in rightful measure – blessed be God for it.'

Then she went out of the monastery, they following and crying upon her, 'You shall be burnt, you false Lollard![3] Here is a cartful of thorns ready for you, and a barrel to burn you with!'

And the creature stood outside the gates of Canterbury – for it was in the evening – with many people wondering at her.

Then people said, 'Take her and burn her!'

And the creature stood still, her body trembling and quaking dreadfully – without any comfort in this world – and she did not know where her husband had gone.

Then she prayed in her heart to our Lord, thinking to herself in this way: 'I came to this place, Lord, for love of you. Blessed Lord, help me and have mercy on me.'

And then, after she had made her prayers in her heart to our Lord, there came two handsome young men and said to her, 'Are you neither a heretic nor a Lollard?'

And she said, 'No, sirs, I am neither heretic nor Lollard.'

Then they asked her where her inn was. She said she didn't know in which street, but anyway it would be at a German man's house. Then these two young men escorted her home to her lodgings and were very nice to her, asking her to pray for them – and there she found her husband.

And many people in N. had maligned her while she was away, and slandered her in respect of many things that she was supposed to have done.

Then after this she was very much at rest in her soul for a long while, and had high contemplation day by day, and many a holy speech and confabulation with our Lord Jesus Christ both morning and afternoon, with many sweet tears of high devotion so abundantly and continually that it was a marvel that her eyes endured, or that her heart could last without being consumed with the ardour of love [4] which was kindled with the holy converse of our

Lord, when he said to her many times, 'Beloved daughter, love me with all your heart, for I love you with all my heart and with all the might of my Godhead, for you were a chosen soul without beginning in my sight and a pillar of Holy Church.[5] My merciful eyes are ever upon you. It would be impossible for you to suffer the scorn and contempt that you will have, were it not for my grace supporting you.'

Chapter 14

Then this creature thought it was a joyous thing to be reproved for God's love. It was great solace and comfort to her when she was chided and scolded for the love of Jesus, for reproving sin, for speaking of virtue, for conversing about scripture, which she learned in sermons and by talking with clerks. She imagined to herself what death she might die for Christ's sake. She thought she would have liked to be slain for God's love but feared the point of death, and therefore she imagined for herself the most easy death, as she thought, because she feared her lack of fortitude – and that was to be tied at her head and her feet to a stake, and her head to be struck off with a sharp axe, for the love of God.

Then our Lord said in her mind, 'I thank you, daughter, that you would be willing to suffer death for my love, for as often as you think so, you shall have the same reward in heaven as if you had suffered that same death. And yet no man shall slay you, nor fire burn you, nor water drown you, nor winds harm you, for I may not forget you and how you are written upon my hands and my feet[1] – I am well pleased with the pains that I have suffered for you. I shall never be angry with you, but I shall love you without end. Though all the world be against you, don't be afraid, for they cannot understand you. I swear to your mind, that if it were possible for me to suffer pain again as I have done before, I would rather suffer as much pain as I ever did for your soul alone, rather than that you should be separated from me without end. And therefore, daughter, just as you see the priest take the child at the font and dip it in the water and wash it from original sin, just so shall I wash you in my precious blood from all your sin.

'And though I sometimes withdraw the feeling of grace from you, either in speaking or in weeping, do not be frightened at this, for I am a hidden God in you,[2] so you should have no vainglory, and should recognize that you may not have tears or spiritual conversing except when God will send them to you, for they are the free gifts of God, distinct from your merit, and he may give them to whom he wishes, and do you no wrong.

'And therefore take them meekly and thankfully when I send them, and suffer patiently when I withdraw them, and seek diligently until you get them, for tears of compunction, devotion and compassion are the highest gifts, and the most secure, that I give on earth.[3]

'And what more should I do for you, unless I were to take your soul out of your body and put it in heaven, and that I will not do yet. Nevertheless, wheresoever God is, heaven is; and God is in your soul, and many an angel is round about your soul to guard it both night and day. For when you go to church, I go with you; when you sit at your meal, I sit with you; when you go to bed, I go with you; and when you go out of town, I go with you.

'Daughter, there was never child so meek to its father as I shall be to you, to help you and look after you. With my grace I sometimes behave towards you as I do with the sun. Sometimes, as you well know, the sun shines so that many people can see it, and sometimes it is hidden behind a cloud so that it cannot be seen, and yet it is the sun nevertheless, in its heat and its brightness. And just so I proceed with you and with my chosen souls.

'Although it may be that you do not always weep when you please, my grace is nevertheless in you. Therefore I prove that you are a daughter indeed to me, and a mother also, a sister, a wife and a spouse, as witness the Gospel where our Lord says to his disciples: "He who does the will of my Father in heaven is both mother, brother, and sister to me." [4] When you strive to please me, then you are a true daughter; when you weep and mourn for my pain and my Passion, then you are a true mother having compassion on her child; when you weep for other people's sins and adversities, then you are a true sister; and when you sorrow because you are kept so long from the bliss of heaven, then you are a true spouse and wife, for it is the wife's part to be with her husband and to have no true joy until she has his company.'

Chapter 15

This creature, when our Lord had forgiven her her sin (as has been written before), had a desire to see those places where he was born, and where he suffered his Passion and where he died, together with other holy places where he was during his life, and also after his resurrection.

While she was feeling these desires, our Lord commanded her in her mind – two years before she went [1] – that she should go to Rome, to Jerusalem, and to Santiago de Compostela, and she would gladly have gone, but she had no money to go with.

And then she said to our Lord, 'Where shall I get the money to go to these holy places with?'

Our Lord replied to her, 'I shall send you enough friends in different parts of England to help you. And, daughter, I shall go with you in every country and provide for you. I shall lead you there and bring you back again in safety, and no Englishman shall die in the ship that you are in. I shall keep you from all wicked men's power. And, daughter, I say to you that I want you to wear white clothes and no other colour, for you shall dress according to my will.'

'Ah, dear Lord, if I go around dressed differently from how

other chaste women dress, I fear people will slander me.[2] They will say I am a hypocrite and ridicule me.'

'Yes, daughter, the more ridicule that you have for love of me, the more you please me.'

Then this creature dared not do otherwise than as she was commanded in her soul. And so she set off on her travels with her husband, for he was always a good and easygoing man with her. Although he sometimes – out of groundless fear – left her on her own for a while, yet he always came back to her again, and felt sorry for her, and spoke up for her as much as he dared for fear of other people. But all others that went along with her forsook her, and they most falsely accused her – through temptation of the devil – of things that she was never guilty of.

And so did one man in whom she greatly trusted, and who offered to travel with her, at which she was very pleased, believing he would give her support and help her when she needed it, for he had been staying a long time with an anchorite, a doctor of divinity and a holy man, and that anchorite was this woman's confessor.

And so his servant – at his own inward stirring – took his leave to travel with this creature; and her own maidservant went with her too, for as long as things went well with them and nobody said anything against them.

But as soon as people – through the enticing of our spiritual enemy, and by permission of our Lord – spoke against this creature because she wept so grievously, and said she was a false hypocrite and deceived people, and threatened her with burning, then this man, who was held to be so holy, and in whom she trusted so much, rebuked her with the utmost force and scorned her most foully, and would not go any further with her. Her maidservant, seeing discomfort on every side, grew obstreperous with her mistress. She would not do as she was told, or follow her mistress's advice. She let her mistress go alone into many fine towns and would not go with her.

And always, her husband was ready when everybody else let her down, and he went with her where our Lord would send her, always believing that all was for the best, and would end well when God willed.

And at this time, he took her to speak with the Bishop of Lincoln, who was called Philip,[3] and they stayed for three weeks before they could speak to him, for he was not at home at his palace. When the Bishop came home, and heard tell of how such a woman had waited so long to speak to him, he then sent for her in great haste to find out what she wanted. And then she came into his presence and greeted him, and he warmly welcomed her and said he had long wanted to speak with her, and he was very glad she had come. And so she asked him if she might speak with him in private and confide in him the secrets of her soul, and he appointed a convenient time for this.

When the time came, she told him all about her meditations and high contemplations, and other secret things, both of the living and the dead, as our Lord revealed to her soul.[4] He was very glad to hear them, and graciously allowed her to say what she pleased, and greatly commended her feelings and her contemplations, saying they were high matters and most devout matters, and inspired by the Holy Ghost, advising her seriously that her feelings should be written down.

And she said that it was not God's will that they should be written so soon, nor were they written for twenty years afterwards and more.

And then she said furthermore, 'My Lord, if it please you, I am commanded in my soul that you shall give me the mantle and the ring,[5] and clothe me all in white clothes. And if you clothe me on earth, our Lord Jesus Christ shall clothe you in heaven,[6] as I understand through revelation.'

Then the Bishop said to her, 'I will fulfil your desire if your husband will consent to it.'

Then she said to the Bishop, 'I pray you, let my husband come into your presence, and you shall hear what he will say.'

And so her husband came before the Bishop, and the Bishop asked him, 'John, is it your will that your wife shall take the mantle and the ring and that you live chaste, the two of you?'

'Yes, my lord,' he said, 'and in token that we both vow to live chaste I here offer my hands into yours,' and he put his hands between the Bishop's hands.

And the Bishop did no more with us on that day, except that he treated us very warmly and said we were most welcome.

Another day this creature came to a meal at the Bishop's request, and she saw him, before he sat down to his meal, give with his own hands to thirteen poor men thirteen pence and thirteen loaves, together with other food. And so he did every day. This creature was stirred to high devotion by this sight, and gave God praise and worship because he gave the Bishop grace to do these good deeds, with such abundant weeping that all the Bishop's household wondered what was wrong with her.

And afterwards she was seated at a meal with many worthy clerks and priests and squires of the Bishop's, and the Bishop himself very kindly sent things to her from his own table.

The clerks asked this creature many hard questions which, through the grace of Jesus, she resolved, so that her answers pleased the Bishop very much, and the clerks were astonished that she answered so readily and pregnantly.

When the Bishop had eaten, he sent for this creature to come into his chamber, saying to her: 'Margery, you and your husband spoke to me about my giving you the mantle and the ring, for which reason I have taken counsel, and I am advised not to profess you in such singular clothing without more consideration. You say, by the grace of God, you will go to Jerusalem. Therefore pray to God that it may wait until you come back from Jerusalem, when you have proved yourself and are recognized.'

The next day this creature went to church and prayed to God with all her spirit that she might know how she should be governed in this matter, and what answer she might give to the Bishop.

Our Lord Jesus Christ answered in her mind in this manner: 'Daughter, say to the Bishop that he is more afraid of the shames of this world than the perfect love of God.[7] Say to him, I would have excused him if he had fulfilled your will as much as I did the children of Israel, when I bade them borrow the goods of the people of Egypt and go away with them. Therefore, daughter, say to him that, though he will not do it now, it shall be done another time when God wills.'

And so she delivered her message to the Bishop of Lincoln as she had been commanded. Then he prayed her to go to the Archbishop of Canterbury – Arundel [8] – 'and pray him to grant leave to me, the Bishop of Lincoln,' to give her the mantle and the ring, inasmuch as she was not from his diocese. He made a pretence of having this reason through the advice of his clerks, because they had no love for this creature.

She said, 'Sir, I will go to my Lord of Canterbury very willingly, because of other reasons and other matters which I have to confide in his reverence. As for this present reason, I shall not go for that, for God does not wish me to ask the Archbishop about it.'

Then she took her leave of the Bishop of Lincoln, and he gave her twenty-six shillings and eight pence to buy her clothes with, and to pray for him.

Chapter 16

Then this creature went on to London with her husband, to Lambeth, where the Archbishop was in residence at that time. And as they came into the hall in the afternoon, there were many of the Archbishop's clerks about and other heedless men, both squires and yeomen, who swore many great oaths and spoke many thoughtless words, and this creature boldly rebuked them, and said they would be damned unless they left off their swearing and the other sins they practised. [1]

And with that there came forward a woman of that town dressed in a pilch [2] who reviled this creature, cursed her, and said very maliciously to her in this way: 'I wish you were in

Smithfield,[3] and I would bring a bundle of sticks to burn you with – it is a pity that you are alive.'

This creature stood still and did not answer, and her husband endured it with great pain and was very sorry to hear his wife so rebuked.

Then the Archbishop sent for this creature to come to him in his garden. When she came into his presence she made her obeisances to him as best she could, praying him, out of his gracious lordship, to grant her authority to choose her confessor and to receive communion every Sunday – if God would dispose her to this – under his letter and his seal throughout all his province. And he granted her with great kindness her whole desire without any silver or gold, nor would he let his clerks take anything for the writing or sealing of the letter.

When this creature found this grace in his sight, she was much comforted and strengthened in her soul, and so she told this worshipful lord about her manner of life, and such grace as God wrought in her mind and in her soul, in order to discover what he would say about it, and if he found any fault with either her contemplation or her weeping.

And she also told him the cause of her weeping, and the manner in which our Lord conversed with her soul. And he did not find fault at all, but approved her manner of life, and was very glad that our merciful Lord Christ Jesus showed such grace in our times – blessed may he be.

Then this creature spoke to him boldly about the correction of his household, saying with reverence, 'My lord, our Lord of all, Almighty God, has not given you your benefice and great worldly wealth in order to maintain those who are traitors to him, and those who slay him every day by the swearing of great oaths. You shall answer for them, unless you correct them or else put them out of your service.'

In the most meek and kindly way he allowed her to say what was on her mind and gave her a handsome answer, she supposing that things would then be better. And so their conversation continued until stars appeared in the sky. Then she took her leave, and her husband too.

Afterwards they went back to London, and many worthy men wanted to hear her converse, for her conversation was so much to do with the love of God that those who heard it were often moved to weep very sadly.

And so she had a very warm welcome there – and her husband because of her – for as long as they wished to stay in the city. Afterwards they returned to Lynn, and then this creature went to the anchorite at the Preaching Friars in Lynn and told him how she had been received, and how she had got on while she was travelling round the country. And he was very pleased at her homecoming and held it to be a great miracle, her coming and going to and fro.

And he said to her: 'I have heard much evil talk of you since you went away, and I have been strongly advised to leave you and not to associate with you any more, and great friendships are promised me on condition that I give you up. And I answered for you in this way: "If you were still the same as you were when we parted, I certainly dared say you were a good woman, a lover of God, and highly inspired with the Holy Ghost. I will not forsake her for any lady in this realm, if speaking with the lady means leaving her, for I would rather leave the lady and speak with Margery, if I might not do both, than do the contrary."' (Read first the twenty-first chapter and then this chapter after that.)

Chapter 17

One day long before this time, while this creature was bearing children and was newly delivered of a child, our Lord Christ Jesus said to her that she should bear no more children, and therefore he commanded her to go to Norwich.

And she said, 'Ah, dear Lord, how shall I go? I am feeling faint and weak.'

'Don't be afraid. I shall make you strong enough. I bid you go to the Vicar of St Stephen's,[1] and say that I greet him warmly, and that he is a high, chosen soul of mine, and tell him he greatly pleases me with his preaching, and tell him the secrets of your soul, and my counsels that I reveal to you.'

Then she made her way to Norwich, and came into his church on a Thursday a little before noon. And the Vicar was walking up and down with another priest who was his confessor, and who was still alive when this book was written. And this creature was dressed in black clothing at that time.

She greeted the Vicar, asking him if she could – in the afternoon, when he had eaten – speak with him for an hour or two of the love of God. He, lifting up his hands and blessing himself, said, 'Bless us! How could a woman occupy one or two hours with the love of our Lord? I shan't eat a thing till I find out what you can say of our Lord God in the space of an hour.'

Then he sat himself down in the church. She, sitting a little to one side, told him all the words which God had revealed to her in her soul. Afterwards she told him the whole manner of her life from her childhood, as closely as it would come to mind – how unkind and unnatural she had been towards our Lord Jesus Christ; how proud and vain she had been in her bearing; how obstinate against the laws of God, and how envious towards her fellow Christians; how she was chastised (later when it pleased our Lord Christ Jesus) with many tribulations and horrible temptations, and how afterwards she was fed and comforted with holy meditations, and specially in the memory of our Lord's Passion.

And, while she conversed on the Passion of our Lord Jesus Christ, she heard so terrible a melody that she could not bear it. Then this creature fell down, as if she had lost her bodily strength, and lay still for a long while, desiring to put it aside, and she could not. Then she knew indeed by her faith that there was great joy in heaven, where the least point of bliss surpasses without any comparison all the joy that ever might be thought or felt in this life. She was greatly strengthened in her faith and the more bold to tell the Vicar her feelings, which she had by revelations about both the living and the dead, and about his own self.

She told him how sometimes the Father of Heaven conversed with her soul as plainly and as certainly as one friend speaks to another through bodily speech. Sometimes the Second Person in Trinity, sometimes all Three Persons in Trinity and one substance in Godhead, spoke to her soul, and informed her in her faith and in his love – how she should love him, worship him and dread him – so excellently that she never heard any book, neither Hilton's book, nor Bride's book, nor *Stimulus Amoris*, nor *Incendium Amoris*, nor any other book that she ever heard read,[2] that spoke so exaltedly of the love of God as she felt highly working in her soul, if she could have communicated what she felt.

Sometimes our Lady spoke to her mind; sometimes St Peter, sometimes St Paul, sometimes St Katherine,[3] or whatever saint in heaven she was devoted to, appeared to her soul and taught her how she should love our Lord and how she should please him. These conversations were so sweet, so holy and so devout, that often this creature could not bear it, but fell down and twisted and wrenched her body about, and made remarkable faces and gestures, with vehement sobbings and great abundance of tears, sometimes saying 'Jesus, mercy,' and sometimes, 'I die.'

And therefore many people slandered her, not believing that it was the work of God, but that some evil spirit tormented her in her body or else that she had some bodily sickness.

Notwithstanding the protests and resentments of people against her, this holy man – Vicar of St Stephen's Church at Norwich, whom God had exalted and through marvellous works had shown and proved to be holy – he always took her side and supported her against her enemies as much as he could, after the time when she at God's command had told him about her manner of life and behaviour, for he faithfully believed that she was learned in the law of God, and endued with the grace of the Holy Ghost, to whom it belongs to inspire where he will. And though his voice be heard, it is not known in this world whence it comes or whither it goes.

This holy Vicar, after this time, was always confessor to this creature when she came to Norwich, and gave her communion with his own hands.

And when on one occasion she was admonished to appear before certain officers of the Bishop, to answer certain charges that would be made against her through the agitation of envious people, the good vicar, preferring the love of God above any shame in this world, went with her to hear her examination, and delivered her from the malice of her enemies. And then it was revealed to this creature that the good Vicar would live for seven more years after this, and then he would pass hence with great grace, and so he did, as she had foreseen.[4]

Chapter 18

This creature was charged and commanded in her soul that she should go to a White Friar in the same city of Norwich, who was called William Southfield,[1] a good man who lived a holy life, to reveal to him the grace that God had wrought in her, as she had done to the good Vicar before. She did as she was commanded and came to the friar one morning, and was with him in a chapel for a long time, and told him her meditations and what God had wrought in her soul, in order to know if she were deceived by any delusions or not.

This good man, the White Friar, all the time that she told him of her feelings, held up his hands and said, 'Jesus, mercy, and thanks be to Jesus.'

'Sister,' he said, 'have no fear about your manner of life, for it is the Holy Ghost plentifully working his grace in your soul. Thank him highly of his goodness, for we are all bound to thank him for you, who now in our times inspires you with his grace, to the help and comfort of all of us who are supported by your prayers and by others such as you. And we are preserved from many misfortunes and troubles which we should deservedly suffer for our trespasses, were there not such good creatures among us. Blessed be Almighty God for his goodness.

'And therefore, sister, I advise you to dispose yourself to receive the gifts of God as lowly and meekly as you can, and put up no obstacle or objections against the goodness of the Holy Ghost, for he may give his gifts where he will, and the unworthy he makes worthy, the sinful he makes righteous. His mercy is always ready for us unless the fault be in ourselves, for he does not dwell in a body subject to sin.[2] He flies from all false pretence and falsehood; he asks of us a low, a meek, and a contrite heart, with a good will.[3] Our Lord says himself, "My spirit shall rest upon a meek man, a contrite man, and one who fears my words."[4]

'Sister, I trust to our Lord that you have these conditions either in your will or in your affections or else in both, and I do not consider that our Lord allows to be endlessly deceived those who place their trust in him, and seek and desire nothing but him only, as I hope you do. And therefore believe fully that our Lord loves you and is working his grace in you. I pray God increase it and continue it to his everlasting worship, for his mercy.'

The said creature was much comforted both in body and in soul by this good man's words, and greatly strengthened in her faith.

And then she was commanded by our Lord to go to an anchoress in the same city who was called Dame Julian.[5] And so she did, and told her about the grace, that God had put into her soul, of compunction, contrition, sweetness and devotion, compassion with holy meditation and high contemplation, and very many holy speeches and converse that our Lord spoke to her soul, and also many wonderful revelations, which she described to the anchoress to find out if there were any deception in them, for the anchoress was expert in such things and could give good advice.

The anchoress, hearing the marvellous goodness of our Lord, highly thanked God with all her heart for his visitation, advising this creature to be obedient to the will of our Lord and fulfil with all her might whatever he put into her soul, if it were not against the worship of God and the profit of her fellow Christians. For if it were, then it were not the influence of a good spirit, but rather of an evil spirit. 'The Holy Ghost never urges a thing against charity, and if he did, he would be contrary to his own self, for he is all charity. Also he moves a soul to all chasteness, for chaste livers are called the temple of the Holy Ghost,[6] and the Holy Ghost makes a soul stable and steadfast in the right faith and the right belief.

'And a double man in soul is always unstable and unsteadfast in all his ways.[7] He that is forever doubting is like the wave of the sea which is moved and borne about with the wind, and that man is not likely to receive the gifts of God.[8]

'Any creature that has these tokens may steadfastly believe that the Holy Ghost dwells in his soul. And much more, when God visits a creature with tears of contrition, devotion or compassion, he may and ought to believe that the Holy Ghost is in his soul. St Paul says that the Holy Ghost asks for us with mourning and weeping unspeakable;[9] that is to say, he causes us to ask and pray with mourning and weeping so plentifully that the tears may not be numbered. No evil spirit may give these tokens, for St Jerome says that tears torment the devil more than do the pains of hell.[10] God and the devil are always at odds, and they shall never dwell together in one place, and the devil has no power in a man's soul.

'Holy Writ says that the soul of a righteous man is the seat of God,[11] and so I trust, sister, that you are. I pray God grant you perseverance. Set all your trust in God and do not fear the talk of the world, for the more contempt, shame and reproof that you have in this world, the more is your merit in the sight of God.[12] Patience is necessary for you, for in that shall you keep your soul.'[13]

Great was the holy conversation that the anchoress and this

creature had through talking of the love of our Lord Jesus Christ for the many days that they were together.

This creature revealed her manner of life to many a worthy clerk, to honoured doctors of divinity, both religious men and others of secular habit, and they said that God wrought great grace in her and bade her not to be afraid – there was no delusion in her manner of living. They counselled her to be persevering, for their greatest fear was that she would turn aside and not keep her perfection. She had so many enemies and so much slander, that it seemed to them that she might not bear it without great grace and a mighty faith.

Others who had no knowledge of her manner of behaving, except through outward observations alone or else through the gossip of other people perverting the judgement of truth, spoke very badly of her and caused her to have much more enmity and distress than she would otherwise have done, if it had not been for their evil talk. Nevertheless, the anchorite of the Preaching Friars in Lynn – who was her principal confessor, as is written before – took the responsibility on his own soul that her feelings were good and sure, and that there was no deception in them. And through the spirit of prophecy he told her that when she went to Jerusalem she would have a great deal of trouble with her maidservant, and that our Lord would try her severely and test her very strictly.

Then she replied, 'Ah, good sir, what shall I do when I am far from home and in strange countries, and my maidservant is against me? My physical comfort would then be all gone, and I would not know where to get spiritual comfort from any confessor such as you are.'

'Daughter, don't be afraid, for our Lord will comfort you himself, whose comfort surpasses all others and, when all your friends have forsaken you, our Lord shall cause a broken-backed man to escort you wherever you wish to go.'

And it happened just as the anchorite had prophesied in every detail and as – I trust – will be written more fully later on.

Then this creature said to the anchorite in a kind of complaining way, 'Good sir, what shall I do? He that is my confessor in your absence is very sharp with me. He won't believe my feelings; he sets no store by them at all; he considers them merely trifles and jokes, and that is most painful to me, for I am very fond of him and would gladly follow his advice.'

The anchorite, answering her, said, 'It is no wonder, daughter, that he can't believe in your feelings so soon. He knows very well that you have been a sinful woman, and therefore he thinks that God would not be on terms of homely familiarity with you in so short a time. After your conversion I would not, for all this world, be so sharp with you as he is. God – because of your deservingness – has appointed him to be your scourge, and he deals with you as a smith with a file makes the iron bright and clear to the sight, which before appeared rusty, dark and nastily coloured. The sharper he is to you the more clearly your soul shines in God's sight, and God has ordained me to be your spiritual fosterer and your comfort. Be humble and meek, and thank God for both the one and the other.'

. . . On one occasion,[14] before this creature went to her prayers to discover what answer she should give to the widow, she was commanded in her spirit to bid the widow leave her current confessor, if she would please God, and go to the anchorite at the Preaching Friars in Lynn and tell him all about her life. When this creature gave this message, the widow would not believe her words, nor her confessor either, unless God would give her the same grace that he gave this creature, and she ordered this creature that she should not come to her place any more. And because this creature told her that she had to feel love and affection for her confessor, therefore the widow said it would have been a good thing for this creature if her love and affection were directed as *hers* were.

Then our Lord commanded this creature to have a letter written and send it to her. A master of divinity wrote a letter at the request of this creature and sent it to the widow, with the following clauses: one clause was that the widow should never have the grace that this creature had; another was that, although this creature were never to come inside her house, it would greatly please God.

Our Lord said again to this creature, 'It would be more profitable for her than this whole world if her love were fixed as yours is. And I command you to go to her confessor, and tell him that, because he will not believe your words, they shall be separated without him noticing, and those who are not confided in by her shall know this before he does, whether he likes it or not. So, daughter, you may see here how hard it is to separate a man from his own will.'

And this whole series of events fell out indeed, as this creature had foretold, twelve years afterwards. Then this creature suffered a great deal of tribulation and unhappiness because she said these words, as our Lord commanded her to. And she was always increasing in the love of God and was bolder than she was before.

Chapter 19

Before this creature went to Jerusalem, our Lord sent her to a very respectable lady, so that she should speak to her confidentially and do his errand to her. The lady would not speak with her unless her confessor were present, and she said she was happy with this. And then, when the lady's confessor had come, the three of them went into a chapel together, and then this creature said with great reverence and many tears, 'Madam, our Lord Jesus Christ bade me tell you that your husband is in purgatory, and that you shall be saved, but that it will be a long time before you get to heaven.'

And then the lady was displeased, and said her husband was a good man – she didn't believe he was in purgatory. Her confessor sided with this creature, and said it might very well be as she said, and backed up her words with many holy tales.

And then this lady sent her daughter, and others of her household with her, to the anchorite who was principal confessor to this creature, in order that he should give her up, or else he would lose her friendship. The anchorite said to the messengers that he would not forsake this creature for any man on earth, for to such persons as would inquire of him about her manner of behaving and what he thought of her, he said she was God's own servant, and he also said she was the tabernacle of God.

And the anchorite said to her, to strengthen her in her faith, 'Though God should take from you all tears and conversings, believe nevertheless that God loves you and that you shall be sure of heaven for what you have had before, for tears with love are the greatest gift that God may give on earth, and all men that love God ought to thank him for you.'

Also, there was a widow who asked this creature to pray for her husband and discover if he had any need of help. And as this creature prayed for him, she was answered that his soul would be thirty years in purgatory, unless he had better friends on earth. She told this to the widow and said, 'If you give three or four pounds for him in masses and in alms-giving to poor folk, you will highly please God and greatly ease the soul.'

The widow took little heed of her words and let it pass. Then this creature went to the anchorite and told him how she had felt, and he said the feeling was from God and the deed in itself was good, even though the soul had no need of it, and advised that it should be fulfilled. Then this creature told this matter to her confessor, in order that he should speak to the widow, and so for a long time this creature heard no more of this matter.

Afterwards our Lord Jesus Christ said to this creature, 'That thing I ordered should be done for the soul is not done. Ask now your confessor.'

And so she did, and he said it was not done.

She replied, 'My Lord Jesus Christ told me as much just now.'

Chapter 20

One day as this creature was hearing mass, a young man and a good priest was holding up the sacrament in his hands over his head, and the sacrament shook and fluttered to and fro just as a dove flutters her wings. And when he held up the chalice with the precious sacrament, the chalice moved to and fro as if it would have fallen out of his hands. When the consecration was done, this creature marvelled at the stirring and moving of the blessed sacrament, wanting to see more consecrations and looking to see if it would do so again.

Then our Lord Jesus Christ said to the creature, 'You will not see it any more in this way; therefore thank God that you have seen it. My daughter Bridget never saw me in this way.'[1]

Then this creature said in her thought, 'Lord, what does this betoken?'

'It betokens vengeance.'

'Ah, good Lord, what vengeance?'

Then our Lord replied to her, 'There shall be an earthquake.[2] Tell whoever you wish, in the name of Jesus. For in truth I tell you, just as I spoke to St Bridget, just so I speak to you, daughter, and I tell you truly that every word that is written in Bridget's book is true, and through you shall be recognized as truth indeed. And you will succeed, daughter, in spite of all your enemies; the more envy they have of you for my grace the better shall I love you. I would not be righteous unless I loved you, for I know you better than you do yourself, whatever people say about you. You say I have great patience with people's sins, and you say truly, but if you saw people's sins as I do, you would marvel much more at my patience, and sorrow much more at people's sin, than you do.'

Then the creature said, 'Alas, beloved Lord, what shall I do for the people?'[3]

Our Lord answered, 'It is enough for you to do as you do.'

Then she prayed, 'Merciful Lord Christ Jesus, in you is all

mercy and grace and goodness. Have mercy, pity and compassion on them. Show your mercy and your goodness upon them, help them, send them true contrition, and let them never die in their sin.'

Our merciful Lord said, 'I may do no more for them in my righteousness, daughter, than I do. I send them preaching and teaching, pestilence and battles, hunger and famine, loss of their goods, with great sickness and many other tribulations, and they will not believe my words nor will they recognize my visitation. And therefore I shall say to them that "I made my servants pray for you, and you despised their deeds and their lives."'

Chapter 21

At the time that this creature had revelations, our Lord said to her, 'Daughter, you are with child.'[1]

She replied, 'Ah, Lord, what shall I do about looking after my child?'

Our Lord said, 'Daughter, don't be afraid, I shall arrange for it to be looked after.'

'Lord, I am not worthy to hear you speak, and still to make love with my husband, even though it is great pain and great distress to me.'

'Therefore it is no sin for you, daughter, because it is reward and merit instead for you, and you will not have any the less grace, for I wish you to bring me forth more fruit.'

Then the creature said, 'Lord Jesus, this manner of life belongs to your holy maidens.'

'Yes, daughter, but rest assured that I love wives also, and specially those wives who would live chaste if they might have their will, and do all they can to please me as you do. For though the state of maidenhood be more perfect and more holy than the state of widowhood, and the state of widowhood more perfect than the state of wedlock, yet I love you, daughter, as much as any maiden in the world.[2] No man may prevent me from loving whom I wish and as much as I wish, for love, daughter, quenches all sin. And therefore ask of me the gifts of love. There is no gift so holy as is the gift of love, nor anything so much to be desired as love, for love may gain what it desires. And therefore, daughter, you may please God no better than to think continually on his love.'

Then this creature asked our Lord Jesus how she should best love him, and our Lord said, 'Be mindful of your wickedness, and think of my goodness.'

She replied, 'I am the most unworthy creature that you ever showed grace to on earth.'

'Ah, daughter,' said our Lord, 'do not be afraid. I take no notice of what a man has been, but I take heed of what he will be.[3] Daughter, you have despised yourself; therefore you will never be despised by God. Bear in mind, daughter, what Mary Magdalene was, Mary of Egypt,[4] St Paul, and many other saints that are now in heaven, for of unworthy, I make worthy, and of sinful, I make righteous. And so I have made you worthy to me, once loved and evermore loved by me. There is no saint in heaven that you wish to speak with, but he shall come to you. Whom God loves, they love. When you please God, you please his mother and all the saints in heaven. Daughter, I take witness of my mother, of all the angels in heaven, and of all the saints in heaven, that I love you with all my heart, and I may not forgo your love.'

Our Lord said then to his blessed mother, 'Blessed Mother, tell my daughter of the greatness of love I have for her.'

Then this creature lay still, weeping and sobbing as if her heart would burst for the sweetness of speech that our Lord spoke to her soul.

Immediately afterwards, the Queen of Mercy, God's mother, chatted to the soul of the creature, saying, 'My beloved daughter, I bring you sure tidings, bearing witness for my sweet son Jesus, with all angels and all saints in heaven who love you most highly.

Daughter, I am your mother, your lady and your mistress, to teach you in every way how you shall please God best.'

She taught this creature and informed her so marvellously that she was embarrassed to tell it to anybody, the matter was so high and so holy, except to the anchorite who was her principal confessor, for he was most knowledgeable in such things. And he charged this creature – by virtue of obedience – to tell him whatever she felt, and so she did.

Chapter 22

As this creature lay in contemplation, weeping bitterly in her spirit, she said to our Lord Jesus Christ, 'Ah, Lord, maidens are now dancing merrily in heaven. Shall I not do so? Because I am no virgin, lack of virginity is now great sorrow to me. I think I wish I had been killed as soon as I was taken from the font, so that I should never have displeased you, and then, blessed Lord, you would have had my virginity without end. Ah, dear God, I have not loved you all the days of my life, and I keenly regret that; I have run away from you, and you have run after me; I would fall into despair, and you would not let me.'

'Ah, daughter, how often have I told you that your sins are forgiven you and that we are united together [in love] without end? To me you are a love unlike any other, daughter, and therefore I promise you that you shall have a singular grace in heaven, daughter, and I promise you that I shall come to your end, at your dying, with my blessed mother, and my holy angels and twelve apostles, St Katherine, St Margaret and St Mary Magdalene, and many other saints that are in heaven, who greatly worship me for the grace that I give to you, your God, your Lord Jesus. You need fear no grievous pains in dying for you shall have your desire, which is to have your mind more on my Passion than on your own pain. You shall not fear the devil of hell, for he has no power over you. He fears you more than you do him. He is angry with you, because you torment him more with your weeping than all the fire in hell does; you win many souls from him with your weeping. And I have promised you that you should have no other purgatory than the slanderous talk of this world, for I have chastised you myself as I would, by many great fears and torments that you have had with evil spirits, both sleeping and waking, for many years. And therefore I shall preserve you at your end through my mercy, so that they shall have no power over you either in body or in soul. It is a great grace and miracle that you still have your wits, considering the vexation that you have had from them in the past.

'I have also, daughter, chastised you with the fear of my Godhead, and many times I have frightened you with great winds and storms, so that you thought vengeance would have fallen on you for sin. I have tested you by many tribulations, many great griefs and many grievous sicknesses, so that you have been anointed for death, and entirely through my grace you have escaped. Therefore don't be at all afraid, daughter, for with my own hands which were nailed to the cross I shall take your soul from your body with great joy and melody, with sweet smells and fragrances, and offer it to my father in heaven, where you shall see him face to face, dwelling with him without end.

'Daughter, you will be very welcome to my father, and to my mother, and to all my saints in heaven, for you have given them drink very many times with the tears of your eyes. All my holy saints shall rejoice at your coming home. You shall be fulfilled with every kind of love that you desire. Then you will bless the time that you were made and the body that has [dearly] redeemed you. He shall rejoice in you and you in him without end.

'Daughter, I promise you the same grace that I promised St Katherine, St Margaret, St Barbara,[1] and St Paul, in that if any person on earth until the Day of Judgement asks any boon of you and believes that God loves you, he shall have his boon or else something better. Therefore those who believe that God loves you shall be blessed without end. The souls in purgatory shall rejoice at your coming home, for they well know that God loves you specially. And men on earth shall rejoice in God for you, for he shall work much grace for you and make all the world to know that God loves you. You have been despised for my love, and therefore you shall be honoured for my love.

'Daughter, when you are in heaven you will be able to ask what you wish, and I shall grant you all your desire. I have told you before that you are a singular lover of God, and therefore you shall have a singular love in heaven, a singular reward and a singular honour. And because you are a maiden in your soul, I shall take you by the one hand in heaven, and my mother by the other, and so you shall dance in heaven with other holy maidens and virgins, for I may call you dearly bought and my own beloved darling. I shall say to you, my own blessed spouse, "Welcome to me, with every kind of joy and gladness, here to dwell with me and never to depart from me without end, but ever to dwell with me in joy and bliss, which no eye may see, nor ear hear, nor tongue tell, nor heart think, that I have ordained for you and for all my servants who desire to love and please me as you do."'

Chapter 23

There once came a vicar to this creature, asking her to pray for him and discover whether he would please God more by leaving his cure of souls and his benefice or by keeping it, because he thought he was of no use among his parishioners. The creature being in her prayers and having this matter in mind, Christ said to her spirit, 'Tell the vicar to keep his cure and his benefice, and be diligent in preaching and teaching to them in person, and sometimes to procure others to teach them my laws and my commandments, so that there is no fault on his part, and if they don't do any better, his reward shall be none the less for it.'

And so she gave her message as she was commanded, and the vicar still kept his cure.

As this creature was once in the Church of St Margaret in the choir, where a corpse was present, and he who was the husband of the dead woman while she was alive was there in good health to make an offering at mass, according to the custom of the place, our Lord said to this creature, 'Lo, daughter, the soul of this body is in purgatory, and he who was her husband is now in good health, and yet he shall be dead within a short time.' And so it happened, as she had felt by revelation.

Also, as this creature once lay in the choir at her prayers, a priest came to her and asked her to pray for a woman who lay at the point of death. As this creature prayed for her our Lord said to her, 'Daughter, it is very necessary to pray for her, because she has been a wicked woman, and she shall die.'

And she replied, 'Lord, as you love me, save her soul from damnation.' And then she wept with abundant tears for that soul. And our Lord granted her mercy for the soul, commanding her to pray for her.

This creature's confessor came to her, urging her to pray for a woman who lay at death's door, as was thought, and then our Lord said she would live and thrive, and so she did.

A good man who was a great friend to this creature, and very helpful to the poor, was seriously ill for many weeks on end. And people were very sorry on his account, for it was not thought he would ever live, his pain was so amazing in all his joints and all over his body. Our Lord Jesus said to her spirit, 'Daughter, don't be afraid for this man – he will live and get on very well.'

And so he lived for many years afterwards in good health and prosperity.

Another good man, who was a dyer, also lay ill, and when this creature prayed for him she was answered in her mind that he would linger a while and then he would die of his illness, and so he did a short time afterwards.

Also, a respectable woman and, as people believed, a holy woman, who was a special friend of this creature, was very ill, and many people thought she would die. Then, while this creature was praying for her, our Lord said, 'She shall not die these ten years, for after this you will celebrate together and have excellent talks, as you have had before.'

And so it was, in truth; this holy woman lived for many years afterwards. Many more such revelations this creature had in feeling; to write them all down would perhaps be to hinder more profitable things. These are written to show the homely intimacy and goodness of our merciful Lord Christ Jesus, and not to commend this creature.

These feelings and others like them, many more than can be written, both of living and of dying, of some to be saved, of some to be damned, were great pain and punishment to this creature. She would rather have suffered any bodily penance than these feelings, if she might have put them aside, such was the fear that she had of delusions and deceptions by her spiritual enemies. She sometimes had such great trouble with such feelings when they did not ring true to her understanding, that her confessor feared that she would fall into despair at them. And then, after her trouble and her great fear, it would be shown to her soul how the feelings should be understood.

Chapter 24

The priest who wrote down this book, in order to test this creature's feelings, asked her questions many different times about things that were to come – things of which the outcome was unsure and uncertain to anybody at that time – asking her, though she was loath and unwilling to do such things, to pray to God and discover when our Lord would visit her with devotion, what the outcome would be, and then truly, without any pretending, tell him how she felt, or else he would not have gladly written the book.

And so this creature, partly compelled by the fear that he would not otherwise have followed her intention in writing this book, did as he asked her and told him her feelings as to what would happen in such matters as he asked her about, if her feelings were true. And in this way he tested them for their truth. And yet he would not always give credence to her words, and that hindered him in the following way.

It happened once that a young man came to this priest, whom the priest had never seen before, bemoaning the poverty and trouble that had befallen him through bad luck, explaining the cause of his misfortune, and also saying he had taken holy orders to be a priest. Because of a little over-hastiness in defending himself – as he had no choice unless he was to be chased and killed by his enemies – he struck a man, or else two, as a result of which, as he said, they were dead or else likely to die. And so he had fallen into an irregular life and might not execute his orders without dispensation of the court of Rome, and for this reason he fled from his friends, and dared not go back to his part of the country for fear of being arrested for their deaths.

The said priest gave credence to the young man's story because he was a likeable person, handsome, well-favoured in looks and manner, sober in talk, priestly in bearing and dress. And feeling sorry for his trouble, and intending to get him some friends to relieve and comfort him, he went to a respectable burgess in Lynn, the equal of any mayor and a compassionate man, who was very ill and had been for a long time. The priest lamented to this man and to his wife, a very good woman, the bad luck of this young man, believing he would receive a generous donation, as he often had previously when he asked on behalf of others.

It so happened that the creature of whom this book is written was present there and heard how the priest put the young man's case and praised him. And she was very much moved in her spirit against that young man, and said they had many poor neighbours whom they knew well enough had great need to be helped and relieved, and it should rather be charity to help those whom they well knew to be well-disposed folk and their own neighbours than other strangers whom they did not know, for many speak and seem very fair outwardly to people's sight – God knows what they are in their souls!

The good man and his wife thought that she spoke very well, and therefore they would give him no charity. At that time the priest was very displeased with this creature, and when he met her alone he repeated how she had hindered him so that he could get no help for the young man, who was a well-disposed man, he thought, and he much commended his behaviour.

The creature said, 'Sir, God knows what his conduct is, for – as far as I know – I never saw him. And yet I have an understanding of what his conduct might be, and therefore, sir, if you will act according to my advice and to what I feel, let him choose and help himself as well as he can, and don't you get involved with him, for he will deceive you in the end.'

The young man was always going to see the priest, flattering him and saying that he had good friends in other places who would help him if they knew where he was – and that in a short time – and also they would thank those people who had supported him in his trouble. The priest, trusting that it would be as this young man told him, willingly lent him silver to help him out. The young man asked the priest to excuse him if he did not see him for two or three days, because he was going a little way away and would return shortly and bring him back his silver, truly. The priest, having confidence in his promise, was quite content, granting him love and leave until the day when he had promised to come back again.

When he was gone, the said creature, having understanding by feeling in her soul that our Lord would show that he was a dishonest man and would not come back any more, she, to prove whether her feeling was true or false, asked the priest where the young man was, that he had praised so much. The priest said he had gone a little way away, and he trusted that he would come back. She said she supposed that he would not see him any more, and nor did he ever again. And then he regretted that he had not done as she advised.

A short time after this happened, another dishonest rascal, an old man, came to the same priest and offered to sell him a breviary, a good little book. The priest went to the aforesaid creature, asking her to pray for him and find out whether God wanted him to buy the book or not, and while she prayed he encouraged the man as well as he could, and afterwards he came back to this creature and asked how she felt.

'Sir,' she said, 'don't buy any book from him, because he is not to be trusted, and that you will know soon enough if you get involved with him.'

Then the priest asked the man if he could see the book. The man said he hadn't got it on him. The priest asked how he came by it. He said he was executor to a priest who had been a relation of his, and who had charged him with disposing of it.

'Father,' said the priest (out of respect for the man's age), 'why do you offer me this book rather than other men or other priests, when there are many better-off priests in the church than I am, and I know very well that you never had any knowledge of me before this time?'

'Truly, sir,' he said, 'no more I had. All the same, I feel good will towards you, and also it was his will who owned it before that, if I knew any young priest whom I thought sober and well-disposed, he should have this book before any other man, and for a lower price than any other man, so that he might pray for him. And these reasons made me come to you rather than to another man.'

The priest asked where he lived.

'Sir,' he said, 'only five miles from this place in Pentney Abbey.' [1]

'I have been there,' said the priest, 'and I have not seen you.'

'No, sir,' he replied, 'I have only been there a little while, and now I have an allowance of food there, thanks be to God.'

The priest asked him if he might have a look at the book and see if they might come to an agreement.

He said, 'Sir, I hope to be here again next week and bring it with me and, sir, I promise that you shall have it before any other man if you like it.'

The priest thanked him for his good will, and so they parted, but the man never came to the priest afterwards, and then the priest well knew that the said creature's feeling was true.

Chapter 25

Here follows, furthermore, a very notable instance of the creature's feeling, and it is written down here for convenience, inasmuch as it is, in feeling, like the matters that have been written before, notwithstanding that it happened long after the matters that follow.

It happened in a notable town where there was one parish church and two chapels annexed, the chapels having and administering all sacraments, except christening and purifications, as allowed by the parson, who was a Benedictine monk sent from the house in Norwich, residing with three of his brethren in this notable town already mentioned.[1]

Through some of the parishioners' desiring to make the chapels like the parish church, pursuing a bull from the Court of Rome, much litigation and much unhappiness occurred between the prior, who was their parson and curate, and these parishioners who wanted to have fonts and purifications in the chapels, as in the parish church. And especially in the one chapel, which was the larger and finer, they wanted to have a font.[2]

A bull was pursued, in which a font was granted to the chapel, provided there was no derogation to the parish church. The bull was put in plea, and various days were spent in litigation to prove whether the font, if it were installed, would be derogation to the parish church or not. The parishioners who pursued the matter were in a very strong position and had the help of lords, and also, above all, they were rich and powerful men, respectable merchants, and had plenty of money, which in every necessity will lead to success – it is a pity that money should succeed before truth.

Nevertheless, the Prior who was their parson,[3] although he was poor, manfully withstood them, through the help of some of his parishioners who were his friends and loved the honour of their parish church. So long was this matter in plea that it began to irk them on both sides, and it was never any nearer to an end.

Then the matter was put to my Lord of Norwich – Alnwick[4] – to see if he might bring it to an end by agreement. He worked very diligently at this matter and, to make the peace, he offered the aforesaid parishioners a great deal of what they wanted, with certain conditions, so that those who held with the parson and with their parish church were very sorry, greatly fearing that those who sued to have a font would gain their desire and so make the chapel equal to the parish church.

Then the priest who afterwards wrote down this book went to the creature whom this treatise mentions, as he had done before in the time of plea, and asked her how she felt in her soul in this matter, whether they should have a font in the chapel or not.

'Sir,' said the creature, 'don't be afraid, for I understand in my soul that, though they should give a bushel of nobles,[5] they should not have it.'

'Ah, mother,' said the priest, 'my Lord Bishop of Norwich has offered it to them, with certain conditions, and they have time to consider whether to say yes or no, and therefore I am afraid they will not refuse it, but be very glad to have it.'

This creature prayed to God that his will might be fulfilled, and inasmuch as she had understood by revelation that they should not have it, she was the more bold to pray our Lord to withstand their intention and to deflate their boasting.

And so, as our Lord willed, they neither obeyed nor liked the conditions which were offered them, for they were completely confident of gaining their object through lordly influence and by process of law; and as God willed, they were disappointed in their intentions, and because they wanted to have everything, they lost everything.

And so – blessed may God be – the parish church still remained in its dignity and its degree as it had done for two hundred years before and more, and the inspiration of our Lord was by experience proved very true and sure in the said creature.

Chapter 26

When the time came [1] that this creature should visit those holy places where our Lord lived and died, as she had seen by revelation years before, she asked the parish priest of the town where she was living [2] to say on her behalf from the pulpit that, if there were any man or woman who claimed any debt against her husband or her, they should come and speak with her before she went, and she, with God's help, would settle up with each of them so that they would hold themselves content. And so she did.

Afterwards, she took leave of her husband and of the holy anchorite, who had told her before the sequence of her going and the great distress that she would suffer along the way and, when all her companions abandoned her, how a broken-backed man would escort her on her way in safety, through the help of our Lord. And so it happened indeed, as it shall be written afterwards.

Then she took her leave of Master Robert and asked him for his blessing, and so took leave of other friends. And then she went on her way to Norwich, and offered at the Trinity, and afterwards she went to Yarmouth, and offered at an image of our Lady,[3] and there she boarded her ship.

And next day they came to a large town called Zierikzee, where our Lord in his high goodness visited this creature with abundant tears of contrition for her own sins, and sometimes for other people's sins as well. And especially, she had tears of compassion at the memory of our Lord's Passion. And she received communion every Sunday, when time and place were convenient for it, with much weeping and violent sobbing, so that many people marvelled and wondered at the great grace that God worked in his creature.

This creature had eaten no meat[4] and drunk no wine for four years before she left England, and now her confessor directed her, by virtue of obedience, that she should both eat meat and drink wine, and so she did for a little while. Afterwards, she prayed to her confessor to excuse her if she ate no meat, and allow her to do as she wished for what time he pleased.

And soon after, because of prompting by some of her companions, her confessor was displeased because she ate no meat, and so were many of the company. And they were most annoyed because she wept so much and spoke all the time about the love and goodness of our Lord, as much at table as in other places. And so they rebuked her shamefully and chided her harshly, and said they would not put up with her as her husband did when she was at home in England.

And she replied meekly to them, 'Our Lord, Almighty God, is as great a lord here as in England, and I have as great cause to love him here as there – blessed may he be.'

At these words her companions were angrier than they were before, and their anger and unkindness were a matter of great unhappiness to this creature, for they were considered very good men, and she greatly desired their love, if she might have had it to the pleasure of God. And then she said to one of them specially, 'You cause me much shame and hurt.'

He replied, 'I pray God that the devil's death may overtake you soon and quickly,' and he said many more cruel words to her than she could repeat. And soon after, some of the company she trusted best, and also her own maidservant, said she should not accompany them any longer, and they said they would take her maidservant away from her so that she would not be prostituted in her company. And then one of them, who was looking after her money, very angrily left her a noble to go where she liked and shift for herself as well as she could – for with them, they said, she could stay no longer, and they abandoned her that night.

Then, on the next morning, one of her company came to her, a man who got on with her well, who asked her to go to his fellow pilgrims and behave meekly to them, and ask them if she might still travel with them until she came to Constance.

And so she did, and went on with them until she came to Constance with great distress and trouble, for they caused her much shame and reproof as they went along, in various places. They cut her gown so short that it only came a little below her knee, and made her put on some white canvas in a kind of sacking apron, so that she would be taken for a fool, and people would not make much of her or hold her in any repute. They made her sit at the end of the table below all the others, so that she scarcely dared speak a word.

And notwithstanding all their malice, she was held in more esteem than they were, wherever they went. And the good man of the house where they were staying, even though she sat at the end of the table, would always do whatever he could to cheer her up before them all and sent her what he had from his own meal, and that annoyed her companions terribly.

As they travelled towards Constance, they were told they would be harmed and have great trouble unless they had great grace. Then this creature came to a church and went in to pray, and she prayed with all her heart, with much weeping and many tears, for help and succour against their enemies.

Then our Lord said to her mind, 'Don't be afraid, daughter, your party will come to no harm while you are in their company.'

And so – blessed may our Lord be in all his works – they went on in safety to Constance.

Chapter 27

When this creature and her companions had arrived at Constance, she heard tell of an English friar, a master of divinity and the Pope's legate, who was in that city. Then she went to that worthy man and unfolded to him the story of her life from the beginning up to that hour, as near as she could in confession, because he was the Pope's legate and a respected clerk.

And afterwards she told him what trouble she was having with her companions. She also told him what grace God gave her of contrition and compunction, of sweetness and devotion, and of many various revelations which our Lord had revealed to her, and the fear that she had of delusions and deceptions by her spiritual enemies, because of which she lived in great fear, desiring to put them aside and to feel none, if she might withstand them.

And when she had spoken, the worthy clerk gave her words of great comfort, and said it was the work of the Holy Ghost, commanding and charging her to obey them and receive them when God would give them and to have no doubts, for the devil has no power to work such grace in a soul. And also he said he would support her against the ill will of her companions.

Afterwards, when her party pleased, they invited this worthy doctor to dinner. And the doctor told this creature, warning her to sit at table in his presence as she did in his absence, and behave in the same way as she did when he was not there.

When the time had come for them to sit at table, everybody took his place where he liked. The worthy legate and doctor sat first, and then the others, and lastly the said creature, sitting at the end of the table and speaking not a word, as she was wont to do when the legate was not there. Then the legate said to her, 'Why are you not merrier?'

And she sat still and did not answer, as he himself had commanded her to do.

When they had eaten, the company made a great deal of complaint about this creature to the legate, and said absolutely that she could no longer be in their party, unless he would order her to eat meat as they did, and leave off her weeping, and that she should not talk so much of holiness.

Then the worthy doctor said, 'No, sirs, I will not make her eat meat while she can abstain and be the better disposed to love our Lord. Whichever of you all who made a vow to walk to Rome barefoot, I would not dispense him of his vow whilst he might fulfil it, and nor will I order her to eat meat while our Lord gives her strength to abstain. As for her weeping, it is not in my power to restrain it, for it is the gift of the Holy Ghost. As for her talking, I will ask her to stop until she comes somewhere that people will hear her more gladly than you do.'

The company was extremely angry. They gave her over to the legate and said absolutely that they would have nothing more to do with her. He very kindly and benevolently received her as though she had been his mother, and took charge of her money – about twenty pounds – and yet one of them wrongfully withheld about sixteen pounds.[1] And they also withheld her maidservant and would not let her go with her mistress, notwithstanding that she had promised her mistress and assured her that she would not forsake her for any necessity.

And the legate made all arrangements for this creature (and organized for her the exchange of her English money into foreign money), as though she had been his mother. Then this creature went into a church and prayed our Lord to arrange for somebody to escort her. And then our Lord spoke to her and said, 'You shall have a very good help and guide.'

And very soon afterwards there came to her an old man with a white beard. He came from Devonshire, and he said, 'Ma'am, will you ask me, for God's love and for our Lady's, to go with you and be your guide, since your fellow countrymen have forsaken you?'

She asked what his name was.

He said, 'My name is William Wever.'

She prayed him, out of reverence of God and of our Lady, to help her in her need, and she would well reward him for his labour. And so they were agreed.

Then she went to the legate and told him how well our Lord had arranged for her, and took her leave of him and of her party who had so unkindly rejected her, and also of her maidservant who was bound to have gone with her. She took leave with a very long face and was very unhappy, because she was in a strange country, and did not know the language or the man who was going to escort her either. And so the man and she went off together in great anxiety and gloom. As they went along together this man said to her, 'I'm afraid you'll be taken from me, and I'll be beaten up because of you and lose my coat.'

She said, 'William, don't be afraid. God will look after us very well.'

And every day this creature remembered the Gospel that tells of the woman who was taken in adultery and brought before our Lord. And then she prayed,

'Lord, as you drove away her enemies, so drive away my enemies, and preserve my chastity that I vowed to you and let me never be defiled, and if I am, Lord, I vow that I will never return to England as long as I live.'

Then they went on day by day and met many excellent people. And they didn't say a bad word to this creature, but gave her and her man food and drink, and the good wives at the lodgings where they put up laid her in their own beds for God's love in many places where they went. And our Lord visited her with great grace of spiritual comfort as she went on her way.

And so God brought her on her way until she came to Bologna. And after she had got there, her former companions who had abandoned her arrived there too. And when they heard tell that she had got to Bologna before them they were amazed, and one of the party came to her asking her to go to his companions and try if they would have her back again in their party. And so she did.

'If you want to travel in our party you must give a new undertaking, which is this: you will not talk of the Gospel where we are, but you will sit and make merry, like us, at all meals.'

She agreed and was received back into their party. Then they went on to Venice and stayed there thirteen weeks.[2] And this creature received communion every Sunday in a great house of nuns – and was very warmly welcomed amongst them – where our merciful Lord Christ Jesus visited this creature with great devotion and plentiful tears, so that the good ladies of the place were greatly amazed at it.

Afterwards it happened, as this creature sat at table with her companions, that she repeated a text of the Gospel which she had learned before with other good words, and then her companions said she had broken her undertaking. And she said, 'Yes, sirs, indeed I can no longer keep this agreement with you, for I must speak of my Lord Jesus Christ, though all this world had forbidden me.'

And then she took to her chamber and ate alone for six weeks, until the time when our Lord made her so ill that she thought she would die, and then he suddenly made her well again. And all the time her maidservant left her alone and prepared the company's food and washed their clothes, and to her mistress, whom she had promised to serve, she would in no way attend.

Chapter 28

Also this company, which had excluded the said creature from their table so that she should no longer eat amongst them, arranged a ship for themselves to sail in. They bought containers for their wine and arranged bedding for themselves, but nothing for her.[1] Then she, seeing their unkindness, went to the man they had been to and provided herself with bedding as they had done, and came where they were and showed them what she had done, intending to sail with them in that ship which they had engaged.

Afterwards, as this creature was in contemplation, our Lord warned her in her mind that she should not sail in that ship, and he assigned her another ship, a galley, that she should sail in.

Then she told this to some of the company, and they told it to others of their party, and then they dared not sail in the ship which they had arranged. And so they sold off the containers which they had got for their wines, and were very glad to come to the galley where she was, and so, though it was against her will, she went on with them in their company, for they did not dare do otherwise.[2]

When it was time to make their beds they locked up her bedclothes, and a priest who was in her party took a sheet away from this creature, and said it was his. She took God to witness that it was her sheet. Then the priest swore a great oath, by the book in his hand, that she was as false as she might be, and despised her and severely rebuked her.

And so she had great and continual tribulation until she came to Jerusalem.[3] And before she arrived there, she said to them that she supposed they were annoyed with her, 'I pray you, sirs, be in charity with me, for I am in charity with you, and forgive me if I have annoyed you along the way. And if any of you have in any way trespassed against me, God forgive you for it, as I do.'

And so they went on into the Holy Land until they could see Jerusalem. And when this creature saw Jerusalem she was riding on an ass – she thanked God with all her heart, praying him for his mercy that, just as he had brought her to see this earthly city of Jerusalem, he would grant her grace to see the blissful city of Jerusalem above, the city of heaven. Our Lord Jesus Christ, answering her thought, granted her her desire.

Then for the joy that she had and the sweetness that she felt in the conversation of our Lord, she was on the point of falling off her ass, for she could not bear the sweetness and grace that God wrought in her soul. Then two German pilgrims went up to her and kept her from falling – one of them was a priest, and he put spices in her mouth to comfort her, thinking she was ill. And so they helped her onwards to Jerusalem, and when she arrived there she said, 'Sirs, I beg you, don't be annoyed though I weep bitterly in this holy place where our Lord Jesus Christ lived and died.'

Then they went to the Church of the Holy Sepulchre in Jerusalem,[4] and they were let in on the one day at evensong time, and remained until evensong time on the next day.[5] Then the friars lifted up a cross and led the pilgrims about from one place to another where our Lord had suffered his pains and his Passion, every man and woman carrying a wax candle in one hand.[6] And the friars always, as they went about, told them what our Lord suffered in every place. And this creature wept and sobbed as plenteously as though she had seen our Lord with her bodily eyes suffering his Passion at that time. Before her in her soul she saw him in truth by contemplation, and that caused her to have compassion. And when they came up on to the Mount of Calvary, she fell down because she could not stand or kneel, but writhed and wrestled with her body, spreading her arms out wide, and cried with a loud voice as though her heart would have burst apart, for in the city of her soul she saw truly and freshly how our Lord was crucified. Before her face she heard and saw in her spiritual sight the mourning of our Lady, of St John and Mary Magdalene, and of many others that loved our Lord.[7]

And she had such great compassion and such great pain to see our Lord's pain, that she could not keep herself from crying and roaring though she should have died for it. And this was the first crying that she ever cried in any contemplation.[8] And this kind of crying lasted for many years after this time, despite anything that anyone might do, and she suffered much contempt and much reproof for it. The crying was so loud and so amazing that it astounded people, unless they had heard it before, or else knew the reason for the cryings. And she had them so often that they made her very weak in her bodily strength, and specially if she heard of our Lord's Passion.[9]

And sometimes, when she saw the crucifix, or if she saw a man had a wound, or a beast, whichever it were, or if a man beat a child before her or hit a horse or other beast with a whip, if she saw or heard it, she thought she saw our Lord being beaten or wounded, just as she saw it in the man or in the beast, either in the fields or in the town, and alone by herself as well as among people.

When she first had her cryings at Jerusalem, she had them often, and in Rome also. And when she first came home to England her cryings came but seldom, perhaps once a month, then once a week, afterwards daily, and once she had fourteen in one day, and another day she had seven, just as God would visit her with them, sometimes in church, sometimes in the street, sometimes in her chamber, sometimes in the fields, when God would send them, for she never knew the time nor hour when they would come. And they never came without surpassingly great sweetness of devotion and high contemplation.

And as soon as she perceived that she was going to cry, she would hold it in as much as she could, so that people would not hear it and get annoyed. For some said it was a wicked spirit tormented her; some said it was an illness; some said she had drunk too much wine; some cursed her; some wished she was in the harbour; some wished she was on the sea in a bottomless boat; and so each man as he thought. Other, spiritually inclined men loved her and esteemed her all the more. Some great clerks said our Lady never cried so, nor any saint in heaven, but they knew very little what she felt, nor would they believe that she could not stop herself from crying if she wanted.

And therefore, when she knew that she was going to cry, she held it in as long as she could, and did all that she could to withstand it or else to suppress it, until she turned the colour of lead, and all the time it would be seething more and more in her mind until such time as it burst out. And when the body might no longer endure the spiritual effort, but was overcome with the unspeakable love that worked so fervently in her soul, then she fell down and cried astonishingly loud. And the more that she laboured to keep it in or to suppress it, so much the more would she cry, and the louder.

And thus she did on the Mount of Calvary, as it is written before: she had as true contemplation in the sight of her soul as if Christ had hung before her bodily eye in his manhood. And when through dispensation of the high mercy of our sovereign saviour, Christ Jesus, it was granted to this creature to behold so truly his precious tender body, all rent and torn with scourges, more full of wounds than a dove-cote ever was of holes,[10] hanging upon the cross with the crown of thorns upon his head, his blessed hands, his tender feet nailed to the hard wood, the rivers of blood flowing out plenteously from every limb, the grisly and grievous wound in his precious side shedding out blood and water for her love and her salvation, then she fell down and cried with a loud voice, twisting and turning her body amazingly on every side, spreading her arms out wide as if she would have died, and could not keep herself from crying and these physical movements, because of the fire of love that burned so fervently in her soul with pure pity and compassion.[11]

It is not to be wondered at if this creature cried out and made astonishing expressions, when we may see every day with our own eyes both men and women – some for loss of worldly wealth, some for love of their family or for worldly friendships, through overmuch study and earthly affection, and most of all for inordinate love and physical feeling, if their friends are parted from them – who will cry and roar and wring their hands as if they were out of their wits and minds, and yet they know well enough that they displease God.

And if anybody advises them to leave off their weeping and crying, they will say that they cannot; they loved their friend so much and he was so gentle and kind to them that they may in no way forget him. How much more might they weep, cry and roar, if their most beloved friends were violently seized in front of their eyes and brought with every kind of reproof before the judge, wrongfully condemned to death, and especially so shameful a death as our merciful Lord suffered for our sake. How would they bear it? No doubt they would both cry and roar and avenge themselves if they could, or else people would say they were no friends.

Alas, alas for sorrow, that the death of a creature who has often sinned and trespassed against his Maker should be so immeasurably mourned and sorrowed over. It is an offence to God and a hindrance to other souls.

And the compassionate death of our Saviour, by which we are all restored to life, is not kept in mind by us unworthy and unkind wretches, nor will we support those whom our Lord has entrusted with his secrets and endued with love, but rather disparage and hinder them as much as we may.

Chapter 29

When this creature with her companions came to the grave where our Lord was buried, then, as she entered that holy place, she fell down with her candle in her hand, as if she would have died for sorrow. And later she rose up again with great weeping and sobbing, as though she had seen our Lord buried right in front of her. Then she thought she saw our Lady in her soul: how she mourned and how she wept for her son's death, and then was our Lady's sorrow her sorrow.

And so wherever the friars led them in that holy place, she always wept and sobbed astonishingly, and specially when she came to where our Lord was nailed on the cross. There she cried out and wept without control, and could not restrain herself. They also came to a marble stone that our Lord was laid on when he was taken down from the cross, and there she wept with great compassion, remembering our Lord's Passion.

Afterwards she received communion on the Mount of Calvary, and then she wept, she sobbed, she cried out so loudly that it was amazing to hear it. She was so full of holy thoughts and meditations, and holy contemplations in the Passion of our Lord Jesus Christ, and holy conversation in which our Lord conversed with her soul, that she could never express them later, so high and so holy they were. Great was the grace that our Lord showed to this creature for the three weeks that she was in Jerusalem.

Another day, early in the morning, they visited the great hills, and her guides told where our Lord bore the cross on his back, and where his mother met with him, and how she swooned, and how she fell down and he fell down also.[1] And so they went on all the morning until they came to Mount Zion, and all the time this creature wept abundantly for compassion of our Lord's Passion. On Mount Zion is a place where our Lord washed his disciples' feet, and a little way from there he celebrated the Last Supper with his disciples.[2]

And therefore this creature had a great desire to receive communion in that holy place where our merciful Lord Christ Jesus first consecrated his precious body in the form of bread, and gave it to his disciples. And so she was with great devotion, with plenteous tears, and with violent sobbings, for in this place there is plenary remission, and so there is in four other places in the Church of the Holy Sepulchre. One is on the Mount of Calvary; another at the grave where our Lord was buried; the third is at the marble stone that his precious body was laid on when it was taken from the cross; the fourth is where the holy cross was buried; and in many other places of Jerusalem.

And when this creature came to the place where the apostles received the Holy Ghost, our Lord gave her great devotion. Afterwards she went to the place where our Lady was buried,[3] and as she knelt on her knees during the hearing of two masses, our Lord Jesus Christ said to her, 'You do not come here, daughter, for any need except merit and reward, for your sins were forgiven you before you came here, and therefore you come here for the increasing of your reward and merit. And I am well pleased with you, daughter, because you are obedient to Holy Church, and you obey your confessor and follow his counsel, who, by authority of Holy Church, has absolved you of your sins and dispensed you, so that you need not go to Rome or to St James at Compostela, unless you wish to yourself. Notwithstanding all this, I command you in the name of Jesus, daughter, that you go to visit these holy places and do as I bid you, for I am above Holy Church, and I shall go with you and keep you safe.'

Then our Lady spoke to her soul in this way, saying, 'Daughter, you are greatly blessed, for my son Jesus will infuse so much grace into you that the whole world will marvel at you. Don't be ashamed, my beloved daughter, to receive the gifts which my son will give you, for I tell you truly they will be great gifts that he will give you. And therefore, dear daughter, don't be ashamed of him who is your God, your Lord and your love, any more than I was ashamed when I saw him hang on the cross – my sweet son Jesus – to cry and to weep for the pain of my sweet son, Jesus Christ. Nor was Mary Magdalene ashamed to cry and weep for my son's love. And therefore, daughter, if you will be a partaker in our joy, you must be a partaker in our sorrow.'

Such was the sweet conversation that this creature had at our Lady's grave, and a great deal more than she could ever repeat.

Afterwards she rode on an ass to Bethlehem, and when she came to the church and to the crib where our Lord was born,[4] she had great devotion, much conversing in her soul, and high spiritual comfort, with much weeping and sobbing, so that her fellow pilgrims would not let her eat in their company. And so she ate her meals alone by herself.

And then the Grey Friars[5] who had led her from place to place took her in with them and seated her with them at meals, so that she should not eat alone. And one of the friars asked one of her party if that was the Englishwoman who, they had heard tell, spoke with God. And when this came to her knowledge, she knew that it was the truth that our Lord said to her before she left England: 'Daughter, I shall make the whole world wonder at you, and many men and women shall speak of me for love of you, and honour me in you.'

Chapter 30

Another time this creature's companions wanted to go to the River Jordan and would not let her go with them. Then this creature prayed our Lord that she might go with them, and he bade that she should go with them whether they wanted her to or not. And then she set forth by the grace of God and didn't ask their permission. When she came to the River Jordan the weather was so hot that she thought her feet would be burnt because of the heat that she felt.

Afterwards she went on with her fellow pilgrims to Mount Quarentyne,[1] where our Lord fasted for forty days. And there she asked her companions to help her up the mountain, and they said 'no,' because they could scarcely help themselves up. Then she was very miserable because she could not get up the mountain. And just then a Saracen, a good-looking man, happened to come by her, and she put a groat into his hand, making signs to him to take her up the mountain. And quickly the Saracen took her under his arm and led her up the high mountain where our Lord fasted forty days. Then she was dreadfully thirsty and got no sympathy from her fellow pilgrims, but then God, of his high goodness, moved the Grey Friars with compassion, and they comforted her, when her fellow countrymen would not acknowledge her.

And so she was ever more strengthened in the love of our Lord and the more bold to suffer shame and rebukes for his sake in every place she went, because of the grace that God wrought in her of weeping, sobbing and crying out, which grace she could not withstand when God would send it. And always she proved her feelings to be true, and those promises that God had made her while she was in England, and in other places also, came to her in effect just as she had sensed before, and therefore she dared the better receive such speeches and conversation, and act the more boldly in consequence.

Afterwards, when this creature had come down from the

Mount, as God willed, she went on to the place where St John the Baptist was born.[2] And later she went to Bethany, where Mary and Martha lived, and to the grave where Lazarus was buried and raised from death to life. And she visited the chapel where our blessed Lord appeared to his blessed mother before all others on the morning of Easter Day.[3] And she stood in the same place where Mary Magdalene stood when Christ said to her, 'Mary, why are you weeping?'[4] And so she was in many more places than are written here, for she was three weeks in Jerusalem and in places thereabouts. And she always had great devotion as long as she was in that country.

And the friars of the Church of the Holy Sepulchre were very welcoming to her and gave her many great relics, wanting her to remain among them if she had wished, because of the belief they had in her. The Saracens also made much of her, and conveyed and escorted her about the country wherever she wanted to go.[5] And she found all people good and gentle to her, except her own countrymen.

And as she went from Jerusalem to Ramleh, she would have liked to return again to Jerusalem, because of the great grace and spiritual comfort that she felt when she was there, and to gain herself more pardon. And then our Lord commanded her to go to Rome, and so on home to England, and said to her, 'Daughter, as often as you say or think "Worshipped be all those holy places in Jerusalem that Christ suffered bitter pain and passion in," you shall have the same pardon as if you were there with your bodily presence, both for yourself and for all those that you will give it to.'

And as she travelled to Venice, many of her companions were very ill, and all the time our Lord said to her, 'Don't be afraid, daughter, no one will die in the ship that you are in.'

And she found her feelings completely true. And when our Lord had brought them all to Venice again in safety, her fellow countrymen abandoned her and went off, leaving her alone. And some of them said that they would not go with her for a hundred pounds.

When they had gone away from her, then our Lord Jesus Christ – who always helps in need and never forsakes his servant who truly trusts in his mercy – said to his creature, 'Don't be afraid, daughter, because I shall provide for you very well, and bring you in safety to Rome and home again to England without any disgrace to your body, if you will be clad in white clothes, and wear them as I said to you while you were in England.'

Then this creature, being in great unhappiness and doubt, answered in her mind, 'If you are the spirit of God that speaks in my soul, and I may prove you to be a true spirit through counsel of the church, I shall obey your will; and if you bring me to Rome in safety, I shall wear white clothes, even though all the world should wonder at me, for your love.'

'Go forth, daughter, in the name of Jesus, for I am the spirit of God, which shall help you in your every need, go with you, and support you in every place – and therefore, do not mistrust me. You never found me deceiving, nor did I ever bid you do anything except what is worship of God and profit to your soul if you will obey; and I shall infuse into you great abundance of grace.'

Just then, as she looked to one side, she saw a poor man sitting there, who had a great hump on his back. His clothes were all very much patched, and he seemed a man of about fifty. Then she went up to him and said, 'Good man, what's wrong with your back?'

He said, 'It was broken in an illness, ma'am.'

She asked what his name was, and where he was from. He said his name was Richard, and he was from Ireland. Then she thought of her confessor's words, who was a holy anchorite, as is written before, who spoke to her while she was in England in this way: 'Daughter, when your own companions have abandoned you, God will provide a broken-backed man to escort you wherever you want to go.'

Then she with a glad spirit said to him, 'Good Richard, guide me to Rome, and you shall be rewarded for your labour.'

'No, ma'am,' he said, 'I know very well that your countrymen have abandoned you, and therefore it would be difficult for me to escort you. Your fellow countrymen have both bows and arrows with which they can defend both you and themselves, and I have no weapon except a cloak full of patches. And yet I fear that my enemies will rob me, and perhaps take you away from me and rape you; and therefore I dare not escort you, for I would not, for a hundred pounds, have you suffer any disgrace while you were with me.'

And then she replied, 'Richard, don't be afraid. God will look after both of us very well, and I shall give you two nobles for your trouble.'

Then he agreed and set off with her. Soon after, there came two Grey Friars and a woman that came with them from Jerusalem, and she had with her an ass, which was bearing a chest containing an image of our Lord.

And then Richard said to this creature, 'You shall go along with these two men and this woman, and I will meet you morning and evening, for I must get on with my occupation and beg my living.'

And so she followed his advice and went along with the friars and the woman. None of them could understand her language, yet they provided her every day with food, drink and lodgings as well as they did for themselves and rather better, so that she was always much obliged to pray for them. And every evening and morning, Richard with the broken back came and cheered her up as he had promised.

The woman who had the image in the chest, when they came into fine cities, took the image out of her chest and set it in the laps of respectable wives. And they would dress it up in shirts and kiss it as though it had been God himself. And when the creature saw the worship and the reverence that they accorded the image, she was seized with sweet devotion and sweet meditations, so that she wept with great sobbing and loud crying. And she was so much the more moved because, while she was in England, she had high meditations on the birth and the childhood of Christ, and she thanked God because she saw each of these creatures have as great faith in what she saw with her bodily eye as *she* had before with her inward eye.

When these good women saw this creature weeping, sobbing and crying out so astonishingly and so powerfully that she was nearly overcome by it, then they arranged a good soft bed and laid her upon it, and comforted her as much as they could for our Lord's love – blessed may he be.

Chapter 31

The said creature had a ring, which our Lord had commanded her to have made while she was at home in England, and to have engraved on it *Jesus est amor meus*.[1] She had much thought how she should keep this ring from being stolen on her travels, for she thought she would not have lost the ring for a thousand pounds and much more, because she had it made at God's command; and also she wore it by his command, for she previously intended, before she had the revelation, never to wear a ring.

And as it happened, she was lodged in a good man's house, and many neighbours came in to welcome her for her perfection and her holiness, and she gave them the measurements of Christ's grave,[2] which they received very devoutly, deriving great joy from it and thanking her very much. Afterwards this creature went to her room and let her ring hang by her purse-string which she carried at her breast. On the morning of the next day, when she would have taken her ring, it was gone – she could not find it. Then she was terribly unhappy, and complained to the good wife of the house in this way: 'Ma'am, my good wedding ring to Jesus Christ – you could call it – is gone!'

The good wife, understanding what she meant, prayed her to pray for her, and her face and expression changed strangely, as though she had been guilty. Then this creature took a candle in her hand and searched all about her bed where she had lain all night, and the good wife of the house took another candle in her hand and also busied herself to look round the bed. And at last she found the ring under the bed on the boards, and with great joy she told the good wife that she had found her ring. Then the good wife very submissively asked this creature for forgiveness as best she could: '*Bone Christian, prey per me.*'[3]

Afterwards this creature came to Assisi, and there she met a Friar Minor,[4] an Englishman, and he was held to be a serious cleric. She told him about her manner of life, her feelings, her revelations, and the grace that God wrought in her soul by holy inspirations and high contemplations, and how our Lord talked to her soul in a kind of conversation. Then the worthy cleric said that she was much beholden to God, for he said he had never heard of anyone living in this world who was on such homely terms with God by love and homely conversation as she was – God be thanked for his gifts, for it is his goodness and no man's merit.

On one occasion, as this creature was in church at Assisi, there was exhibited our Lady's kerchief [5] – which she wore here on earth – with many lights and great reverence. Then this creature had great devotion. She wept, she sobbed, she cried, with great abundance of tears and many holy thoughts.[6] She was there also on Lammas Day,[7] when there is great pardon with plenary remission,[8] in order to obtain grace, mercy and forgiveness for herself, for all her friends, for all her enemies, and for all the souls in purgatory.

And there was a lady who had come from Rome to obtain her pardon. Her name was Margaret Florentyne, and she had with her many Knights of Rhodes, many gentlewomen, and a very fine equipage.

Then Richard, the broken-backed man, went to her, asking her if this creature could go with her to Rome – and himself too – so as to be kept safe from the danger of thieves. And then that worthy lady received them into her party and let them go with her to Rome, as God willed. When this creature came to Rome, those who were her fellow pilgrims before and excluded her from their company were also in Rome, and when they heard tell that such a woman had arrived they were greatly surprised at how she came there safely.

And then she went and got her white clothes and was clad all in white, just as she was commanded to do years before in her soul by revelation, and now it was fulfilled in effect.

Then this creature was taken in at the Hospital of St Thomas of Canterbury in Rome,[9] and there she received communion every Sunday with great weeping, violent sobbing and loud crying, and was highly beloved by the Master of the Hospital and all his brethren.

And then, through the stirring of her spiritual enemy, there came a priest, who was held to be a holy man in the Hospital and also in other places in Rome, and who was one of her companions and one of her own countrymen. And notwithstanding his holiness, he spoke so badly of this creature and slandered her name so much in the Hospital that, through his evil tongue, she was put out of the Hospital, so that she could no longer be shriven or receive communion there.

Chapter 32

When this creature saw she was abandoned, and ejected from amongst those good men, she was very miserable, most of all because she had no confessor and could not then be shriven as she wished. Then, with great abundance of tears, she prayed to our Lord, of his mercy, that he would dispose for her as was most pleasing to him.

And later she called to her Richard with the broken back, asking him to go over to a church opposite the Hospital[1] and inform the parson of the church of her manner of behaving, and what sorrow she had, and how she wept because she might not be shriven or receive communion, and what compunction and contrition she had for her sins.

Then Richard went to the parson and told him about this creature, and how our Lord gave her contrition and compunction with great abundance of tears, and how she wanted to receive communion every Sunday if she could, and she had no priest to be shriven to. And then the parson, hearing of her contrition and compunction, was very glad and bade that she should come to him in the name of Jesus and say her '*Confiteor*', and he would give her communion himself, for he could not understand any English.

Then our Lord sent St John the Evangelist to hear her confession,[2] and she said '*Benedicite*', and he said '*Dominus*' truly in her soul, so that she saw him and heard him in her spiritual understanding as she would have done another priest by her bodily sense. Then she told him all her sins and all her unhappiness with many sorrowful tears, and he heard her very meekly and kindly. And afterwards he enjoined on her the penance that she should do for her trespass, and absolved her of her sins with sweet and humble words, highly strengthening her to trust in the mercy of our Lord Jesus Christ, and bade her that she should receive the sacrament of the altar, in the name of Jesus. And then he passed away from her.

When he was gone, she prayed with all her heart all the time, as she heard mass, 'Lord, as surely as you are not angry with me, grant me a well of tears,[3] through which I may receive your precious body with all manner of tears of devotion to your worship and the increasing of my merit; for you are my joy, Lord, my bliss, my comfort, and all the treasure that I have in this world, for I covet no other worldly joy, but only you. And therefore, my dearest Lord and my God, do not forsake me.'

Then our blessed Lord Christ Jesus answered to her soul and said, 'My beloved daughter, I swear by my high majesty that I will never forsake you. And, daughter, the more shame, contempt and rebuke that you suffer for my love, the better I love you, for I behave like a man who greatly loves his wife: the more envy that other men have of her, the better he will dress her to spite his enemies. And just so, daughter, shall I behave with you. In anything that you do, daughter, or say, you cannot please God better than by believing that he loves you; for if it were possible for me to weep with you, I would weep with you, daughter, for the compassion that I have for you. The time shall come when you will consider yourself well pleased, for in you shall be proved true the common proverb that men say: "He is blessed indeed who can sit in his chair of happiness and talk about his chair of unhappiness." And so shall you do, daughter, and all your weeping and your sorrow shall turn into joy and bliss which you shall never lack.'

Chapter 33

Another time, while this creature was at the church of St John Lateran, before the altar, hearing mass, she thought that the priest who said mass seemed a good and devout man. She was greatly moved in spirit to speak with him. Then she asked her man with the broken back to go to the priest and ask him to speak with her. The priest understood no English and did not know what she was saying, and she knew no other language than English, and therefore they spoke through an interpreter, a man who told each of them what the other said.

Then she prayed the priest, in the name of Jesus, that he should make his prayers to the blessed Trinity, to our Lady, and to all the blessed saints in heaven, also urging others who loved our Lord to pray for him, so that he might have grace to understand her language and her speech in such things as she, through the grace of God, would say to him.

The priest was a good man, German by birth, a good clerk and a learned man, highly beloved, well esteemed and much trusted in Rome, and he had one of the greatest offices of any priest in Rome.

Desiring to please God, he followed the advice of this creature, and he prayed to God as devoutly as he could every day, that he might have grace to understand what this creature would say to him, and he also got other lovers of our Lord to pray for him. They prayed in this way for thirteen days. And after thirteen days the priest came back to her to test the effect of their prayers, and then he understood what she said in English to him, and she understood what he said. And yet he did not understand the English that other people spoke; even though they spoke the same words that she spoke, he still did not understand them unless she spoke herself.

Then she was confessed to this priest of all her sins, as near as her memory would serve her, from her childhood up until that hour, and received her penance very joyfully. And afterwards she told him about the secret things of revelations and of high contemplations, and how she had such thought of his Passion, and such great compassion when God would give it, that she fell down because of it and could not bear it. Then she wept bitterly, she sobbed violently and cried out so loud and horribly that people were often afraid and greatly astonished, thinking she had been troubled with some evil spirit or a sudden illness not believing it was the work of God, but rather some evil spirit, or a sudden illness, or else pretence and hypocrisy, something she put on deceitfully herself.

The priest had great trust that it was the work of God and, when he had doubts, our Lord sent him such tokens through this creature of his own misconduct and his manner of living – which nobody knew but God and he, as our Lord showed her by revelation and bade her tell him – that he knew very well because of this that her feelings were true.

And then the priest received her very meekly and reverently, as if she were his mother and his sister, and said he would support her against her enemies. And so he did, as long as she was in Rome, and endured much evil talk and much tribulation. And also he gave up his office, because he wanted to support her in her sobbing and in her crying when all her countrymen had abandoned her; for they were always her greatest enemies, and caused her much unhappiness in every place they went, because they wanted her never to sob or cry. And she was quite unable to choose; but that they would not believe. They were always against her, and against the good man who supported her.

Then this good man, seeing this woman sobbing and crying so astonishingly, and especially on Sundays when she was to receive communion amongst all the people, made up his mind to prove whether it were the gift of God, as she said, or else her own hypocritical pretence, as people said. He took her alone on another Sunday into another church when mass was over and everybody gone home, no one knowing about it except himself and the clerk. And when he was about to give her communion, she wept so copiously, and sobbed and cried so loud that he was astonished himself, because it seemed to his hearing that she had never previously cried so loud. And then he fully believed that it was the working of the Holy Ghost and neither any pretending nor hypocrisy of her own.

Then afterwards he was not embarrassed to take her part and to speak against those who wanted to defame her and speak evil of her, until he was detracted by the enemies of virtue almost as much as she was, and it pleased him very much to suffer tribulation for God's cause. Many people in Rome who were disposed to virtue loved him all the more, and her too, and often invited her to meals and made her very welcome, asking her to pray for them.

Her own countrymen were always obdurate, and especially a priest who was amongst them. He stirred up many people against her and said many evil things about her, because she wore white clothing more than did others who were holier and better than she ever was, as he thought. The cause of his malice was that she would not obey him. And she well knew it was against the health of her soul to obey him as he wanted her to do.

Chapter 34

Then the good man, the German priest who confessed her, through the agitating of the English priest who was her enemy, asked her if she would be obedient to him or not.

And she said, 'Yes, sir.'

'Will you then do as I shall order you to do?'

'Very willingly, sir.'

'I charge you then to leave off your white clothes and wear your black clothes again.'

And she did what he commanded, and then she felt that she pleased God with her obedience. But then she endured much scorn from women in Rome. They asked her if highwaymen had robbed her, and she said, 'No, ma'am.'

Afterwards when she went on pilgrimage she happened to meet the priest who was her enemy, and he greatly rejoiced that she had been deflected from her intention, and said to her, 'I am glad that you go about in black clothes as you used to do.'

And she answered him, 'Sir, our Lord would not be displeased though I wore white clothes, for he wills that I do so.'

Then the priest replied to her, 'Now I well know that you have a devil inside you, for I hear him speak in you to me.'

'Ah, good sir, I pray you, drive him away from me, for God knows I would very gladly do well and please him if I could.'

And then he was very angry, and said very many sharp words to her.

And she said to him, 'Sir, I hope I have no devil within me, for if I had a devil within me I should be angry with you, you know. And sir, I don't think I am at all angry with you for anything that you can do to me.' And then the priest went away from her with a very gloomy expression.

Then our Lord spoke to this creature in her soul and said: 'Daughter, do not be afraid of whatever he says to you, for though he ran every year to Jerusalem, I have no liking for him; for as long as he speaks against you he speaks against me, for I am in

you and you are in me. And from this you may know that I
endure many sharp words, for I have often said to you that I
should be crucified anew in you by sharp words, for you shall be
slain in no other way than by suffering sharp words. As for this
priest who is your enemy, he is just a hypocrite.'

Then the good priest, her confessor, ordered her by virtue of
obedience, and also as part of her penance, that she should serve
an old woman, a poor creature, in Rome. And so she did for six
weeks. She served her as she would have done our Lady. And she
had no bed to lie in, nor any bedclothes to be covered with except
her own mantle. Then she was full of vermin and suffered a lot of
pain as a result. She also fetched home water and sticks on her
neck for the poor woman, and begged for both meat and wine for
her; and when the poor woman's wine was sour, this creature
herself drank that sour wine, and gave the poor woman good
wine that she had bought for her own self.

Chapter 35

As this creature was in the church of the Holy Apostles at Rome [1]
on St Lateran's Day,[2] the Father of Heaven said to her, 'Daughter,
I am well pleased with you, inasmuch as you believe in all the
sacraments of Holy Church and in all faith involved in that, and
especially because you believe in the manhood of my son, and
because of the great compassion that you have for his bitter
Passion.'

The Father also said to this creature, 'Daughter, I will have you
wedded to my Godhead, because I shall show you my secrets and
my counsels, for you shall live with me without end.'

Then this creature kept silence in her soul and did not answer
to this, because she was very much afraid of the Godhead; and
she had no knowledge of the conversation of the Godhead, for all

her love and affection were fixed on the manhood of Christ, and of that she did have knowledge and would not be parted from that for anything.

She had so much feeling for the manhood of Christ, that when she saw women in Rome carrying children in their arms, if she could discover that any were boys, she would cry, roar and weep as if she had seen Christ in his childhood. And if she could have had her way, she would often have taken the children out of their mothers' arms and kissed them instead of Christ. And if she saw a handsome man, she had great pain to look at him, lest she might see him who was both God and man. And therefore she cried many times and often when she met a handsome man, and wept and sobbed bitterly for the manhood of Christ as she went about the streets of Rome, so that those who saw her were greatly astonished at her, because they did not know the reason.

Therefore it was not surprising if she was still and did not answer the Father of Heaven, when he told her that she should be wedded to his Godhead. Then the Second Person, Christ Jesus, whose manhood she loved so much, said to her, 'What do you say to my Father, Margery, daughter, about these words that he speaks to you? Are you well pleased that it should be so?'

And then she would not answer the Second Person, but wept amazingly much, desiring to have himself still, and in no way to be parted from him. Then the Second Person in Trinity answered his Father for her, and said, 'Father, excuse her, for she is still only young and has not completely learned how she should answer.'

And then the Father took her by the hand [spiritually] in her soul, before the Son and the Holy Ghost, and the Mother of Jesus, and all the twelve apostles, and St Katherine and St Margaret and many other saints and holy virgins, with a great multitude of angels, saying to her soul, 'I take you, Margery, for my wedded wife, for fairer, for fouler, for richer, for poorer, provided that you are humble and meek in doing what I command you to do. For, daughter, there was never a child so kind to its mother as I shall be to you, both in joy and sorrow, to help you and comfort you. And that I pledge to you.'

And then the Mother of God and all the saints that were present there in her soul prayed that they might have much joy together. Then this creature with high devotion, with great abundance of tears, thanked God for this spiritual comfort, holding herself in her own feeling very unworthy of any such grace as she felt, for she felt many great comforts, both spiritual comforts and bodily comforts. Sometimes she sensed sweet smells in her nose; they were sweeter, she thought, than any earthly sweet thing ever was that she smelled before, nor could she ever tell how sweet they were, for she thought she might have lived on them if they had lasted.

Sometimes she heard with her bodily ears such sounds and melodies that she could not hear what anyone said to her at that time unless he spoke louder. These sounds and melodies she had heard nearly every day for twenty-five years when this book was written, and especially when she was in devout prayer, also many times while she was at Rome, and in England too.

She saw with her bodily eyes many white things flying all about her on all sides, as thickly in a way as specks in a sunbeam; they were very delicate and comforting, and the brighter the sun shone, the better she could see them. She saw them at many different times and in many different places, both in church and in her chamber, at her meals and at her prayers, in the fields and in town, both walking and sitting. And many times she was afraid what they might be, for she saw them at night in darkness as well as in daylight. Then when she was afraid of them, our Lord said to her, 'By this token, daughter, believe it is God who speaks in you, for wherever God is, heaven is, and where God is, there are many angels, and God is in you and you are in him. And therefore, don't be afraid, daughter, for these betoken that you have many angels around you, to keep you both day and night so that no devil shall have power over you, nor evil men harm you.'[3]

Then from that time forward she used to say when she saw them coming: 'Benedictus qui venit in nomine Domini.'[4]

Our Lord also gave her another token which lasted about

sixteen years, and increased ever more and more, and that was a flame of fire of love – marvellously hot and delectable and very comforting, never diminishing but ever increasing; for though the weather were never so cold she felt the heat burning in her breast and at her heart, as veritably as a man would feel the material fire if he put his hand or his finger into it.[5]

When she first felt the fire of love burning in her breast she was afraid of it, and then our Lord answered in her mind and said, 'Daughter, don't be afraid, because this heat is the heat of the Holy Ghost, which will burn away all your sins, for the fire of love quenches all sins. And you shall understand by this token that the Holy Ghost is in you, and you know very well that wherever the Holy Ghost is, there is the Father, and where the Father is, there is the Son, and so you have fully in your soul all of the Holy Trinity. Therefore you have great cause to love me well, and yet you shall have greater cause than you ever had to love me, for you shall hear what you never heard, and you shall see what you never saw, and you shall feel what you never felt.

'For, daughter, you are as sure of the love of God, as God is God. Your soul is more sure of the love of God than of your own body, for your soul will part from your body, but God shall never part from your soul, for they are united together without end. Therefore, daughter, you have as great reason to be merry as any lady in this world; and if you knew, daughter, how much you please me when you willingly allow me to speak in you, you would never do otherwise, for this is a holy life and the time is very well spent. For, daughter, this life pleases me more than wearing the coat of mail for penance, or the hair-shirt, or fasting on bread and water; for if you said a thousand *paternosters* every day you would not please me as much as you do when you are in silence and allow me to speak in your soul.'

Chapter 36

'Fasting, daughter, is good for young beginners, and discreet penance, especially what their confessor gives them or enjoins them to do. And to pray many beads is good for those who can do no better, yet it is not perfect. But it is a good way towards perfection. For I tell you, daughter, those who are great fasters and great doers of penance want it to be considered the best life; those also who give themselves over to saying many devotions would have that to be the best life; and those who give very generous alms would like that considered the best life.

'And I have often told you, daughter, that thinking, weeping, and high contemplation is the best life on earth. You shall have more merit in heaven for one year of thinking in your mind than for a hundred years of praying with your mouth; and yet you will not believe me, for you will pray many beads whether I wish it or not. And yet, daughter, I will not be displeased with you whether you think, say or speak, for I am always pleased with you.

'And if I were on earth as bodily as I was before I died on the cross, I would not be ashamed of you, as many other people are, for I would take you by the hand amongst the people and greet you warmly, so that they would certainly know that I loved you dearly.

'For it is appropriate for the wife to be on homely terms with her husband. Be he ever so great a lord and she ever so poor a woman when he weds her, yet they must lie together and rest together in joy and peace. Just so must it be between you and me, for I take no heed of what you have been but what you would be, and I have often told you that I have clean forgiven you all your sins.

'Therefore I must be intimate with you, and lie in your bed with you. Daughter, you greatly desire to see me, and you may boldly, when you are in bed, take me to you as your wedded husband, as your dear darling, and as your sweet son, for I want to be loved as a son should be loved by the mother, and I want you to love me, daughter, as a good wife ought to love her husband. Therefore you can boldly take me in the arms of your soul and kiss my mouth, my head, and my feet as sweetly as you want. And as often as you think of me or would do any good deed to me, you shall have the same reward in heaven as if you did it to my own precious body which is in heaven, for I ask no more of you but your heart, to love me who loves you, for my love is always ready for you.'

Then she gave thanks and praise to our Lord Jesus Christ for the high grace and mercy that he showed to her, unworthy wretch.

This creature had various tokens in her hearing. One was a kind of sound as if it were a pair of bellows blowing in her ear. She – being dismayed at this – was warned in her soul to have no fear, for it was the sound of the Holy Ghost. And then our Lord turned that sound into the voice of a dove, and afterwards he turned it into the voice of a little bird which is called a redbreast, that often sang very merrily in her right ear. And then she would always have great grace after she heard such a token. She had been used to such tokens for about twenty-five years at the time of writing this book.

Then our Lord Jesus Christ said to his creature, 'By these tokens you may well know that I love you, for you are to me a true mother and to all the world, because of that great charity which is in you; and yet I am cause of that charity myself, and you shall have great reward for it in heaven.'

Chapter 37

'Daughter, you are obedient to my will, and cleave as fast to me as the skin of the stockfish sticks to man's hand when it is boiled, and you will not forsake me for any shame that any man can do you.

'And you also say that, though I stood before you in my own person and said to you that you should never have my love, never come to heaven, nor ever see my face, yet you say, daughter, that you would never forsake me on earth, never love me the less, nor ever be less busy to please me, though you should lie in hell without end, because you cannot go without my love on earth nor have any other comfort but me alone, who am I, your God, and am all joy and all bliss to you.

'Therefore I say to you, beloved daughter, it is impossible that any such soul should be damned or parted from me, who has such great meekness and charity towards me. And therefore, daughter, never be afraid, for all the great promises that I have promised to you and yours, and to all your confessors, shall always be true and truly fulfilled when the time comes. Have no doubt about it.'

Another time while she was in Rome, a little before Christmas,[1] our Lord Jesus Christ commanded her to go to her confessor, Wenslawe by name, and ask him to give her leave to wear her white clothes once again, for he had made her stop doing so, by virtue of obedience, as is written before. And when she told him the will of our Lord he did not dare once say 'no'. And so she wore white clothes ever after.

Then our Lord bade her that she should at Christmas go home again to her host's house where she was lodged before. And then she went to a poor woman whom she served at the time at the bidding of her confessor, as is written before, and told the poor woman how she must leave her. Then the poor woman was very sorry and greatly bemoaned her departure. This creature told her how it was the will of God that it should be so, and then she took it more easily.

Afterwards, while this creature was in Rome, our Lord bade her give away all her money and make herself destitute for his love. And she immediately, with a fervent desire to please God, gave away such money as she had, and such also as she had borrowed from the broken-backed man who went with her. When he found out how she had given away his money, he was greatly moved and displeased that she had given it away, and spoke very sharply to her. And then she said to him, 'Richard, by the grace of God, we shall come home to England very well. And you shall come to me in Bristol in Whitsun week, and there I shall pay you well and truly, by the grace of God, for I trust faithfully that he who bade me give it away for his love will help me to pay it back.'

And so he did.[2]

Chapter 38

After this creature had thus given away her money and had not a penny to help herself with, as she lay in St Marcellus's Church in Rome,[1] thinking and concentrating as to where she could get her living, inasmuch as she had no silver to keep herself with, our Lord answered to her mind and said, 'Daughter, you are not yet as poor as I was when I hung naked on the cross for your love, for you have clothes on your body and I had none. And you have advised other people to be poor for my sake, and therefore you must follow your own advice.

'But do not be afraid, daughter, for money will come to you, and I have promised you before that I would never fail you. I shall pray my own mother to beg for you, for you have many times begged for me, and for my mother also. And therefore do not be afraid. I have friends in every country, and I shall cause my friends to comfort you.'

When our Lord had talked sweetly to her soul in this way, she thanked him for this great comfort, completely trusting that it would be as he said. Afterwards she got up and went out into the street and by chance met a good man. And so they fell into edifying conversation as they went along together, and she repeated to him many good tales and many pious exhortations until God visited him with tears of devotion and compunction, so that he was highly comforted and consoled. And then he gave her money, by which she was relieved and comforted for a good while.

Then one night she saw in a vision how our Lady, she thought, sat at table with many worthy people and asked for food for her. And then this creature thought that our Lord's words were fulfilled spiritually in that vision, for he promised this creature a little before that he would pray his mother to beg for her.

And very shortly after this vision she met up with a worthy lady, Dame Margaret Florentyne, the same lady who brought her from Assisi to Rome, and neither of them could understand the other very well, except by signs and tokens and a few common words. And then the lady said to her, '*Margerya in poverté?*'

She, understanding what the lady meant, answered, '*Yea, grand poverté, madame.*' [2]

Then the lady commanded her to eat with her every Sunday and seated her at her own table above herself, and served her her food with her own hands. Then this creature sat and wept bitterly, thanking our Lord that she was thus encouraged and cherished for his love by those who could not understand her language.

When they had eaten, the good lady used to give her a hamper with other stuff which she could make stew from for herself, enough to serve her with two days' food, and filled her bottle with good wine. And sometimes she gave her eight bolendine coins [3] as well.

Then another man in Rome, who was called Marcelle, asked her to meals two days a week. His wife was about to have a baby, and she very much wanted this creature to be godmother to her child when it was born, but she did not stay in Rome long enough.

And also there was a pious single lady who gave this creature her food on Wednesdays. Other days, when she was not provided for, she begged for her food from door to door.

Chapter 39

Another time, just as she came by a poor woman's house, the poor woman called her into her house and made her sit by her little fire, giving her wine to drink in a stone cup. And she had a little boy-child sucking at her breast some of the time; at another time it ran to this creature, the mother meanwhile sitting full of sorrow and sadness. Then this creature burst out crying, as though she had seen our Lady and her son at the time of his Passion, and she had so many holy thoughts that she could never tell half of them, but always sat and wept plentifully for a long time, so that the poor woman, feeling sorry for her weeping, begged her to stop, not knowing why she wept.

Then our Lord Jesus Christ said to this creature, 'This place is holy.' And then she got up and went about in Rome and saw much poverty among the people; then she thanked God highly for the poverty that she was in, trusting by means of it to be a partner with them in merit.

Then there was a great gentlewoman in Rome, praying this creature to be godmother to her child, and naming it after St Bridget, for they knew her during her lifetime.[1] And so she did. Afterwards, God gave her grace to have great love in Rome, both from men and women, and great favour amongst the people.

When the Master and Brothers of the Hospital of St Thomas – where she was previously refused, as is written before – heard tell of what love and favour she had in the city, they asked her if she would go to them again, and she should be more welcome than she ever was before, because they were very sorry that they had barred her from them. And she thanked them for their charity and did as they commanded. When she had come back to them, they received her warmly and were very glad she had come.

Then she found there the girl who was her maidservant previously, and rightly should still have been so, living in the Hospital in great wealth and prosperity, for she was the keeper of their wine. And this creature sometimes went to her out of humility and begged her for food and drink, and the girl gave it to her willingly, and sometimes a groat as well. Then she complained to her maidservant, and said she felt great sorrow at their separation, and what slander and evil talk people spoke of her because they were apart – but the girl never wanted to be with her again.

Afterwards this creature spoke with St Bridget's former maid-servant[2] in Rome, but she could not understand what she said. Then she had a man who could understand her language, and that man told St Bridget's maid what this creature said, and how she asked after St Bridget, her lady. Then the maidservant said that her lady, St Bridget, was kind and meek with everybody, and that she had a laughing face. And the good man where this creature was lodged also told her that he knew St Bridget himself, but he little thought that she had been as holy a woman as she was, because she was always homely and kind with everybody who wanted to talk to her.

She was in the chamber that St Bridget died in,[3] and heard a German priest preach of her there, and of her revelations and of her manner of life. She knelt also on the stone on which our Lord appeared to St Bridget and told her what day she should die on.[4] And this was one of St Bridget's days[5] when this creature was in her chapel, which previously was her chamber that she died in. Our Lord sent such storms of winds and rains, and various atmospheric disturbances, that those who were in the fields and at their work outdoors were compelled to enter houses to avoid danger and injury to themselves. Through such tokens this creature supposed that our Lord wished that his holy saint's day should be hallowed, and the saint held in more respect than she was at that time.

And sometimes, when this creature would have done the Stations of Rome,[6] our Lord warned her at night in her bed that she should not go out far from her lodging, for he would send great storms that day of thunder and lightning. And so it was indeed. There were such great storms that year of thunder and lightning, heavy rain and stormy weather, that very old men living in Rome at that time said they had never seen anything like it before; the flashes of lightning were so frequent and shone so brightly inside their houses, that they truly believed that their houses would be burnt with the contents.

Then they cried on this creature to pray for them, fully believing that she was the servant of Almighty God, and that through her prayers they would be helped. This creature praying our Lord for mercy at their request, he answered in her soul saying, 'Daughter, do not be afraid, for no weather, no storm, shall harm you, and therefore do not distrust me, for I shall never deceive you.'

And our merciful Lord Christ Jesus, as it pleased him, withdrew the storms, preserving the people from all misfortunes.

Chapter 40

Then, through the provision of our merciful Lord Christ Jesus, a priest, a good man, came from England to Rome with other companions, asking and inquiring diligently after the said creature, whom he had never seen before, nor she him. But while he was in England he heard tell of such a woman who was at Rome, with whom he highly longed to speak, if God would grant him grace. While he was still in his own country, and intending to see this creature whenever he, through the permission of our Lord, might come to where she was, he provided himself with money to bring to relieve her if she needed it. Then, by inquiring, he came to the place where she was, and very humbly and meekly he called her 'mother', praying her out of charity to receive him as her son. She said that he was as welcome to God and to her, as to his own mother.

So by holy conversation and communing she felt sure he was a good man. And then she, disclosing the secrets of her heart, revealed what grace God wrought in her soul through his holy inspiration, and also something of her manner of life. Then he would no longer allow her to beg her food from door to door, but asked her to eat with him and his party, unless good men and women by way of charity and for spiritual comfort would ask her to meals. Then he wished that she would accept in the name of our Lord; but otherwise she ate with him and his party every day, and he gave her enough money to return to England. And then was fulfilled what our Lord said to her a little before: 'Money will come to you.' And so it did, indeed, thanks be to Almighty God.

Then some of her companions, with whom she had been to Jerusalem, came to this good priest who had newly arrived in Rome, complaining about her and saying that she had been confessed by a priest who could not understand her language or her confession. Then this good priest, trusting in her as if in his own mother, and desiring the health of her soul, asked her if her confessor understood her when she spoke to him or not.

'Good son, I beg you, ask him to dine with you and your companions, and let me be present, and then you will know the truth.'

Her confessor was asked to dinner and, when the time came, was seated and served with this good priest and his party – the said creature being present – and the good English priest chatting and conversing in their own language, English. The German priest, a worthy cleric as is written before, confessor to the said creature, sat quietly in a sort of gloom, because he did not understand what they said in English, but only when they spoke Latin. And they did it on purpose, unbeknown to him, to prove whether he understood English or not.

At last, the said creature – seeing and well understanding that her confessor did not understand their language, and that it was tedious to him – partly to cheer him up and partly, or much more, to prove the work of God, told him in her own language, in English, a story of Holy Writ, which she had learned from clerics while she was at home in England, for she would not talk of any vanity or fantasies.

Then they asked her confessor if he understood what she had said, and he straightaway in Latin told them the same words that she said before in English, for he could neither speak English nor understand English except from her tongue. And then they were astonished, for they knew that he understood what she said, and she understood what he said, and yet he could not understand any other English person. So blessed may God be, who made a foreigner to understand her when her own countrymen had abandoned her, and would not hear her confession unless she would leave off her weeping and talking of holiness.

And yet she could not weep except when God gave it to her, and often he gave it so abundantly that she could not withstand it. But the more she tried to withstand it or put it aside, the more strongly it worked in her soul with such holy thoughts that she could not stop. She would sob and cry very loudly, all against her will, so that many men, and women too, were amazed at her because of it.

Chapter 41

Sometimes when the said creature was at sermons where Germans and other men preached, teaching the laws of God, sudden sorrow and heaviness filling her heart caused her to complain with mournful expression at her lack of understanding, desiring to be refreshed with some crumb of spiritual understanding of her most trusted and most entirely beloved sovereign, Christ Jesus, whose melodious voice, sweetest of all savours, softly sounding in her soul, said, 'I shall preach to you and teach you myself, for your will and your desire are acceptable to me.'

Then her soul was so delectably fed with the sweet converse of our Lord, and so fulfilled with his love, that like a drunk she turned herself first on one side and then on the other, with great weeping and sobbing, powerless to keep herself steady because of the unquenchable fire of love which burned very strongly in her soul.

Then many people were amazed at her, asking her what was wrong with her; to which she, like a creature all wounded with love, and in whom reason had failed, cried with a loud voice: 'The Passion of Christ slays me.'

The good women, feeling sorry for her sorrows and astonished at her weeping and crying, loved her much the more as a result. And therefore they, wanting to cheer her up after her spiritual labour, through signs and tokens – for she did not understand their language – prayed her, and in a way compelled her, to come home with them, not wanting her to leave them.

Then our Lord sent her grace to have great love and great favour from many persons in Rome, both religious men and others. Some religious came to such of her countrymen as loved her and said, 'This woman has sown much good seed in Rome since she came here; that is to say, shown a good example to the people, through which they love God more than they did before.'

One time, this creature was in a church at Rome where the body of St Jerome lies buried,[1] which was miraculously translated from Bethlehem to that place and is now held in great reverence there, beside the place where St Laurence lies buried.[2] To this creature's inward sight St Jerome appeared and said to her soul, 'Blessed are you, daughter, in the weeping that you weep for people's sins, for many shall be saved thereby. And daughter, don't be at all afraid, for it is a singular and a special gift that God has given you – a well of tears which man shall never take from you.'[3]

With such manner of conversing he highly comforted her spirits. And he also gave great praise and thanks to God for the grace that he wrought in her soul, for unless she had had such spiritual comfortings it would have been impossible for her to have borne the shames and wonderings which she suffered patiently and meekly for the grace that God showed in her.

Chapter 42

When Eastertime had come and gone,[1] and this creature and her companions were intending to go back to their own native land, they were told there were many thieves along the way who would relieve them of their goods and perhaps kill them.

Then the said creature, with many a bitter tear in her eye, prayed to our Lord Jesus Christ, saying, 'Christ Jesus, in whom is all my trust, as you have promised me many times before that no one should be harmed in my company, and as I was never deceived or disappointed in your promises as long as I fully and faithfully trusted in you, so hear the prayers of your unworthy servant all wholly trusting in your mercy, and grant that I and my companions, without hindrance to our bodies or possessions – for over our souls, Lord, they have no power – may go home again to our land just as we came here, for your love, and never let our enemies have any power over us, Lord, if it please you. As you will, so may it be.'

Then our Lord Jesus Christ said to her mind, 'Don't be afraid, daughter, for you and everybody in your company shall go as safe as if they were in St Peter's church.'

Then she thanked God with all her spirit, and was bold enough to go where God willed, and took her leave of her friends in Rome and especially of her confessor, who for our Lord's love had supported her and succoured her very tenderly against the wicked storms of her envious enemies, and with whom her parting was very miserable, as was witnessed by the teardrops running down the cheeks of both of them. She, falling on her knees, received the benefit of his blessing and so they parted, whom charity had joined in one, and through which they trusted to meet again, when our Lord willed, in their common homeland, after they had passed this wretched worldly exile.

And thus she and her party set off for England, and when they were a little way out of Rome, the good priest, whom as is written before this creature had received for her own son, had great fear of enemies, and so he said to her, 'Mother, I fear being killed by enemies.'

She said, 'No, son, you will make good progress and travel safely by the grace of God.'

And he was much comforted by her words for he greatly trusted in her feelings, and along their route he treated her as warmly as if he had been her own son, born of her body.

And so they reached Middelburg,[2] and then her party continued their journey over to England on the Sunday. Then the good priest came to her, saying, 'Mother, will you go with your companions or not on this good day?'

And she said, 'No, son, it is not my Lord's will that I should go so soon hence.'

And so she stayed with the good priest and some others of her party until the Saturday after, but many of her companions took ship on the Sunday. On the Friday after, this creature went out into the fields for a break, with some of her own countrymen with her, whom she instructed in the laws of God as well as she could – and she spoke to them sharply because they swore great oaths and broke the commandment of our Lord God.

And as she was talking to them, our Lord Jesus Christ bade her go home quickly to her lodging, because a great and perilous storm was coming. Then she hurried homewards with her companions, and as soon as they got home to their lodging the storm broke, as she had felt by revelation. And many times, as she went by the way and in the fields, there were great flashes of lightning with terrifying thunder, such that she feared she would be struck and killed, and very heavy storms of rain which caused her great fear and grief.

Then our Lord Jesus Christ said to her, 'Why are you afraid while I am with you? I am as mighty to keep you safe here in the fields as in the strongest church in all this world.'

And after that time she was not so very afraid as she was before, for she always greatly trusted in his mercy – blessed may he be, who comforted her in every sorrow.

Afterwards an Englishman happened to come to this creature

and swore a great oath. She, hearing that oath, wept, mourned, and sorrowed immeasurably, quite powerless to restrain herself from weeping and sorrowing, because she saw her brother was offending our Lord God Almighty, and would pay little heed to his own fault.

Chapter 43

Early the next day[1] the good priest who was like a son to this creature came to her and said, 'Mother, good news! We have a good wind, God be thanked.'

And straightaway she gave praise to our Lord, and prayed him of his mercy to grant them that the good wind and weather should last so that they might reach home in safety. And it was answered and commanded in her soul that they should go their way in the name of Jesus.

When the priest knew that she would in any case depart, he said, 'Mother, there is no proper ship here; there is only a little smack.'

She replied, 'Son, God is as mighty in a little boat as in a big ship, for I will go in that boat, by God's leave.'

And when they were in that small ship, the weather began to turn very stormy and dark. Then they cried to God for mercy and grace, and then the storms ceased, and they had fair weather, and sailed all through the night and the next day till evensong time, and then they came to land. And when they were on land, the said creature fell down on her knees kissing the ground, highly thanking God who had brought them home in safety.

Then this creature had neither penny nor halfpenny in her purse, and so they happened to meet up with other pilgrims, who gave her three halfpence because she had, in conversation, told them some holy tales. And then she was very glad and cheerful,

for she had some money with which she could make an offering
in reverence of the Trinity when she came to Norwich, as she did
when she was on her way out of England.

And so when she got there she very gladly made an offering,
and afterwards she went with her companions to the Vicar of St
Stephen's, Master Richard Caister, who was still alive at that
time. He led them with him to the place where he took his meals
and made them very welcome.

And he said to this creature, 'Margery, I am amazed how you
can be so merry, when you have had such great troubles and
travelled so far.'

'Sir, it is because I have great cause to be merry and rejoice in
our Lord, who has helped me and succoured me and brought me
home again in safety – blessed and worshipped may he be.'

And so they talked of our Lord for a good while and had much
good cheer. And then they took their leave, and she went to an
anchorite,² who was a monk from far away and lived in the
Chapel-in-the-Fields.³ He had a name for great perfection and
previously had loved this creature very much. But afterwards,
through evil talk that he heard about her, he turned completely
against her, and therefore she went to him on purpose, to humble
herself and draw him to charity if she could.

When she came to him, he welcomed her home shortly, and
asked her what she had done with her child which was conceived
and born while she was abroad, as he had heard tell.

And she said, 'Sir, the same child that God has sent me I have
brought home, for God knows I never did anything since I went
abroad through which I should have a child.'

And he would not believe her for anything that she could say.
Yet nevertheless she humbly and meekly told him, because of the
trust that she had in him, how it was our Lord's will that she
should be clad in white clothing. And he said 'God forbid', for she
would make everybody amazed at her. And she replied, 'Sir, I
don't care, so long as God is pleased with it.'

Then he bade her come again to him and be governed by him,
and by a good priest called Sir Edward.⁴ And she said she would

find out if it were the will of God or not, and with that she took her leave at that time. And as she went away from him, our Lord said to her soul as she went along, 'I do not wish that you should be governed by him,' and she sent him word what answer she had from God.

Chapter 44

And then she prayed to God, saying, 'As surely, Lord, as it is your will that I should be clad in white, as surely grant me a token of lightning, thunder and rain – provided it neither hinders nor harms anything – so that I, unworthy, may the sooner fulfil your will.'

Then our Lord answered and said to his unworthy servant, 'Daughter, have no doubt, you shall have that token by the third day.'

And so it was. On the Friday next following, early in the morning, as she lay in her bed, she saw great lightning, and heard great thunder and great rain following, and just as quickly it all passed away and the weather was fine again. Then she fully resolved to wear white clothes, except that she had neither gold nor silver to buy her clothing with.

And then our Lord said to her soul, 'I shall provide for you.'

Later she went to a worthy man in Norwich with whom she was very welcome. And as they sat together telling holy tales our Lord said continually in her soul, 'Speak to this man, speak to this man.'

Then she said to that worthy man, 'Would to God, sir, that I might find a good man who would lend me two nobles till I could pay him back, to buy myself clothes with.'

And he said, 'I will do that gladly. What sort of clothes do you want to wear?'

'Sir,' she said, 'white clothes, by God's leave.'

So this good man bought white cloth, and had a gown made for her from it, and also a hood, a kirtle and a cloak. And on the Saturday, which was the next day, he brought her this clothing in the evening and gave it to her for God's love, and showed a great deal more kindness to her for our Lord's love – Christ Jesus be his reward and have mercy upon his soul, and on all Christians.

And on the Trinity Sunday following,[1] she received communion all in white, and since then she has suffered much contempt and much shame in many divers countries, cities and towns – thanks be to God for everything.

Soon after, her husband came from Lynn to Norwich to see how she was and how she had got on, and so they went home together to Lynn. And she, shortly afterwards, fell very ill, so much so that she was anointed, because it was feared she might die. And she desired, if it were the will of God, that she might visit Santiago before she died, and suffer more shame for his love, as he had promised her before that she should do.

Then our Lord Jesus Christ said to her in her soul that she would not die yet, but she herself believed she would not live, for her pain was so great. And quickly afterwards she was in good health again.

And then winter drew on, and she was so cold that she did not know what she could do, for she was poor and had no money, and also she was greatly in debt. Then she suffered shame and abuse for wearing her white clothes, and because she cried so loud when our Lord put her in mind of his Passion. Because of the compassion that she had for our Lord's Passion she cried so astonishingly loud, and as they had never heard her crying previously it was all the more amazing to them, for she had her first crying at Jerusalem, as is written before.

And many said there was never saint in heaven that cried as she did, and from that they concluded that she had a devil within her which caused that crying. And this they said openly, and much more evil talk. She took everything patiently for our Lord's love, for she knew very well that the Jews said much worse of his own person than people did of her, and therefore she took it the more meekly.

Some said she had epilepsy, for while she cried she wrested her body about, turning from one side to the other,[2] and turned all blue and grey, like the colour of lead. Then people spat at her in horror at the illness, and some scorned her and said that she howled like a dog, and cursed her, and said that she did a lot of harm among the people. And then those who before had given her food and drink for God's love now spurned her, and ordered her not to come to their places, because of the unfavourable tales that they heard about her.

And afterwards, when the time came that she should go to Santiago, she went to the best friends that she had in Lynn and told them of her intention, how she proposed to go to Santiago if she could get the money to go with, but she was poor and much in debt. And her friends said to her, 'Why have you given away your money and other people's as well? Where will you now get as much money as you owe?'

And she replied, 'Our Lord God will help very well, for he never failed me in any country, and therefore I trust in him.'

And suddenly a good man came and gave her forty pence, and with some of that she bought herself a furred coat. And our Lord God always said to her, 'Daughter, don't concentrate on getting money, because I shall provide for you, but always concentrate on loving and remembering me, because I shall go with you wherever you go, as I have promised before.'

And afterwards there came a woman, a good friend to this creature, and gave her seven marks[3] to pray for her when she got to Santiago. Then she took leave of her friends in Lynn, intending to set off as quickly as she could.

And it was said in Lynn that there were many thieves along the way. Then she was greatly afraid that they would rob her and take her gold away from her. And our merciful Lord, comforting her, said to her, 'Go forth, daughter, in the name of Jesus. No thief shall have power over you.'

Then she set off, and came to Bristol on the Wednesday in Whitsun week, and there she found the broken-backed man who had been with her at Rome, and whom she left in Rome when she came away from there two years previously. And while they were in Rome she borrowed some money from him, and at God's bidding she then gave away to poor people all the money that she had, and what she had borrowed from him as well, as is written before. And then, while she was in Rome, she promised to pay him back in Bristol at this time, and so he had come there for his payment.

And our Lord Jesus Christ had so provided for her, as she went towards Bristol, that she was given so much money that she could easily pay the said man all she owed him. And so she did – blessed be our Lord for it.

And then she remained in Bristol six weeks, by God's command, to wait for a ship, in that there were no English ships that could sail for Santiago, because they were requisitioned for the King.[4]

Other pilgrims who were at Bristol, and wanted to speed up their journey, went about from port to port, but they were not any more successful and returned to Bristol, while she stayed where she was and did better than them despite all their efforts.

And while she remained at Bristol in this way at God's command, our merciful Lord Christ Jesus visited his creature with many holy meditations and many high contemplations and many sweet comforts. And she received communion there every Sunday with plentiful tears and violent sobbings, with loud crying and shrill shriekings; and therefore many men and women were astonished at her, scorned her and despised her, cursed her, spoke much evil of her, slandered her, and accused her of saying something she never said.

Then she wept sorely for her sins, praying God for mercy and forgiveness for them, saying to our Lord, 'Lord, as you said, hanging on the cross, for your crucifiers, "Father, forgive them; they know not what they do," so, I beseech you, forgive these people all the scorn and slanders, and all their trespasses, if it be your will, for I have deserved much more, and of much more am I worthy.'

Chapter 45

On Corpus Christi Day afterwards,[1] as the priests bore the sacrament about the town in solemn procession, with many candles and great solemnity, as was worthy to be done, the said creature followed, full of tears and devotion, with holy thoughts and meditation, bitter weeping and violent sobbing. And then a good woman came up to this creature and said, 'God give us grace to follow the steps of our Lord Jesus Christ.'

Then those words had such an effect in her heart and mind that she could not bear it, and had to go into a house. Then she cried out, 'I die, I die,' and roared so astonishingly that people were amazed at her, and wondered very much what was wrong with her. And yet our Lord made some people love and cherish her greatly, and invite her home both to eat and to drink, and have great joy to hear her converse of our Lord.

And so there was a man from Newcastle[2] – his name was Thomas Marchale – who often invited this creature to meals in order to hear her talk. He was so drawn by the good words that God put it into her head to say of contrition and compunction, of sweetness and of devotion, that he was utterly moved, as though he had been a new man, with tears of contrition and compunction both day and night, as our Lord would visit his heart with grace, so that sometimes, as he walked in the fields, he wept so sorely for his sins and his trespasses that he fell down and could not bear it. He told the said creature that he had been a very heedless and misdirected man, and he bitterly repented that – thanks be to God. And then he blessed the time when he knew this creature and fully resolved to be a good man.

Also, he said to this creature, 'Mother, I have here ten marks. I pray you that it be yours, as your own, for I will help you to get to Santiago with God's grace. And whatever you bid me give to any poor man or woman I will do your bidding – always one penny for you, another for myself.'

Then, as it pleased our Lord, he sent a ship from Brittany to

Bristol, which ship was made ready to sail to Santiago, and then the said Thomas Marchale went and paid the master for himself and for the said creature. Then there was a rich man of Bristol who would not let the said creature sail in that ship, for he held her to be no good woman. And she said to that rich man, 'Sir, if you put me out of the ship, my Lord Jesus shall put you out of heaven, for I tell you, sir, our Lord Jesus has no liking for a rich man unless he will be a good man and a meek man.'

And so she said many sharp words to him, without any flattery. Then our Lord said to her in her soul, 'You shall have your will and go to Santiago at your desire.'

And immediately afterwards, she was summoned to appear before the Bishop of Worcester, who was staying three miles outside Bristol.[3] She rose early the next day and went to the place where he was – he being still in bed – and happened to meet one of his worthiest men in the town, and so they talked of God. And when he had heard her talk for a good while, he asked her to eat with him, and afterwards he brought her into the Bishop's hall.

When she came into the hall, she saw many of the Bishop's men in clothes very fashionably slashed and cut into points. Lifting up her hand, she blessed herself. And then they said to her, 'What the devil's wrong with you?'

She replied, 'Whose men are you?'

They answered, 'The Bishop's men.'

Then she said, 'No, truly, you are more like the devil's men.'

Then they were annoyed and rebuked her, and spoke angrily to her, and she put up with it very meekly. And afterwards she spoke so seriously against sin and their misconduct that they were silent, and held themselves well pleased with her talk – thanks be to God – before she left.

Then she went into the church and waited for the Bishop to come; and when he came she knelt down and asked what was his will, and why was she summoned to come before him; it was very inconvenient for her, inasmuch as she was a pilgrim, intending by the grace of God to go to Santiago.

Then the Bishop said, 'Margery, I have not summoned you, for

I know well enough you are John of Brunham's daughter from Lynn. I beg you not to be angry, but be pleasant with me, and I shall be pleasant with you, for you shall eat with me today.'

'Sir,' she said, 'I beg you to excuse me, because I have promised a good man in town to eat with him today.'

And then he said, 'You shall both eat with me.'

And so she remained with him till God sent wind so that she could sail, and she was made very welcome by him, and by his household as well. Afterwards, she was shriven by the Bishop, and then he asked her to pray for him to die in charity, for he had been warned by a holy man, who had understood by revelation that this Bishop would be dead within the space of two years. And so it happened, indeed. And therefore he lamented to this creature, and asked her to pray for him, that he might die in charity.

At last she took her leave of him, and he gave her gold and his blessing, and commanded his household to escort her on her way. And he also asked her, when she came back again from Santiago, to come to him.

And so she set off for her ship. Before she entered the ship, she said her prayers that God would guard and preserve them from vengeance, storms and perils on the sea, so that they might go and return in safety. For she had been told that, if they had any storm, they would throw her into the sea, for they said it would be because of her; and they said the ship was the worse for her being in it.

And therefore in her prayers she said in this way: 'Almighty God, Christ Jesus, I beseech you for your mercy: if you wish to chastise me, spare me till I come back to England again. And when I get back, chastise me just as you will.'

And then our Lord granted her her boon, and so she took ship in the name of Jesus and sailed forth with her companions, whom God sent fair wind and weather, so that they reached Santiago on the seventh day.[4]

And then those who were against her when they were in Bristol were now very nice to her. And so they stayed there for fourteen days in that country, and there she had great happiness, both bodily and spiritually, high devotion, and many loud cryings at the memory of our Lord's Passion, with abundant tears of compassion.

And afterwards they came home again to Bristol in five days, and she did not stay there long, but went on to see the Blood of Hailes,[5] and there was shriven and had loud cryings and violent sobbings.

And then the religious men took her in amongst them, and made her very welcome, except that they swore many great and horrible oaths. And she rebuked them for it in accordance with the Gospel, and at that they were very surprised. Nevertheless, some were very well pleased – God be thanked for his goodness.

Chapter 46

Afterwards she went on to Leicester with a good man, Thomas Marchale, of whom is written before. And there she came into a fine church where she beheld a crucifix, which was piteously portrayed and lamentable to behold, and through beholding of which, the Passion of our Lord entered her mind, whereupon she began to melt and utterly dissolve with tears of pity and compassion. Then the fire of love kindled so quickly in her heart that she could not keep it secret for, whether she liked it or not, it caused her to break out in a loud voice and cry astonishingly, and weep and sob very terribly, so that many men and women wondered at her because of it.

When it was overcome, and she was going out of the church door, a man took her by the sleeve and said, 'Woman, why are you weeping so bitterly?'

'Sir,' she said, 'it is not to be told to you.'

And so she and the good man, Thomas Marchale, went on and found lodgings for themselves and ate a meal there. When they had eaten, she asked Thomas Marchale to write a letter and send it to her husband, so that he might fetch her home. And while the letter was being written, the innkeeper came up to her room in great haste and took away her bag, and ordered her to come quickly and speak with the Mayor.[1] And so she did. Then the Mayor asked her from which part of the country she came, and whose daughter she was.

'Sir,' she said, 'I am from Lynn in Norfolk, the daughter of a good man of the same Lynn, who has been five times mayor of that worshipful borough, and also an alderman for many years; and I have a good man, also a burgess of the said town of Lynn, for my husband.'

'Ah,' said the Mayor, 'St Katherine told of what kindred she came, and yet you are not alike, for you are a false strumpet, a false Lollard, and a false deceiver of the people, and therefore I shall have you in prison.'

And she replied, 'I am as ready, sir, to go to prison for God's love, as you are ready to go to church.'

When the Mayor had rebuked her for a long time and said many evil and horrible words to her, and she – by the grace of Jesus had reasonably answered him in everything that he could say, then he commanded the gaoler's man to lead her to prison. The gaoler's man, having compassion for her with weeping tears, said to the Mayor, 'Sir, I have no place to put her in, unless I put her in among men.'

Then she – moved with compassion for the man who had compassion for her, praying for grace and mercy to that man as to her own soul – said to the Mayor, 'I beg you, sir, not to put me among men, so that I may keep my chastity, and my bond of wedlock to my husband, as I am bound to do.'

And then the gaoler himself said to the Mayor, 'Sir, I will undertake to keep this woman in my own safekeeping until you want to see her again.'

Then there was a man from Boston, who said to the good wife where she was lodging, 'Truly,' he said, 'in Boston this woman is held to be a holy woman and a blessed woman.'

Then the gaoler took her into his custody, and led her home to his own house and put her into a fine room, locking the door with a key, and ordering his wife to keep the key safe. Nevertheless, he let her go to church when she wished, and let her eat at his own table, and made her very welcome for our Lord's love – thanks be to Almighty God for it.

Chapter 47

Then the Steward of Leicester, a good-looking man, sent for the said creature to the gaoler's wife, and she – because her husband was not at home – would not let her go to any man, Steward or otherwise. When the gaoler knew about this he came himself, and brought her before the Steward. As soon as he saw her, the Steward spoke Latin to her, many priests standing about to hear what she would say, and other people too. She said to the Steward, 'Speak English, if you please, for I do not understand what you are saying.'

The Steward said to her, 'You lie most falsely, in plain English.'

Then she replied to him, 'Sir, ask what question you will in English, and through the grace of my Lord Jesus Christ I shall answer you very reasonably.'

And then he asked many questions, to which she answered readily and reasonably, so that he could get no cause against her.

Then the Steward took her by the hand and led her into his chamber, and spoke many foul, lewd words to her, intending and desiring, as it seemed to her, to overcome her and rape her. And then she had great fear and great sorrow, begging him for mercy. She said, 'Sir, for the reverence of Almighty God, spare me, for I am a man's wife.'

And then the Steward said: 'You shall tell me whether you get this talk from God or from the devil, or else you shall go to prison.'

'Sir,' she said, 'I am not afraid to go to prison for my Lord's love, who suffered much more for my love than I may for his. I pray you, do as you think best.'

The Steward, seeing her boldness in that she was not afraid of any imprisonment, struggled with her, making filthy signs and giving her indecent looks, through which he frightened her so much that she told him how she had her speech and conversing from the Holy Ghost and not from her own knowledge.

And then he, completely astonished at her words, left off his lewdness, saying to her as many a man had done before, 'Either you are a truly good woman or else a truly wicked woman,' and delivered her up again to her gaoler, and he led her home again with him.

Afterwards they took two of her companions who went with her on pilgrimage – one was Thomas Marchale, aforesaid, the other a man from Wisbech – and put them both in prison because of her. Then she was grieved and sorry for their distress, and prayed to God for their deliverance. And then our merciful Lord Christ Jesus said to his creature, 'Daughter, I shall, for your love, so dispose for them that the people will be very glad to let them go, and not detain them for long.'

And on the next day following, our Lord sent such storms of thunder and lightning, and continuous rain, that all the people in the town were so afraid they didn't know what to do. They feared it was because they had put the pilgrims in prison.

And then those who governed the town went in great haste and took out the two pilgrims, who had lain in prison all the night before, leading them to the Guildhall, there to be examined before the Mayor and the reputable men of the town, compelling them to swear if the said creature were a woman of true faith and true belief, chaste and pure of body, or not.

As far as they knew, they swore, as certainly as God should help them at the Day of Judgement, that she was a good woman of true faith and true belief, pure and chaste in all her conduct as far as they knew, in manner and expression, in word and deed.

And then the Mayor let them go wherever they wished. And

soon the storm ceased, and the weather was fair – worshipped be our Lord. Those pilgrims were glad that they were released, and dared not stay in Leicester any longer, but went ten miles away and stayed there, so that they could get information as to what would be done with the said creature. For when they were both put in prison, they had told her themselves that they supposed that, if the Mayor could have his way, he would have her burnt.

Chapter 48

On a Wednesday, the said creature was brought into a church of All Saints in Leicester,[1] in which place, before the high altar, were seated the Abbot of Leicester[2] with some of his canons, and the Dean of Leicester,[3] a worthy cleric. There were also many friars and priests; also the Mayor of the same town with many other lay people. There were so many people that they stood upon stools to look at her and marvel at her.

The said creature knelt down, saying her prayers to Almighty God that she might have grace, wit and wisdom, so to answer that day as might be most pleasure and honour to him, most profit to her soul, and best example to the people.

Then a priest came to her and took her by the hand, and brought her before the Abbot and his assessors sitting at the altar, who made her swear on a book that she should answer truly to the Articles of the Faith, just as she felt about them. And first they repeated the blessed sacrament of the altar, charging her to say exactly what she believed about it.[4]

Then she said, 'Sirs, I believe in the sacrament of the altar in this way: that whatever man has taken the order of priesthood, be he never so wicked a man in his manner of life, if he duly say those words over the bread that our Lord Jesus Christ said when he celebrated the Last Supper sitting among his disciples, I believe that it is his very flesh and his blood, and no material bread; nor may it ever be unsaid, be it once said.'

And so she went on answering on all the articles, as many as they wished to ask her, so that they were well pleased.

The Mayor, who was her deadly enemy said, 'Truly, she does not mean with her heart what she says with her mouth.'

And the clerics said to him, 'Sir, she answers us very well.'

Then the Mayor severely rebuked her and repeated many reproving and indecent words, which it is more fitting to conceal than express.

'Sir,' she said, 'I take witness of my Lord Jesus Christ, whose body is here present in the sacrament of the altar, that I never had part of any man's body in this world in actual deed by way of sin, except my husband's body, to whom I am bound by the law of matrimony, and by whom I have borne fourteen children. For I would have you know, sir, that there is no man in this world that I love so much as God, for I love him above all things, and, sir, I tell you truly, I love all men in God and for God.'

Also, furthermore, she said plainly to his face, 'Sir, you are not worthy to be a mayor, and that shall I prove by Holy Writ, for our Lord God said himself before he would take vengeance on the cities, "I shall come down and see," [5] and yet he knew all things. And that was for nothing else, sir, but to show men such as you are that you should not carry out punishments unless you have prior knowledge that they are appropriate. And, sir, you have done quite the contrary to me today, for, sir, you have caused me much shame for something I am not guilty of. I pray God forgive you it.'

Then the Mayor said to her, 'I want to know why you go about in white clothes, for I believe you have come here to lure away our wives from us, and lead them off with you.' [6]

'Sir,' she said, 'you shall not know from my mouth why I go about in white clothes; you are not worthy to know it. But, sir, I will gladly tell it to these worthy clerks by way of confession. Let them consider whether they will tell it to you.'

Then the clerks asked the Mayor to go down from among them

with the other people. And when they had gone, she knelt on her knees before the Abbot, and the Dean of Leicester, and a Preaching Friar, a worthy cleric, and told these three clerics how our Lord by revelation warned her and bade her wear white clothes before she went to Jerusalem.

'And so I have told my confessors. And therefore they have charged me that I should go about like this, for they dare not go against my feelings for fear of God; and if they dared, they would do so very gladly. And therefore, sirs, if the Mayor wants to know why I go about in white, you may say, if you please, that my confessors order me to do so; and then you will tell no lies, yet he will not know the truth.'

So the clerics called the Mayor up again, and told him in confidence that her confessors had charged her to wear white clothes, and she had bound herself in obedience to them.

Then the Mayor called her to him, saying, 'I will not let you go from here in spite of anything you can say, unless you go to my Lord Bishop of Lincoln for a letter, inasmuch as you are in his jurisdiction, so that I may be discharged of responsibility for you.'

She said, 'Sir, I certainly dare speak to my Lord of Lincoln, for I have been very kindly received by him before now.'

And then other men asked her if she were in charity with the Mayor, and she said, 'Yes, and with all whom God has created.' And then she, bowing to the Mayor and weeping tears, prayed him to be in charity with her, and forgive her anything in which she had displeased him. And he spoke fine words to her for a while, so that she believed all was well, and that he was her good friend, but afterwards she well knew it was not so.

And thus she had leave from the Mayor to go to my Lord Bishop of Lincoln, and fetch a letter by which the Mayor should be excused responsibility.

Chapter 49

So she went first to Leicester Abbey [1] and into the church, and as soon as the Abbot had espied her he, out of his goodness, with many of his brethren, came to welcome her.

When she saw them coming, at once in her soul she beheld our Lord coming with his apostles, and she was so ravished into contemplation with sweetness and devotion, that she could not stand until they came, as courtesy demanded, but leaned against a pillar in the church and held on to it tightly for fear of falling, for she would have stood and she could not, because of the abundance of devotion which was the reason that she cried and wept very bitterly.

When she had overcome her crying, the Abbot asked his brethren to take her in with them and comfort her, and so they gave her very good wine and were extremely nice to her.

Then she got herself a letter from the Abbot to my Lord of Lincoln, putting on record what controversy she had been in during the time that she was in Leicester. And the Dean of Leicester was also ready to provide a record and act as witness for her, for he had great confidence that our Lord loved her, and therefore he comforted her very highly in his own place.

And so she took leave of her said son [Thomas Marchale], intending to travel to Lincoln with a man called Patrick, who had been with her to Santiago previously. And at this time he was sent by the said Thomas Marchale, from Melton Mowbray to Leicester, to inquire and see how things stood with the same creature. For the said Thomas Marchale was very afraid that she would have been burnt, and therefore he sent this man Patrick to find out the truth.

And so she and Patrick, together with many good folk of Leicester who had come to encourage her, thanking God who had preserved her and given her victory over her enemies, went out to the edge of the town, and there they gave her a good send-off, promising her that, if she ever came back, she would receive a much better welcome amongst them than she had before.

Then she had forgotten and left behind in the town a staff made with a piece of Moses' rod, which she had brought back from Jerusalem, and would not have lost for forty shillings. Then Patrick went into the town again for her staff and her bag and happened to meet the Mayor, and the Mayor would have put him in prison, so that in the end he got away with difficulty and left her bag there.

The said creature was waiting for this man in a blind woman's house in a very gloomy mood, dreading what had happened to him because he was so long. At last this man came riding past where she was. When she saw him she cried, 'Patrick, son, where have you been so long away from me?'

'Yes, yes, mother,' he said, 'I have been in great danger for you. I was on the point of being put in prison because of you, and the Mayor has greatly harassed me because of you, and he has taken away your bag from me.'

'Ah, good Patrick,' she said, 'don't be upset, for I shall pray for you, and God will well reward you for your trouble; it is all for the best.'

Then Patrick set her upon his horse and brought her home to his own house in Melton Mowbray where Thomas Marchale was, as previously mentioned, who took her down from the horse, highly thanking God that she was not burnt. So they rejoiced in our Lord all that night.

And afterwards she went on to the Bishop of Lincoln, where he was staying at that time. She, not exactly knowing where he was, met a very respectable man with a furred hood, a very worthy officer of the Bishop's, who said to her, 'Woman, don't you recognize me?'

'No, sir,' she said, 'truly.'

'And yet you have been beholden to me,' he said, 'because I was once very good to you.'

'Sir, I trust that what you did you did for God's love, and therefore I hope he will well reward you. And I beg you to excuse me, for I take little heed of a man's good looks or of his face, and therefore I forget him much the sooner.'

And then he kindly told her where she would find the Bishop, and so she got herself a letter from the Bishop to the Mayor of Leicester, admonishing him that he should not trouble her, nor hinder her from coming and going when she wanted.

Then there occurred great storms of thunder and lightning and heavy rain, so that people believed it was for revenge of the said creature, greatly desiring that she had been out of that part of the country. And she would in no way leave until she had her bag again.

When the said Mayor received the Bishop's letter, he sent her her bag and let her go in safety wherever she wanted. For three weeks she was delayed in her journey by the Mayor of Leicester, before he would let her leave that district.[2] Then she hired the said man Patrick to go with her through the country, and so they went on to York.

Chapter 50

When she came to York, she went to an anchoress who had greatly loved her before she went to Jerusalem, in order to have knowledge of her spiritual progress; also desiring, for the purpose of more spiritual communication, to eat with the anchoress that day nothing else but bread and water, for it was on Our Lady's Eve.[1] And then the anchoress would not receive her, because she had heard so much evil talked about her. So she went on to other strange folk, and they made her very welcome for our Lord's love.

One day, as she sat in a church in York, our Lord Jesus Christ said in her soul, 'Daughter, there is much tribulation coming to you.'

She was somewhat depressed and dismayed at this, and so she remained sitting still, and did not answer. Then our blessed Lord said again, 'What, daughter, are you displeased to suffer more tribulation for my love? If you do not wish to suffer any more, I shall take it away from you.'

And then she replied, 'No, good Lord, let me be at your will, and make me mighty and strong to suffer all that you ever wish me to suffer, and grant me meekness and patience as well.'

And so from that time forward, as she knew it was our Lord's will that she should suffer more tribulation, she received it gladly when our Lord would send it, and thanked him highly for it, being very glad and cheerful on that day when she suffered any distress. And in the process of time, that day on which she suffered no tribulation, she was not as cheerful and glad as that day when she suffered tribulation.

Afterwards, as she was in the Minster at York, a cleric came to her, saying, 'How long will you stay here, woman?'

'Sir,' she said, 'I intend to stay for fourteen days.'

And so she did. And in that time many good men and women asked her to meals and made her very welcome, and were very glad to hear her conversation, greatly marvelling at her talk because it was spiritually fruitful.

And also she had many enemies who slandered her, scorned her, and despised her, of whom one priest came to her while she was in the said Minster, and taking her by the collar of her gown, said, 'You wolf, what is this cloth that you have on?'[2]

She stood still and would not answer in her own defence. Children of the monastery going past said to the priest, 'Sir, it is wool.'

The priest was annoyed because she would not answer, and began to swear many great oaths. Then she began to speak for God's cause – she was not afraid. She said, 'Sir, you should keep the commandments of God, and not swear as negligently as you do.'

The priest asked her who kept the commandments.

She said, 'Sir, they who keep them.'

Then he said, 'Do you keep them?'

She replied, 'Sir, it is my will to keep them, for I am bound to do so, and so are you and every man who will be saved at the last.'

After he had wrangled with her for a long time, he slipped away before she noticed, so that she did not know where he went.

Chapter 51

Another time a great cleric came to her asking how these words should be understood: *Crescite et multiplicamini.*[1]

She answering said, 'Sir, these words are not only to be understood as applying to the begetting of children physically, but also to the gaining of virtue, which is spiritual fruit, such as by hearing the words of God, by giving a good example, by meekness and patience, charity and chastity, and other such things – for patience is more worthy than miracle-working.' And she, through the grace of God, so answered that cleric that he was well pleased. And our Lord, of his mercy, always made some men love her and support her.

And so in this city of York, there was a doctor of divinity, Master John Aclom,[2] also a canon of the Minster, Sir John Kendale,[3] and another priest who sang by the Bishop's tomb[4] – these were her good friends among the ecclesiastics.

So she stayed in that city for fourteen days, as she had said before, and somewhat more, and on Sundays she received communion in the Minster with much weeping, violent sobbing, and loud crying, so that many people wondered very much what was wrong with her. So afterwards there came a priest – a worthy cleric he seemed – and said to her, 'Woman, you said when you first came here that you would only stay fourteen days.'

'Yes, sir, with your leave, I said that I would stay here fourteen days, but I did not say that I should neither stay here more nor less. But now, sir, I tell you truly that I am not leaving yet.'

Then he set her a day, commanding her to appear before him in the Chapterhouse.[5] And she said that she would obey his injunction with a good will.

She went then to Master John Aclom, the said doctor of divinity, begging him to be there on her side. And so he was, and he found great favour amongst them all. Another master of divinity had also promised her to be there with her, but he drew back till he knew how the cause should go, whether with her or against her.

There were many people that day in the Chapterhouse of the Minster to hear and see what would be said or done to the said creature. When the day came, she was all ready in the Minster to come and answer for herself. Then her friends came to her and urged her to be cheerful. Thanking them, she said that so she would.

And immediately a priest came and very kindly took her by the arm to help her through the press of people, and brought her before a worthy doctor, the one who had ordered her to appear before him in the Chapterhouse on this day in York Minster. And with this doctor sat many other very reverend and worthy clerics, of whom some had great love for the said creature.

Then the worthy doctor said to her, 'Woman, what are you doing here in this part of the country?'

'Sir, I come on pilgrimage to offer here at St William's shrine.'[6]

Then he went on, 'Do you have a husband?'

She said, 'Yes.'

'Do you have a letter recording his permission?'

'Sir,' she said, 'my husband gave me permission with his own mouth. Why do you proceed in this way with me more than you do with other pilgrims who are here, and who have no letter any more than I have? Sir, them you let go in peace and quiet, and undisturbed, and yet I may not be left alone amongst you. And sir, if there be any cleric here amongst you all who can prove that I have said any word otherwise than as I ought to do, I am ready to put it right very willingly. I will neither maintain error nor heresy, for it is my will entirely to hold as Holy Church holds, and fully to please God.'

Then the clerks examined her in the articles of the faith and on many other points, as they pleased, to all of which she answered well and truly, so that they might have no occasion in her words to harm her, thanks be to God.

And then the doctor who sat there as a judge summoned her to appear before the Archbishop of York – and told her what day – at a town called Cawood,[7] commanding her to be kept in prison till the day of her appearing came.

Then the secular people answered for her, and said she should not go to prison, for they would themselves undertake for her and go to the Archbishop with her. And so the clerics said no more to her at that time, for they rose up and went wherever they wanted, and let her go wherever she wanted – worship be to Jesus!

And soon after there came a cleric to her – one of the same that had sat against her – and said, 'Woman, I beg you not to be annoyed with me, though I sat with the doctor against you; he kept on at me so, that I dared not do otherwise.'

And she said, 'Sir, I am not annoyed with you for that.'

Then he said, 'I pray you then, pray for me.'

'Sir,' she said, 'I will, very readily.'

Chapter 52

There was a monk who was going to preach in York, and who had heard much slander and much evil talk about the said creature. And when he was going to preach, there was a great crowd of people to hear him, and she present with them. And so when he was launched into his sermon, he repeated many matters so openly that people saw perfectly well it was on account of her, at which her friends who loved her were very sorry and upset because of it, and she was much the merrier, because she had something to try her patience and her charity, through which she trusted to please our Lord Christ Jesus.

When the sermon was over, a doctor of divinity who had great love for her, together with many other people as well, came to her and said, 'Margery, how have you got on today?'

'Sir,' she said, 'very well indeed, God be blessed. I have reason to be very happy and glad in my soul that I may suffer anything for his love, for he suffered much more for me.'

Shortly afterwards, a man who was also devoted to her

came with his wife and other people, and escorted her seven miles from there to the Archbishop of York, and brought her into a fair chamber, where there came a good cleric, saying to the good man who had brought her there, 'Sir, why have you and your wife brought this woman here? She will steal away from you, and then she will have brought shame upon you.'

The good man said, 'I dare well say she will remain and answer for herself very willingly.'

On the next day she was brought into the Archbishop's chapel, and many of the Archbishop's household came there scorning her, calling her 'Lollard' and 'heretic', and swore many a horrible oath that she should be burned. And she, through the strength of Jesus, replied to them, 'Sirs, I fear you will be burned in hell without end, unless you correct yourselves of your swearing of oaths, for you do not keep the commandments of God. I would not swear as you do for all the money in this world.'

Then they went away, as if they were ashamed. She then, saying her prayers in her mind, asked for grace to behave that day as was most pleasure to God, and profit to her own soul, and good example to her fellow Christians. Our Lord, answering her, said that everything would go well.

At last the said Archbishop[1] came into the chapel with his clerics, and he said to her abruptly, 'Why do you go about in white clothes? Are you a virgin?'

She, kneeling before him, said, 'No, sir, I am no virgin; I am a married woman.'

He ordered his household to fetch a pair of fetters and said she should be fettered, for she was a false heretic, and then she said, 'I am no heretic, nor shall you prove me one.'

The Archbishop went away and left her standing alone. Then for a long while she said her prayers to our Lord God Almighty to help her and succour her against all her enemies both spiritual and bodily, and her flesh trembled and quaked amazingly, so that she was glad to put her hands under her clothes so that it should not be noticed.

Afterwards the Archbishop came back into the chapel with

many worthy clerics, amongst whom was the same doctor who had examined her before, and the monk who had preached against her a little while before in York. Some of the people asked whether she were a Christian woman or a Jew; some said she was a good woman, and some said not.

Then the Archbishop took his seat, and his clerics too, each according to his degree, many people being present. And during the time that people were gathering together and the Archbishop was taking his seat, the said creature stood at the back, saying her prayers for help and succour against her enemies with high devotion, and for so long that she melted all into tears. And at last she cried out loudly, so that the Archbishop, and his clerics, and many people, were all astonished at her, for they had not heard such crying before.

When her crying was passed, she came before the Archbishop and fell down on her knees, the Archbishop saying very roughly to her, 'Why do you weep so, woman?'

She answering said, 'Sir, you shall wish some day that you had wept as sorely as I.'

And then, after the Archbishop had put to her the Articles of our Faith – to which God gave her grace to answer well, truly and readily, without much having to stop and think, so that he could not criticize her – he said to the clerics, 'She knows her faith well enough. What shall I do with her?'

The clerics said, 'We know very well that she knows the Articles of the Faith, but we will not allow her to dwell among us, because the people have great faith in her talk, and perhaps she might lead some of them astray.' Then the Archbishop said to her: 'I am told very bad things about you. I hear it said that you are a very wicked woman.'

And she replied, 'Sir, I also hear it said that you are a wicked man. And if you are as wicked as people say, you will never get to heaven, unless you amend while you are here.'

Then he said very roughly, 'Why you! . . . What do people say about me?'

She answered, 'Other people, sir, can tell you well enough.'

Then a great cleric with a furred hood said, 'Quiet! You speak about yourself, and let him be.'

Afterwards the Archbishop said to her, 'Lay your hand on the book here before me, and swear that you will go out of my diocese as soon as you can.'

'No, sir,' she said, 'I pray you, give me permission to go back into York to take leave of my friends.'

Then he gave her permission for one or two days. She thought it was too short a time, and so she replied, 'Sir, I may not go out of this diocese so hastily, for I must stay and speak with good men before I go; and I must, sir, with your leave, go to Bridlington and speak with my confessor, a good man, who was the good Prior's confessor, who is now canonized.'[2]

Then the Archbishop said to her, 'You shall swear that you will not teach people or call them to account in my diocese.'

'No, sir, I will not swear,' she said, 'for I shall speak of God and rebuke those who swear great oaths wherever I go, until such time that the Pope and Holy Church have ordained that nobody shall be so bold as to speak of God, for God Almighty does not forbid, sir, that we should speak of him. And also the Gospel[3] mentions that, when the woman had heard our Lord preach, she came before him and said in a loud voice, "Blessed be the womb that bore you, and the teats that gave you suck." Then our Lord replied to her, "In truth, so are they blessed who hear the word of God and keep it." And therefore, sir, I think that the Gospel gives me leave to speak of God.'

'Ah, sir,' said the clerics, 'here we know that she has a devil in her, for she speaks of the Gospel.'[4]

A great cleric quickly produced a book and quoted St Paul for his part against her, that no woman should preach.[5] She, answering to this, said, 'I do not preach, sir; I do not go into any pulpit. I use only conversation and good words, and that I will do while I live.'

Then a doctor who had examined her before said, 'Sir, she told me the worst tale about priests that I ever heard.'

The Archbishop commanded her to tell that tale.

'Sir, by your reverence, I only spoke of one priest, by way of example, who, as I have learned it, went astray in a wood – through the sufferance of God, for the profit of his soul – until night came upon him. Lacking any shelter, he found a fair arbour in which he rested that night, which had a beautiful pear-tree in the middle, all covered in blossom, which he delighted to look at. To that place came a great rough bear, ugly to behold, that shook the pear-tree and caused the blossoms to fall. Greedily this horrible beast ate and devoured those fair flowers. And when he had eaten them, turning his tail towards the priest, he discharged them out again at his rear end.

'The priest, greatly revolted at that disgusting sight and becoming very depressed for fear of what it might mean, wandered off on his way all gloomy and pensive. He happened to meet a good-looking, aged man like a pilgrim, who asked the priest the reason for his sadness. The priest, repeating the matter written before, said he felt great fear and heaviness of heart when he beheld that revolting beast soil and devour such lovely flowers and blossoms, and afterwards discharge them so horribly at his rear end in the priest's presence – he did not understand what this might mean.

'Then the pilgrim, showing himself to be the messenger of God, thus addressed him, "Priest, you are yourself the pear-tree, somewhat flourishing and flowering through your saying of services and administering of sacraments, although you act without devotion, for you take very little heed how you say your matins and your service, so long as it is babbled to an end. Then you go to your mass without devotion, and you have very little contrition for your sin. You receive there the fruit of everlasting life, the sacrament of the altar, in a very feeble frame of mind. All day long afterwards, you spend your time amiss: you give yourself over to buying and selling, bartering and exchanging, just like a man of the world. You sit over your beer, giving yourself up to gluttony and excess, to the lust of your body, through lechery and impurity. You break the commandments of God through swearing, lying, detraction and backbiting gossip, and the practice of other such sins. Thus, through your misconduct, just like the loathsome bear, you devour and destroy the flowers and blossoms of virtuous living, to your own endless damnation and to the hindrance of many other people, unless you have grace for repentance and amending." '

Then the Archbishop liked the tale a lot and commended it, saying it was a good tale. And the cleric who had examined her before in the absence of the Archbishop, said, 'Sir, this tale cuts me to the heart.'

The said creature said to the cleric, 'Ah, worthy doctor, sir, in the place where I mostly live is a worthy cleric, a good preacher, who boldly speaks out against the misconduct of people and will flatter no one. He says many times in the pulpit: "If anyone is displeased by my preaching, note him well, for he is guilty." And just so, sir,' she said to the clerk, 'do you behave with me, God forgive you for it.'

The cleric did not know what he could say to her, and afterwards the same cleric came to her and begged her for forgiveness that he had been so against her. He also asked her specially to pray for him.

And then afterwards the Archbishop said, 'Where shall I get a man who could escort this woman from me?'

Many young men quickly jumped up, and everyone of them said, 'My lord, I will go with her.'

The Archbishop answered, 'You are too young: I will not have you.'

Then a good, sober man of the Archbishop's household asked his lord what he would give him if he would escort her. The Archbishop offered him five shillings, and the man asked for a noble.[6] The Archbishop answering said, 'I will not spend so much on her body.'

'Yes, good sir,' said this creature, 'Our Lord shall reward you very well for it.'

Then the Archbishop said to the man, 'See, here is five shillings, and now escort her fast out of this area.'

She, kneeling down on her knees, asked his blessing. He, asking her to pray for him, blessed her and let her go.

Then she, going back again to York, was received by many people, and by very worthy clerics, who rejoiced in our Lord, who had given her – uneducated as she was – the wit and wisdom to answer so many learned men without shame or blame, thanks be to God.

Chapter 53

Afterwards that good man who was her escort brought her out of the town, and they went on to Bridlington to her confessor, who was called Sleytham, and spoke with him and with many other good men who had encouraged her previously and done much for her. Then she would not stay there, but took her leave to walk on upon her journey. And then her confessor asked her if she dared not stay because of the Archbishop of York, and she said, 'No, truly.'

Then the good man gave her silver, begging her to pray for him. And so she went on to Hull. And there, on one occasion, as they went in procession, a great woman treated her with utter contempt, and she said not a word in reply. Many other people said that she ought to be put in prison and made great threats. And notwithstanding all their malice, a good man still came and asked her to a meal, and made her very welcome. Then the malicious people who had despised her before came to this good man, and told him that he ought not do her any kindness, for they considered that she was not a good woman. On the next day, in the morning, her host escorted her out to the edge of town, for he dared not keep her with him any longer.

And so she went to Hessle and would have crossed over the Humber. Then she happened to find there two Preaching Friars, and two yeomen of the Duke of Bedford's.[1] The friars told the yeomen which woman she was, and the yeomen arrested her as she was about to board her boat, and also arrested a man who travelled with her.

'For our lord,' they said, 'the Duke of Bedford, has sent for you, and you are held to be the greatest Lollard in all this part of the country, or around London either. We have sought you in many a part of the land, and we shall have a hundred pounds for bringing you before our lord.'

She said to them, 'With a good will, sirs, I shall go with you wherever you will lead me.'

Then they brought her back to Hessle, and there men called her Lollard, and women came running out of their houses with their distaffs, crying to the people, 'Burn this false heretic.'

So as she went on towards Beverley with the said yeomen and friars, they many times met with men of that district who said to her, 'Woman, give up this life that you lead, and go and spin, and card wool, as other women do, and do not suffer so much shame and so much unhappiness. We would not suffer so much for any money on earth.'

Then she said to them, 'I do not suffer as much sorrow as I would do for our Lord's love, for I only suffer cutting words, and our merciful Lord Christ Jesus – worshipped be his name – suffered hard strokes, bitter scourgings, and shameful death at the last, for me and for all mankind, blessed may he be. And therefore, it is truly nothing that I suffer, in comparison to what he suffered.'

And so, as she went along with the said men, she told them good stories, until one of the Duke's men who had arrested her said to her, 'I rather regret that I met with you, for it seems to me that you speak very good words.'

Then she said to him, 'Sir, do not regret nor repent that you met with me. Do your lord's will, and I trust that all shall be for the best, for I am very well pleased that you met with me.'

He replied, 'If ever you're a saint in heaven, lady, pray for me.'

She answered, saying to him, 'Sir, I hope you will be a saint yourself, and every man that shall come to heaven.'

So they went on till they came into Beverley, where lived the wife of one of the men who had arrested her. And they escorted her there and took away from her her purse and her ring. They provided her with a nice room and a decent bed in it, with all the necessaries, locking the door with a key, and bearing the key away with them.

Afterwards they took the man whom they arrested with her, who was the Archbishop of York's man, and put him in prison. And soon after, that same day, came news that the Archbishop had come to the town where his man was put in prison. The Archbishop was told of his man's imprisonment, and he immediately had him let out. Then that man went to the said creature with an angry face, saying, 'Alas that I ever knew you! I have been imprisoned because of you.'

She, comforting him, replied, 'Have meekness and patience, and you shall have great reward in heaven for it.'

So he went away from her. Then she stood looking out at a window, telling many edifying tales to those who would hear her, so much so that women wept bitterly, and said with great heaviness of heart, 'Alas, woman, why should you be burned?'

Then she begged the good wife of the house to give her a drink, for she was terribly thirsty. And the good wife said her husband had taken away the key, because of which she could not come in to her, nor give her a drink. And then the women took a ladder and set it up against the window, and gave her a pint of wine in a pot, and also a cup, begging her to conceal the pot and cup, so that when the good man came back he might not notice it.

Chapter 54

The said creature, lying in her bed on the following night, heard with her bodily ears a loud voice calling, 'Margery.' With that voice she awoke, greatly frightened, and, lying still in silence, she said her prayers as devoutly as she could at that time. And soon our merciful Lord, everywhere present, comforting his unworthy servant, said to her, 'Daughter, it is more pleasing to me that you suffer scorn and humiliation, shame and rebukes, wrongs and distress, than if your head were struck off three times a day every day for seven years. And therefore, daughter, do not fear what any man can say to you. But in my goodness, and in your sorrows that you have suffered, you have great cause to rejoice, for when you come home to heaven, then shall every sorrow be turned into joy for you.'

On the next day she was brought into the Chapterhouse of Beverley,[1] and there was the Archbishop of York, and many great clerics with him, priests, canons, and secular men. Then the Archbishop said to this creature, 'What, woman, have you come back again? I would gladly be rid of you.'

And then a priest brought her before him, and the Archbishop said, in the hearing of all present, 'Sirs, I had this woman before me at Cawood, and there I with my clerics examined her in her faith and found no fault in her. Furthermore, sirs, I have since that time spoken with good men who hold her to be a perfect woman[2] and a good woman. Notwithstanding all this, I gave one of my men five shillings to lead her out of this part of the country, in order to quieten the people down. And as they were going on their journey they were taken and arrested, my man put in prison because of her; also her gold and her silver was taken away from her, together with her beads and her ring, and she is brought before me again here. Is there any man here who can say anything against her?'

Then other men said, 'Here is a friar who knows many things against her.'

The friar came forward and said that she disparaged all men of Holy Church – and he uttered much evil talk about her that time. He also said that she would have been burnt at Lynn, had his order – that was the Preaching Friars – not been there. 'And, sir, she says that she may weep and have contrition when she will.'

Then came the two men who had arrested her, saying with the friar that she was Cobham's daughter,[3] and was sent to carry letters about the country. And they said she had not been to Jerusalem, nor in the Holy Land, nor on other pilgrimage, as she had been in truth.[4] They denied all truth, and maintained what was wrong, as many others had done before. When they had said enough for a long while, they held their peace.

Then the Archbishop said to her, 'Woman, what do you say to all this?'

She said, 'My lord, saving your reverence, all the words that they say are lies.'

Then the Archbishop said to the friar, 'Friar, the words are not heresy; they are slanderous words and erroneous.'

'My lord,' said the friar, 'she knows her faith well enough. Nevertheless, my lord of Bedford is angry with her, and he will have her.'

'Well, friar,' said the Archbishop, 'and you shall escort her to him.'

'No, sir,' said the friar, 'it is not a friar's job to escort a woman about.'

'And I will not have it,' said the Archbishop, 'that the Duke of Bedford be angry with me because of her.'

Then the Archbishop said to his men, 'Watch the friar until I want to see him again,' and commanded another man to guard the said creature as well, until he wanted to see her another time, when he pleased. The said creature begged his lordship that she not be put amongst men, for she was a man's wife. And the Archbishop said, 'No, you shall come to no harm.'

Then he who was charged with her took her by the hand and led her home to his house, and made her sit with him to eat and drink, making her very welcome. Many priests and other men came there to see her and talk to her, and many people were very sorry that she was being so badly treated.

A short time afterwards the Archbishop sent for her, and she was led into his chamber, and even up to his bedside. Then she, bowing, thanked him for his gracious favour that he had shown her before.

'Yes, yes,' said the Archbishop, 'I am told worse things of you than I ever was before.'

She said, 'My lord, if you care to examine me, I shall avow the truth, and if I be found guilty, I will be obedient to your correction.'

Then a Preaching Friar came forward, who was Suffragan to the Archbishop, to whom the Archbishop said, 'Now, sir, as you said to me when she was not present, say now while she is present.'

'Shall I do so?' said the Suffragan.

'Yes,' said the Archbishop.

Then the Suffragan said to this creature, 'Woman, you were at my Lady Westmorland's.' [5]

'When, sir?' said she.

'At Easter,' said the Suffragan.

She, not replying, said, 'Well, sir?'

Then he said, 'My Lady herself was well pleased with you and liked your talk, but you advised my Lady Greystoke to leave her husband, [6] and she is a baron's wife, and daughter to my Lady of Westmorland. And now you have said enough to be burned for.' And so he multiplied many sharp words in front of the Archbishop – it is not fitting to repeat them.

At last she said to the Archbishop, 'My lord, if it be your will, I have not seen my Lady Westmorland these two years and more. Sir, she sent for me before I went to Jerusalem [7] and, if you like, I will go to her again for a testimonial that I prompted no such matter.'

'No,' said those who stood round about, 'let her be put in prison, and we will send a letter to the noble lady, and, if it be the truth that she is saying, let her go free, without any grudging.'

And she said she was quite satisfied that it should be so.

Then a great cleric who stood a little to one side of the Archbishop said, 'Put her in prison forty days, and she will love God the better for the rest of her life.'

The Archbishop asked her what tale it was that she told the Lady of Westmorland when she spoke with her.

She said, 'I told her a good tale of a lady who was damned because she would not love her enemies, and of a bailiff who was saved because he loved his enemies and forgave them their trespasses against him, and yet he was held to be an evil man.'

The Archbishop said it was a good tale. Then his steward said, and many others with him, crying with a loud voice to the Archbishop, 'My lord, we pray you, let her go from here this time, and if she ever comes back again, we will burn her ourselves.'

The Archbishop said, 'I believe there was never woman in England so treated as she is, and has been.'

Then he said to this creature, 'I do not know what I shall do with you.'

She said, 'My lord, I pray you, let me have your letter and your seal as a record that I have vindicated myself against my enemies, and that nothing admissible is charged against me, neither error nor heresy that may be proved against me, our Lord be thanked. And let me have John, your man, again to bring me over the water.'

And the Archbishop very kindly granted her all she desired – our Lord grant him his reward – and delivered to her her purse with her ring and beads, which the Duke of Bedford's men had taken from her before. The Archbishop was amazed at where she got the money to travel about the country with, and she said good men gave it her so that she would pray for them.

Then she, kneeling down, received his blessing and took her leave with a very glad heart, going out of his chamber. And the Archbishop's household asked her to pray for them, but the Steward was angry because she laughed and was so cheerful, saying to her, 'Holy folk should not laugh.'[8]

She said, 'Sir, I have great cause to laugh, for the more shame and scorn I suffer, the merrier I may be in our Lord Jesus Christ.'

Then she came down into the hall, and there stood the Preaching Friar who had caused her all that unhappiness. And so she passed on with a man of the Archbishop's, bearing the letter which the Archbishop had granted her for a record, and he brought her to the River Humber, and there he took his leave of her, returning to his lord and bearing the said letter with him again, and so she was left alone, without any knowledge of the people.

All the aforesaid trouble befell her on a Friday, God be thanked for everything.[9]

Chapter 55

When she had crossed the River Humber, she was immediately arrested as a Lollard and led towards prison. There happened to be a person there who had seen her before the Archbishop of York, and he got her leave to go where she wanted, and excused her to the bailiff, and undertook for her that she was no Lollard. And so she escaped away in the name of Jesus.

Then she met a man from London, and his wife who was with him. And so she went on with them until she came to Lincoln, and there she suffered much scorn and many annoying words, answering back in God's cause without any hindrance, wisely and discreetly, so that people were amazed at her knowledge.

There were men of law who said to her, 'We have gone to school many years, and yet we are not sufficient to answer as you do. From whom do you get this knowledge?'

And she said, 'From the Holy Ghost.'

Then they asked, 'Do you have the Holy Ghost?'

'Yes, sirs,' said she, 'no one may say a good word without the gift of the Holy Ghost, for our Lord Jesus Christ said to his disciples, "Do not study what you shall say, for it shall not be your spirit that shall speak in you, but it shall be the spirit of the Holy Ghost."' [1]

And thus our Lord gave her grace to answer them, worshipped may he be.

Another time there came a great lord's men to her, and they swore many great oaths, saying, 'We've been given to understand that you can tell us whether we shall be saved or damned.'

She said, 'Yes, truly I can, for as long as you swear such horrible oaths, and break God's commandment as knowingly as you do, and will not leave your sin, I dare well say you shall be damned. And if you will be contrite, and shriven of your sin, willingly do penance and leave sin while you may, with a will to turn back to it no more, I dare well say you shall be saved.'

'What! Can't you tell us anything other than this?'

'Sirs,' she said, 'this is very good, I think.'

And then they went away from her.

After this she went on homewards again, until she came to West Lynn.[2] When she was there, she sent into Bishop's Lynn for her husband, for Master Robert, her confessor, and for Master Aleyn, a doctor of divinity, and told them in part of her tribulations. And afterwards she told them that she could not come home to Bishop's Lynn until such time as she had been to the Archbishop of Canterbury for his letter and his seal.

'For when I was before the Archbishop of York,' she said, 'he would give no credence to my words, inasmuch as I didn't have my Lord of Canterbury's letter and seal. And so I promised him that I would not come to Bishop's Lynn until I had my Lord of Canterbury's letter and seal.'

And then she took her leave of the said clerks, asking their blessing, and went on with her husband to London. When she got there, she was soon successful over her letter from the Archbishop of Canterbury.[3] And so she stayed in the city of London a long time, and was very well received by many worthy men.

Afterwards, she was coming towards Ely on her way home to Lynn, and she was three miles from Ely, when a man came riding after them at a great speed, and arrested her husband and her also, intending to take them both to prison. He cruelly rebuked them and utterly reviled them, repeating many reproving words. And at last she asked her husband to show him my Lord of Canterbury's letter. When the man had read the letter he spoke handsomely and kindly to them, saying, 'Why didn't you show me your letter before?'

And so they parted from him, and then came to Ely, and from there home to Lynn, where she suffered much humiliation, much reproof, many a scorn, many a slander and many a curse.

And on one occasion a reckless man, caring little for his own shame, deliberately and on purpose threw a bowlful of water on her head as she was coming along the street. She, not at all disturbed by it, said, 'God make you a good man,' highly thanking God for it, as she did of many other things at different times.

Chapter 56

Afterwards God punished her with many great and various illnesses. She had dysentery for a long time, until she was anointed, expecting to be dead. She was so weak that she could not hold a spoon in her hand. Then our Lord Jesus Christ spoke to her in her soul and said that she should not die yet. Then she recovered again for a little while.

And shortly afterwards she had a great sickness in her head, and later in her back, so that she feared to lose her wits because of it. Afterwards, when she was recovered from all these illnesses, another illness followed within a short time, which settled in her right side, lasting over a period of eight years, all but eight weeks, at different times. Sometimes she had it once in a week, lasting sometimes thirty hours, sometimes twenty, sometimes ten, sometimes eight, sometimes four, sometimes two, so hard and so sharp that she must discharge everything that was in her stomach, as bitter as if it had been gall, neither eating nor drinking while the sickness lasted, but always groaning until it was gone.

Then she would say to our Lord, 'Ah, blissful Lord, why would you become man and suffer so much pain for my sins and for all men's sins that shall be saved, and we are so unkind, Lord, to you; and I, most unworthy, cannot suffer this little pain? Ah, Lord, because of your great pain, have mercy on my little pain; for the great pain that you suffered, do not give me as much as I am worthy of, for I may not bear as much as I am worthy of. And if you wish, Lord, that I should bear it, send me patience, for otherwise I may not endure it.

'Ah, blissful Lord, I would rather suffer all the cutting words that people might say about me, and all clerics to preach against me for your love (provided it were no hindrance to any man's soul), than this pain that I have. For to suffer cruel words for your love hurts me not at all, Lord, and the world may take nothing from me but respect and worldly goods, and on the respect of the world I set no value at all.

'And all manner of worldly goods and dignities, and all manner of loves on earth, I pray you, Lord, forbid me, especially all those loves and possessions of any earthly thing which would decrease my love towards you, or lessen my merit in heaven. And all manner of loves and goods which you know in your Godhead should increase my love towards you, I pray you, grant me for your mercy to your everlasting worship.'

Sometimes, notwithstanding that the said creature had great bodily sickness, the Passion of our merciful Lord Christ Jesus still so worked in her soul that at that time she did not feel her own illness, but wept and sobbed at the memory of our Lord's Passion, as though she saw him with her bodily eye suffering pain and Passion before her.

Afterwards, when eight years were passed, her sickness abated, so that it did not come week by week as it did before, but then her cries and weeping increased so much that priests did not dare to give her communion openly in the church, but privately, in the Prior's chapel at Lynn, out of people's hearing.

And in that chapel she had such high contemplation and so much confabulation with our Lord, inasmuch as she was put out of church for his love, that she cried at the time when she should receive communion as if her soul and her body were going to be parted, so that two men held her in their arms till her crying ceased, for she could not bear the abundance of love that she felt in the precious sacrament, which she steadfastly believed was very God and man in the form of bread.

Then our blessed Lord said to her mind, 'Daughter, I will not have my grace hidden that I give you, for the busier people are to hinder it and prevent it, the more I shall spread it abroad and make it known to all the world.'

Chapter 57

Then it so happened that another monk came to Lynn at the time of removing [1] – as was the custom amongst them – who had no love for the said creature, nor would allow her to come into their chapel, as she had done before he came there.

Then the Prior of Lynn, Dom Thomas Hevyngham, [2] meeting the said creature and Master Robert Spryngolde, who was her confessor at that time, asked them to excuse him if she no longer received communion in his chapel; 'for there has come,' he said, 'a new brother of mine who will not come into our chapel as long as she is in it. And therefore, please provide yourselves with another place.'

Master Robert answered, 'Sir, we must then give her communion in the church – we may not choose, for she has my Lord of Canterbury's letter and seal, in which we are commanded, by virtue of obedience, to hear her confession and administer the sacrament to her as often as we are required.' [3]

Then after this time she received communion at the high altar in St Margaret's Church, and our Lord visited her with such great grace when she should receive communion that she cried so loudly that it could be heard all round the church, and outside as well, as if she would have died because of it, so that she could not receive the sacrament from the priest's hands, the priest turning back again to the altar with the precious sacrament until her crying had ceased. And then he, turning back to her, would minister to her as he ought to do. And thus it happened many times when she was to receive communion; and sometimes she would weep very softly and silently in receiving the precious sacrament without any violence, just as our Lord would visit her with his grace.

One Good Friday, as the said creature beheld priests kneeling and other worthy men with torches burning in their hands before the Easter Sepulchre, representing the lamentable death and doleful burying of our Lord Jesus Christ according to the good

custom of Holy Church,[4] the memory of our Lady's sorrows, which
she suffered when she beheld his precious body hanging on the
cross and then buried before her eyes, suddenly filled the heart of
this creature. Her mind was drawn wholly into the Passion of our
Lord Christ Jesus, whom she beheld with her spiritual eye in the
sight of her soul as truly as if she had seen his precious body
beaten, scourged and crucified with her bodily eye, which sight
and spiritual beholding worked by grace so fervently in her mind,
wounding her with pity and compassion, so that she sobbed,
roared and cried, and, spreading her arms out wide, said with a
loud voice, 'I die, I die,' so that many people were astonished at
her, and wondered what was the matter with her. And the more
she tried to keep herself from crying, the louder she cried, for it
was not in her power to take it or leave it, but as God would send
it. Then a priest took her in his arms and carried her into the
Prior's Cloister to let her get the air, supposing she would not
otherwise have lasted, her affliction was so great. Then she turned
all blue like lead, and sweated dreadfully.[5]

And this manner of crying lasted for a period of ten years, as is
written before.[6] And every Good Friday in all these years she was
weeping and sobbing five or six hours together, and also cried
loudly many times, so that she could not restrain herself from
doing so, which made her very weak and feeble in her bodily
strength. Sometimes she wept for an hour on Good Friday for the
sins of the people, having more sorrow for their sins than for her
own, inasmuch as our Lord forgave her her own sins before she
went to Jerusalem.

Nevertheless, she wept for her own sins most plentifully when
it pleased our Lord to visit her with his grace. Sometimes she wept
another hour for the souls in purgatory; another hour for those
who were in misfortune, in poverty, or in any distress; another
hour for Jews, Saracens, and all false heretics, that God out of his
great goodness should set aside their blindness, so that they might
through his grace be turned to the faith of Holy Church and be
children of salvation.

Many times, when this creature would say her prayers, our

Lord said to her, 'Daughter, ask what you wish, and you shall have it.' [7]

She said, 'I ask for absolutely nothing, Lord, except what you may well give me, and that is mercy, which I ask for the people's sins. Often during the year you say to me that you have forgiven me my sins. Therefore I now ask mercy for the sins of the people, as I would do for my own, for, Lord, you are all charity, and charity brought you into this wretched world and caused you to suffer hard pains for our sins. Why should I not then have charity for the people and desire forgiveness of their sins?

'Blessed Lord, I think you have shown very great charity to me, unworthy wretch that I am. You are as gracious to me as though I were as pure a maiden as any is in this world, and as though I had never sinned.

'Therefore, Lord, I wish I had a well of tears to constrain you with, so that you would not take utter vengeance on man's soul, to part him from you without end; for it is a hard thing, to think that any earthly man should ever do any sin through which he should be parted from your glorious face without end.

'If I could, Lord, give the people contrition and weeping as good as that which you gave me for my own sins and other men's sins also, and as easily as I could give a penny out of my own purse, I should soon fill men's hearts with contrition so that they might cease from their sin. I wonder very much in my heart, Lord, that I – who have been so sinful a woman, and the most unworthy creature that you ever showed your mercy to in all this world – should have such great charity towards my fellow Christian souls. I think that, though they had ordained for me the most shameful death that any man or woman might ever suffer on earth, yet I would forgive them it for your love, Lord, and have their souls saved from everlasting damnation.

'And therefore, Lord, I shall not cease, when I may weep, to weep for them abundantly, prosper if I may. And if you wish, Lord, that I cease from weeping, I pray you, take me out of this world. What should I do there, unless I might profit? For though it were possible that all this world might be saved through the tears of my eyes, I would not be worthy of thanks. Therefore, all praising, all honour, all worship be to you, Lord. If it were your will, Lord, I would for your love, and for the magnifying of your name, be chopped up as small as meat for the pot.'

Chapter 58

On one occasion, as the said creature was in her contemplation, she hungered very much for God's word, and said, 'Alas, Lord! as many clerics as you have in this world, and you will not send me one of them who might fill my soul with your word and with reading of Holy Scripture, for all the clerics that preach may not satisfy me, for I think that my soul is always just as hungry. If I had money enough, I would give a noble every day to have a sermon, for your word is worth more to me than all the money in this world. And therefore, blessed Lord, take pity on me, for you have taken away from me the anchorite who was a singular solace and comfort to me, and many times refreshed me with your holy word.'

Then our Lord Jesus Christ answered in her soul, saying, 'There shall come someone from far away who shall fulfil your desire.'

So, many days after this answer, there came a priest to Lynn who had never known her before and, when he saw her going along the streets, he was greatly moved to speak with her, and inquired of other people what sort of woman she was. They said they trusted to God that she was a very good woman.

Afterwards, the priest sent for her, asking her to come and speak with him and with his mother, for he had hired a room for his mother and for himself, and so they lived together. Then the creature came to learn his will, and she spoke with his mother and with him, and was very kindly received by them both.

Then the priest took a book and read in it how our Lord, seeing the city of Jerusalem, wept over her, rehearsing the misfortunes and sorrows that should come upon her, for she did not know the time of her visitation.[1] When the said creature heard it read how our Lord wept, then she wept bitterly and cried loudly, neither the priest nor his mother knowing any reason for her weeping. When her crying and her weeping were ceased, they rejoiced and were very merry in our Lord. Afterwards she took her leave and parted from them at that time.

When she was gone, the priest said to his mother, 'I am amazed at why this woman weeps and cries so. Nevertheless, I think she is a good woman, and I greatly desire to speak more with her.'

His mother was well pleased, and advised that he should do so. And afterwards this same priest loved her and trusted her greatly, and blessed the time that he ever knew her, for he found great spiritual comfort in her, and was caused to look up much good scripture, and many a good doctor, at which he would not have looked at that time, had it not been for her.

He read to her many a good book of high contemplation, and other books, such as the Bible with doctors' commentaries on it, St Bride's book, Hilton's book, Bonaventura's *Stimulus Amoris*, *Incendium Amoris*,[2] and others similar. And then she knew it was a spirit sent from God which said to her these words, as is written a little before, when she complained of a lack of reading: 'There shall come someone from far away who shall fulfil your desire.' And thus she knew by experience that it was a very true spirit.

The said priest read books to her for the most part of seven or eight years, to the great increase of his knowledge and of his merit, and he suffered many an evil word for her love, inasmuch as he read her so many books, and supported her in her weeping and her crying. Afterwards he became beneficed and had a large cure of souls, and then he was very pleased that he had read so much before.

Chapter 59

Thus, through listening to holy books and through listening to holy sermons, she was always increasing in contemplation and holy meditation. It would be impossible to write all the holy thoughts, holy speeches, and high revelations which our Lord showed to her, both concerning herself and other men and women, and also concerning many souls, some to be saved and some to be damned.

This was a great punishment and a sharp chastisement to her. To know of those who would be saved, she was very glad and joyful, because she longed as much as she dared for all men to be saved; and when our Lord revealed to her any who would be damned, she had great pain.[1] She would not hear it, nor believe that it was God who showed her such things, and put it out of her mind as much as she could. Our Lord blamed her for this, and bade her believe that it was his high mercy and his goodness to reveal to her his secret counsels, saying to her mind, 'Daughter, you must hear of the damned as well as of the saved.'

She would give no credence to the counsel of God, but rather believed it was some evil spirit out to deceive her. Then for her forwardness and her unbelief, our Lord withdrew from her all good thoughts and all good recollections of holy speeches and conversation, and the high contemplation which she had been used to before, and allowed her to have as many evil thoughts as she previously had good thoughts. And this affliction lasted twelve days altogether, and just as previously she had four hours in the morning of holy speeches and confabulation with our Lord, so she now had as many hours of foul thoughts and foul recollections of lechery and all uncleanness, as though she would have prostituted herself with all manner of people.

And so the devil deluded her, dallying with her with accursed thoughts, just as our Lord dallied with her previously with holy thoughts. And just as before she had many glorious visions and high contemplation upon the manhood of our Lord, upon our

Lady, and upon many other holy saints, even so now she had horrible and abominable visions – despite anything she could do – of seeing men's genitals, and other such abominations.

She saw, as she really thought, various men of religion, priests and many others, both heathen and Christian, coming before her eyes so that she could not avoid them or put them out of her sight, and showing her their naked genitals.

And with that the devil ordered her in her mind to choose which of them she would have first, and she must prostitute herself to them all.

And he said she liked one of them better than all the others. She thought he spoke the truth; she could not say no; and she had to do his bidding, and yet she would not have done it for all this world. But yet she thought it should be done, and she thought that these horrible sights and accursed thoughts were delicious to her against her will. Wherever she went or whatever she did, these accursed thoughts remained with her. When she would see the sacrament, say her prayers, or do any other good deed, such abomination was always put into her mind. She was shriven and did all that she could, but she found no release, until she was nearly in despair. It cannot be written what pain she felt, and what sorrow she was in.

Then she said, 'Alas, Lord, you have said before that you would never forsake me. Where is now the truthfulness of your word?'

And immediately afterwards her good angel came to her, saying, 'Daughter, God has not forsaken you, nor ever shall forsake you, as he has promised you. But because you do not believe that it is the spirit of God that speaks in your soul and reveals to you his secret counsels, of some that shall be saved and some that shall be damned, therefore God chastises you in this way, and this chastising shall endure twelve days until you will believe that it is God who speaks to you and no devil.'

Then she said to her angel, 'Ah, I pray you, pray for me to my Lord Jesus Christ, that he will vouchsafe to take from me these accursed thoughts, and speak to me as he did before now, and I shall make a promise to God that I shall believe that it is God who has spoken to me before, for I may no longer endure this great pain.'

Her angel said to her again, 'Daughter, my Lord Jesus will not take it away from you until you have suffered it twelve days, for he wishes that you should know by that means whether it is better that God speak to you or the devil. And my Lord Christ Jesus is never the angrier with you, though he allow you to feel this pain.'

So she suffered that pain until twelve days were passed, and then she had as holy thoughts, as holy reflections, and as holy desires, as holy speeches and conversation with our Lord Jesus Christ as she ever had before, our Lord saying to her, 'Daughter, now believe indeed that I am no devil.'

Then she was filled with joy, for she heard our Lord speaking to her as he used to do. Therefore she said, 'I shall believe that every good thought is the speech of God. Blessed may you be, Lord, that you do not disdain to comfort me again. I would not, Lord, for all this world suffer such another pain as I suffered these twelve days, for I thought I was in hell – blessed may you be that it is past. Therefore, Lord, I will now lie still and be obedient to your will. I pray you, Lord, speak in me what is most pleasing to you.'

Chapter 60

The good priest who was written about before, and who was her reader, fell very ill, and she was stirred in her soul to look after him, on God's behalf. And when she lacked such thing as was needful for him, she went about to good men and good women and got what was necessary for him. He was so ill that people had no confidence that he would live, and his sickness was long continuing.

Then on one occasion, as she was in church hearing mass and

prayed for the same priest, our Lord said to her that he should live and get on very well. Then she was stirred to go to Norwich, to St Stephen's Church, where the good Vicar is buried who died only shortly before that time,[1] and for whom God showed high mercy to his people, to thank him for the recovery of this priest.

She took leave of her confessor, and set off for Norwich. When she came into the churchyard of St Stephen's, she cried, she roared, she wept, she fell down to the ground, so fervently did the fire of love burn in her heart.

Afterwards she rose up again and went on weeping into the church and up to the high altar, and there she fell down with violent sobbings, weepings and loud cries beside the grave of the good Vicar, all ravished with spiritual comfort in the goodness of our Lord, who worked such great grace for his servant who had been her confessor, and many times heard her confession of all her life, and administered to her at various times the precious sacrament of the altar. And her devotion was all the more increased, in that she saw our Lord work such special grace for such a creature as she had been conversant with in his lifetime.

She had such holy thoughts and such holy memories that she could not control her weeping nor her crying. And therefore people were astonished at her, supposing that she had wept because of some fleshly or earthly affection, and said to her, 'What is wrong with you, woman? Why are you behaving like this? We knew him as well as you.'

Then there were priests in the same place who knew her way of behaving, and they very charitably took her to a tavern and made her have a drink, and made her very welcome with much kindness.

There was also a lady who wanted to have the said creature to a meal. And therefore, as decency required, she went to the church where this lady heard her service, and where this creature saw a beautiful image of our Lady called a *pietà*.[2] And through looking at that *pietà* her mind was wholly occupied with the Passion of our Lord Jesus Christ and with the compassion of our Lady, St Mary, by which she was compelled to cry out very loudly and weep very bitterly, as though she would have died.

Then the lady's priest came to her, saying, 'Woman, Jesus is long since dead.'

When her crying had ceased, she said to the priest, 'Sir, his death is as fresh to me as if he had died this same day, and so, I think, it ought to be to you and to all Christian people. We ought always to remember his kindness, and always think of the doleful death that he died for us.'

Then the good lady, hearing what she had said, declared, 'Sir, it is a good example to me, and to other people also, the grace that God works in her soul.'

And so the good lady was her advocate and answered for her. Afterwards she took her home with her to eat, and showed her great warmth and kindness as long as she wanted to remain there. And soon after, she came home again to Lynn, and the said priest, for whom she went most specially to Norwich, and who had read to her for about seven years,[3] recovered and went about where he liked – Almighty God be thanked for his goodness.

Chapter 61

Then a friar came to Lynn who was held to be a holy man and a good preacher.[1] His name and his skill in preaching were very widely known. Good men came to the said creature in their charity and said, 'Margery, now you will have enough preaching, for one of the most famous friars in England has come to this town to be in their establishment here.'

Then she was happy and glad, and thanked God with all her heart that so good a man had come to dwell amongst them. A short time afterwards, he preached a sermon in a chapel of St James in Lynn,[2] where many people gathered to hear the sermon. And before he went to the pulpit, the parish priest of the place where he was going to preach went to him and said, 'Sir, I pray you be not displeased. A woman will come here to your sermon who often, when she hears of the Passion of our Lord or of any high devotion, weeps, sobs and cries, but it does not last long. And therefore, good sir, if she should make any noise at your sermon, bear with it patiently and do not be dismayed by it.'

The good friar went forward to preach the sermon, and spoke most holily and most devoutly, and said much about our Lord's Passion, so that the said creature could no longer bear it. She kept herself from crying as long as she could, and then at last she burst out with a great cry, and cried amazingly bitterly. The good friar bore with it patiently, and said not a word about it at that time.

A short time afterwards he preached again in the same place. The said creature being present, and noticing how much people came running to hear the sermon, she had great joy in her soul, thinking in her mind, 'Ah, Lord Jesus, I believe, if you were here to preach in person, people would have great joy to hear you. I pray you, Lord, make your holy word to settle in their souls as I would that it would do in mine, and may as many be turned by his voice, as would be by your voice if you preached yourself.'

And with such holy thoughts and reflections, she asked grace for the people at that time. And afterwards, what with the holy sermon, and what with her meditation, grace of devotion worked so intensely in her mind that she fell into violent weeping.

Then the good friar said, 'I wish this woman were out of the church; she is annoying people.'

Some people that were her friends replied, 'Sir, do excuse her. She can't control it.'

Then many people turned against her and were very glad that the good friar held against her. Then some men said that she had a devil within her, and they had said so many times before, but now they were bolder, for they thought that their opinion was much strengthened by this good friar. Nor would he allow her to hear his sermons unless she would leave off her sobbing and her crying.

There was then a good priest who had read to her much good scripture and knew the cause of her crying. He spoke to another good priest, who had known her many years, and told him his idea: how he proposed to go to the good friar, and try if he could humble his heart.

The other good priest said he would willingly go with him, to obtain grace, if he might. So they went, both priests together, and begged the good friar with all their hearts that he would allow the said creature to come quietly to his sermon, and bear with her patiently if she happened to sob or cry, as other good men had borne with her before.

He answered shortly, that if she came into any church where he was going to preach, and made any noise as she was used to do, he would speak out against her sharply – he would not allow her to cry in any way.

Afterwards, a worthy doctor of divinity, a White Friar – a very serious-minded cleric and elderly doctor, and very well thought-of – who had known the said creature many years of her life, and believed the grace that God worked in her, took with him another worthy man, a bachelor of law, a man well grounded and long practised in scripture, who was confessor to the said creature,[3] and went to this friar as the good priests did before, and sent for wine to cheer him with, praying him of his charity to look favourably on the works of our Lord in the said creature, and grant her his benevolence in supporting her, if she happened to cry or sob while he was in the middle of his sermon. And these worthy clerics told him that it was a gift of God, and that she could not have it but when God would give it, nor could she withstand it when God would send it, and God would withdraw it when he willed – for that she had through revelation, and that was unknown to the friar.

Then he, neither giving credence to the doctor's words nor the bachelor's, trusting a great deal on the favour of the people, said he would not look favourably on her crying for anything that anyone might say or do, for he would not believe that it was a gift of God. But, he said, if she could not withstand it when it came, he believed it was a heart condition, or some other sickness, and if she would acknowledge this to be so, he said, he would have compassion on her and urge people to pray for her. And, on this condition, he would have patience with her and allow her to cry enough, if she would say it was a natural illness.

And she herself well knew by revelation and by experience that it was no sickness, and therefore she would not for all this world say otherwise than as she felt. And therefore they could not agree. Then the worthy doctor and her confessor advised her that she should not go to his sermon, and that was a great pain to her.

Then another man went – a most worthy burgess, who a few years after was Mayor of Lynn – and asked him as the worthy clerics had done before, and he was answered as they were.

Then she was charged by her confessor that she should not go where he preached, but when he preached in one church she should go into another. She felt so much sorrow that she did not know what she could do, for she was excluded from the sermon, which was to her the highest comfort on earth when she could hear it, and equally, the contrary was to her the greatest pain on earth, when she could not hear it. When she was alone by herself in one church, and he preaching to people in another, she had as loud and as astonishing cries as when she was amongst people.

For years she was not allowed to come to his sermons, because she cried so when it pleased our Lord to put her in mind and true beholding of his bitter Passion. But she was not excluded from any other cleric's preaching, but only from the good friar's, as is said before; notwithstanding that in the meantime there preached many worthy doctors and other worthy clerks, both religious and secular, at whose sermons she cried very loudly and sobbed very violently many times and often. And yet they put up with it very patiently, and some who had spoken with her before, and had knowledge of her manner of life, excused her to the people when they heard any clamour or grumbling against her.

Chapter 62

Afterwards, on St James's Day,[1] the good friar preached in St James's Chapel yard in Lynn – he was at that time neither bachelor nor doctor of divinity – where there were many people and a great audience, for he had a holy name and great favour amongst the people, in so much that some men, if they knew that he would preach in the district, would go with him or else follow him from town to town, such great delight had they to hear him, and so – blessed may God be – he preached most holily and devoutly.

Nevertheless, on this day he preached a great deal against the said creature, not mentioning her name, but so conveying his thoughts that people well understood that he meant her. Then there was much protest amongst the people, for many men and many women trusted and loved her very much, and were very sad and sorry that he spoke so much against her as he did, wishing that they had not heard him that day.

When he heard the murmuring and grumbling of the people, and supposing he would be gainsaid another day by those who were her friends, he, striking his hand on the pulpit, said, 'If I hear these matters repeated any more, I shall so strike the nail on the head,' he said, 'that it shall shame all her supporters.'

And then many of those who pretended friendship to her hung back out of a little vain dread that they had of his words, and dared not very well speak with her. Among these people was the same priest who afterwards wrote down this book, and he was resolved never again to believe her feelings.

And yet our Lord drew him back in a short time – blessed may he be – so that he loved her more, and trusted more in her weeping and her crying than he ever did before. For afterwards he read of a woman called Mary of Oignies,[2] and of her manner of life, of the wonderful sweetness that she had in hearing the word of God, of the wonderful compassion that she had in thinking of his Passion, of the abundant tears that she wept, which made her so weak and feeble that she could not endure to look upon the cross, nor hear our Lord's Passion repeated, without dissolving into tears of pity and compassion.

Of the plentiful grace of her tears, it treats especially in the book before mentioned, in the eighteenth chapter which begins *Bonus est, domine, sperantibus in te*, and also in the nineteenth chapter, where it tells how she, at the request of a priest that he should not be troubled or disturbed at his mass by her weeping and sobbing, went out at the church door, crying with a loud voice, such that she could not restrain herself.

And our Lord also visited the priest when at mass with such grace and such devotion when he should read the Holy Gospel, that he wept amazingly, so that he wetted his vestments and the ornaments of the altar, and could not control his weeping or his sobbing, it was so abundant; nor could he restrain it, or very well stand at the altar because of it.

Then he well believed that the good woman, for whom he had previously had little affection, could not restrain her weeping, her sobbing, nor her crying, and that she felt much more abundance of grace than he ever did, beyond comparison. Then he well knew that God gave his grace to whom he would.

Then the priest who wrote this treatise, through the prompting of a worthy clerk, a bachelor of divinity, had seen and read the matter before written much more seriously and in greater detail than it is written in this present treatise. (For here is included only a little of the purpose of it, because he did not have a very clear memory of the said matter when he wrote this treatise, and therefore he wrote less about it.)

Then he drew towards and inclined more steadfastly to the said creature, whom he had fled and avoided because of the friar's preaching, as is written before. The same priest also read afterwards in a treatise which is called *The Prick of Love*,[3] the second chapter, that Bonaventura wrote these following words about himself: 'Ah, Lord, what shall I more cry out and call? You delay and do not come, and I, weary and overcome with desire, begin to go mad, for love governs me, and not reason. I run with a hasty course wherever you wish. I submit, Lord. Those who see me are irked and have pity, not knowing me to be drunk with your love. "Lord," they say, "see, that mad man cries out in the streets," but they do not perceive how great is the desire of my heart.'

He also read similar material about Richard of Hampole,[4] the hermit, in the *Incendium Amoris*, which prompted him to give credence to the said creature. Elizabeth of Hungary[5] also cried with a loud voice, as is written in her treatise.

And many others, who had forsaken her because of the friar's preaching, repented and turned to her once more by process of time, notwithstanding that the friar kept his opinion. He would always in his sermons have a part against her, whether she were there or not, and caused many people to think very badly of her for many long days.

For some said that she had a devil within her, and some said to her own face that the friar should have driven those devils out of her. Thus was she slandered, and eaten and gnawed by people's talk, because of the grace that God worked in her of contrition, of devotion, and of compassion, through the gift of which graces she wept, sobbed, and cried very bitterly against her will – she might not choose, for she would rather have wept softly and privately than openly, if it had been in her power.

Chapter 63

Then some of her friends came to her and said it would be more comfortable for her to go out of the town than stay there, because so many people were against her. And she said she would stay there as long as God wanted.

'For here,' she said, 'in this town I have sinned. Therefore it is fitting that I suffer sorrow in this town because of it. And yet I do not have as much sorrow or shame as I have deserved, for I have trespassed against God. I thank Almighty God for whatever he sends me, and I pray God that all manner of wickedness that any man shall say of me in this world may stand towards remission of my sins, and any good thing that any man shall say about the grace that God works in me, may turn to worship and to praising of God, and magnifying of his holy name without end, for all manner of worship belongs to him, and all contempt, shame and reproof belongs to me, and that I have well deserved.'

Another time, her confessor came to her in a chapel of our Lady, called the Gesine,[1] saying, 'Margery, what will you do now? There can be no more against you but the moon and seven stars. There is scarcely anyone on your side except only myself.'

She said to her confessor, 'Sir, cheer up, for everything will be quite all right in the end. And I tell you truly, my Lord Jesus gives me great comfort in my soul, and otherwise I should fall into despair. My blissful Lord Christ Jesus will not let me despair for any holy name that the good friar has,[2] for my Lord tells me that he is angry with him, and he says to me it were better if he were never born, for he despises his works in me.'

Also our Lord said to her, 'Daughter, if he be a priest that despises you, well knowing why you weep and cry, then he is accursed.'

And one time, when she was in the Prior's Cloister and dared not stay in the church for fear of disturbing people with her crying, our Lord said to her, she being in great heaviness of heart, 'Daughter, I bid you to go back into church, for I shall take away from you your crying, so that you will no longer cry so loudly, nor in that kind of way that you have done before, even if you wanted to.'

She obeyed the commandment of our Lord, and told her confessor exactly how she felt, and it happened in truth as she felt. She afterwards no longer cried so loud, nor in the way that she had done before, but later she did sob remarkably and wept as bitterly as she ever did before, sometimes loud and sometimes quiet, as God would control it himself.

Then many people believed that she dared no longer cry out because of the way the good friar preached against her and would not endure her in any way. Then they held him to be a holy man, and her a false, pretending hypocrite. And just as some spoke badly of her before because she cried, so some now spoke badly of her because she did not cry. And so slander and bodily anguish befell her on every side, and all was to the increasing of her spiritual comfort.

Then our merciful Lord said to his unworthy servant, 'Daughter, I must comfort you, for now you have the true way to heaven. By this way I came to heaven and all my disciples, for now you will know all the better what sorrow and shame I suffered for your love, and you will have the more compassion when you think upon my Passion. Daughter, I have told you many times that the friar should say evil things about you. Therefore, I warn you not to tell him of the secret counsels which I have revealed to you, for I do not wish him to hear it from your mouth. And daughter, I tell you truly, he shall be chastised sharply. As his name is now, it shall be thrown down, and yours shall be raised up. And I shall make as many men love you for my love as have despised you for my love. Daughter, you shall be in church when he shall be outside. In this church you have suffered much shame and rebuke for the gifts that I have given you and for the grace and goodness that I have worked in you, and therefore in this church and in this place I will be worshipped in you.[3] Many a man and woman shall say, "It is clear to see that God loves her well." Daughter, I shall work so much grace for you, that all the world shall wonder and marvel at my goodness.'

Then the said creature said to our Lord with great reverence, 'I am not worthy that you should show such grace to me. Lord, it is enough for me that you save my soul from endless damnation by your great mercy.'

'It is my worship, daughter, that I shall perform, and therefore I wish you to have no will but my will. The less price that you set on yourself, the more price I set on you, and the better will I love you, daughter. See that you have no sorrow for earthly goods. I have tried you in poverty, and I have chastised you as I would myself, both inwardly within your soul, and outwardly through people's slander. See, daughter, I have granted you your own desire – that you should have no other purgatory than in this world alone.

'Daughter, you often say to me in your mind that rich men have great cause to love me well, and you say most truly, for you say I have given them many goods with which they may serve me and love me. But, good daughter, I pray you, love me with all your heart, and I shall give you goods enough to love me with, for heaven and earth should rather fail, than I should fail you. And if other men fail, you shall not fail. And though all your friends forsake you, I shall never forsake you. You made me once steward of your household, and executor of all your good works,[4] and I will be a true steward and a true executor in the fulfilling of all your will and all your desire. And I shall provide for you, daughter, as for my own mother and as for my own wife.'

Chapter 64

The creature said to her Lord Christ Jesus, 'Ah, blessed Lord, I wish I knew in what I might best love you and please you, and that my love were as sweet to you as I think your love is to me.'

Then our sweet Lord Jesus, answering his creature, said, 'Daughter, if you knew how sweet your love is to me, you would never do anything else but love me with all your heart. And therefore, do believe, daughter, that my love is not so sweet to you as your love is to me. Daughter, you do not know how much I love you, for it may not be known in this world how much it is, nor be felt as it is, for you would fail and burst and never endure it, for the joy that you would feel. And therefore I measure it as I wish to your greatest ease and comfort.

'But daughter, you shall well know in another world how much I loved you on earth, for there you will have great reason to thank me. There you will see without end every good day that I ever gave you on earth of contemplation, of devotion, and of all the great charity that I have given you to the profit of your fellow Christians. For this shall be your reward when you come home into heaven.

'There is no clerk in all this world who can, daughter, teach you better than I can do, and, if you will be obedient to my will, I shall be obedient to your will. Where is a better token of love than to weep for your Lord's love? You know very well, daughter, that the devil has no charity, for he is very angry with you, and he might hurt you somewhat, but he shall not injure you, except a little, in this world, in sometimes making you afraid, so that you should pray all the more strongly to me for grace, and direct your love all the more towards me. There is no clerk who can speak against the life which I teach you, and, if he does so, he is not God's clerk, he is the devil's clerk. I tell you truly that there is no man in this world – if he would willingly suffer as much humiliation for my love as you have done, and cleave as steadfastly to me, not willing to forsake me for anything that may be said or done against him – but I shall treat him fairly and show him much grace, both in this world, and in the other.'

Then the creature said, 'Ah, my beloved Lord, you should show this life to religious men and priests.'

Our Lord replied to her, 'No, no, daughter, for that thing which I love best they do not love – and that is shame, contempt, scorn and rebukes from people – and therefore they shall not have this grace. For, daughter, I tell you, he that dreads the shame of the world may not perfectly love God. And, daughter, under the habit of holiness is covered much wickedness. Daughter, if you saw the wickedness that is done in the world as I do, you would be amazed that I do not take utter vengeance upon them. But, daughter, I desist because of your love. You weep so every day for mercy that I have to grant it, and people will not believe the goodness that I work in you for them.

'Nevertheless, daughter, there shall come a time when they shall be very glad to believe the grace that I have given you for them. And I shall say to them when they are passed out of this world, "Look, I ordained her to weep for her sins, and you held her in great contempt, but her charity for you would never cease." And therefore, daughter, those who are good souls shall highly thank me for the grace and goodness that I have given you, and those who are wicked shall protest and have great pain to endure the grace that I show to you. And therefore I shall chastise them as it were for myself.'

She prayed, 'No, beloved Lord Jesus, do not chastise any creature for me. You well know, Lord, that I desire no vengeance, but I ask mercy and grace for all men if it be your will to grant it. Nevertheless, Lord, rather than that they should be separated from you without end, chastise them as you wish yourself. It seems, Lord, in my soul, that you are full of charity, for you say you do not wish the death of a sinful man. And you also say that you wish all men to be saved. Then Lord, since you wish all men to be saved, I must wish the same, and you say yourself that I must love my fellow Christians as my own self.[1] And, Lord, you know that I have wept and sorrowed many years because I would be saved, and so must I do for my fellow Christians.'

Chapter 65

Our Lord Jesus Christ said to this creature, 'Daughter, you shall well see when you are in heaven with me that no man is damned unless he is well worthy to be damned, and you shall hold yourself well pleased with all my works. And therefore, daughter, thank me highly for this great charity that I work in your heart, for it is myself, Almighty God, that makes you weep every day for your own sins; for the great compassion that I give you for my bitter Passion; and for the sorrows that my mother had here on earth, for the anguish that she suffered and for the tears that she wept;

and also, daughter, for the holy martyrs in heaven (when you hear of them, you give me thanks with crying and weeping for the grace that I have showed to them, and, when you see any lepers, you have great compassion on them, giving me thanks and praises that I am more favourable to you than to them); and also, daughter, for the great sorrow that you have for all this world, that you might help them as well as you would help yourself both spiritually and physically; and furthermore, for the sorrows that you have for the souls in purgatory, that you would be so pleased that they were out of their pain, so that they might praise me without end.

'And all this is my own goodness that I give to you, because of which you are bound to thank me. And nevertheless, I still thank you for the great love you have for me, and because you have so great a will and desire that all men and women should love me well. For, as you think, they all – holy and unholy – want money to live with, as is lawful for them to do, but they will not all busy themselves to love me, as they do to get themselves temporal goods.

'Also, daughter, I thank you because you think it such a long time that you are kept out of my blessed presence. Furthermore, I thank you especially, daughter, because you cannot allow any man to break my commandments, nor to swear by me, without it being a great pain to you, and because you are always ready to reprove them about their swearing, for my love. And therefore you have endured many a cutting word and many a rebuke, and because of this you shall have many a joy in heaven.

'Daughter, I once sent St Paul to you to strengthen you and comfort you,[1] so that you should boldly speak in my name from that day forward. And St Paul said to you that you had suffered much tribulation because of his writing, and he promised you that because of this you should have as much grace for his love as you ever had shame or reproof for his love. He also told you of many joys of heaven, and of the great love that I had for you.

'And, daughter, I have often said to you that there is no saint in heaven who, if you will speak with him, is not ready to comfort you and speak to you in my name. My angels are ready to offer your holy thoughts and your prayers to me, and the tears of your eyes as well, for your tears are angels' drink, and are truly to the angels like spiced and honeyed wine.

'Therefore, my beloved daughter, do not be weary of me on earth, to sit alone by yourself and think of my love, for I am not weary of you, and my merciful eye is ever upon you. Daughter, you may boldly say to me *Jesus est amor meus*, that is to say, "Jesus is my love". Therefore, daughter, let me be all your love, and all the joy of your heart.

'Daughter, if you will think things over to yourself, you have great cause to love me above all things, because of the great gifts that I have given you before now. And yet you have another great cause to love me, because you have your will in the matter of chastity as if you were a widow, although your husband is still living and in good health.

'Daughter, I have drawn the love of your heart from all men's hearts into my heart. At one time, daughter, you thought it had been in a way impossible to be so, and at that time you suffered very great pain in your heart with earthly affections. And then you could well cry to me saying, "Lord, for all your smarting wounds, draw all the love of my heart into your heart."

'Daughter, for all these reasons, and many other causes and benefits which I have shown you on this side of the sea and beyond the sea, you have great cause to love me.'

Chapter 66

'Now, daughter, I wish that you should eat meat again as you used to do, and that you should be meek and obedient to my will and my bidding, and leave your own will, and tell your confessors to let you act according to my will. And you will have none the less grace, but so much the more, for you shall have the same reward in heaven as though you still fasted according to your own will. Daughter, I commanded you first that you should give up meat and eat none, and you have obeyed my will for many years and abstained in accordance with my advice. Therefore I now order you to take up eating meat again.'

The said creature with reverent dread said, 'Ah, blessed Lord, the people who have known of my abstinence over so many years and who now see me returning to eating meat, will be astonished and will, I suppose, despise me and scorn me because of this.'

Our Lord replied to her, 'You shall take no heed of their scorn, but let every man say what he will.'

Then she went to her confessors and told them what our Lord had said to her. When her confessors knew the will of God, they charged her by virtue of obedience to eat meat, as she had done many years before. Then she had much scorn and many a rebuke because she ate meat again.

She had also made a vow to fast one day in the week, as long as she lived, in worship of our Lady, which vow she kept for many years. Our Lady, appearing to her soul, bade her go to her confessor and say that she would have her discharged of her vow, so that she should be sufficiently strong to bear her spiritual labours, for without bodily strength they could not be endured. Then her confessor, perceiving with discretion that this was the appropriate thing to do, commanded her by virtue of obedience to eat moderately, as other people did, when God wished her to eat. And her grace was not decreased but rather increased, for she would rather have fasted than eaten, if it had been the will of God.

Furthermore, our Lady said to her, 'Daughter, you are weak enough from weeping and crying, for both make you weak and feeble. I can thank you more for eating meat for my love than for fasting, so that you may endure your perfection of weeping.'

Chapter 67

On one occasion there happened to be a great fire in Bishop's Lynn,[1] which burned down the Guildhall of the Trinity. This same terrible and serious fire was very likely to have burned down the parish church – dedicated in honour of St Margaret, a stately place and richly honoured – and also the whole town as well, had there been no grace or miracle.

The said creature being present there, and seeing the dangerous plight of the whole town, cried out very loudly many times that day, and wept most abundantly, praying for grace and mercy for all the people. And notwithstanding that at other times they could not endure her crying and weeping because of the plentiful grace that our Lord worked in her, on this day, in order to lessen their physical danger, they allowed her to cry and weep as much as she liked, and nobody would order her to stop, but instead begged her to continue, fully trusting and believing that through her crying and weeping our Lord would take them to mercy.

Then her confessor[2] came to her and asked if it were best to carry the sacrament towards the fire, or not.

She said, 'Yes, sir, yes! For our Lord Jesus Christ told me it will be well.'

So her confessor, parish priest of St Margaret's Church, took the precious sacrament and went before the fire as devoutly as he could and afterwards brought it back into the church again – and the sparks of the fire flew about the church. The said creature, desiring to follow the precious sacrament to the fire, went out at the church door, and as soon as she saw the terrible flames of the fire, she immediately cried with a loud voice and much weeping, 'Good Lord, make everything all right!'

These words worked in her mind, inasmuch as our Lord had said to her before that he would make everything all right, and therefore she cried, 'Good Lord, make everything all right, and send down some rain or storm that may through your mercy quench this fire and ease my heart.'

Afterwards she went back into the church, and then she saw how the sparks were coming into the choir through the lantern of the church. Then she had a new sorrow, and cried very loudly again for grace and mercy, with great abundance of tears. Soon after, three worthy men came in to her with snow on their clothes, saying to her, 'Look, Margery, God has shown us great grace and sent us a fair snowstorm to quench the fire with. Be now of good cheer, and thank God for it.'

And with a great cry she gave praise and thanks to God for his great mercy and his goodness, especially because he had said to her before that everything would be well, when it was most unlikely to be well, except through a miracle and special grace. And now that she saw that all was well indeed, she thought she had great reason to thank our Lord.

Then her confessor came to her and said he believed that because of her prayers God granted them to be delivered out of their great danger, for without devout prayers it could not happen that the air, being bright and clear, should so soon be changed into clouds and darkness, and send down great flakes of snow, through which the fire was hindered in its natural working – blessed may our Lord be.

Notwithstanding the grace that he showed for her, still, when the dangers were past, some people slandered her because she cried, and some said that our Lady never cried. 'Why do you cry in this way?' – and she said, because she could not do otherwise.

Then she fled from people into the Prior's Chapel, so that she should give them no further occasion. When she was there, she had such intense recollection of the Passion of our Lord Jesus Christ, and of his precious wounds, and how dearly he bought her, that she cried and roared amazingly, so that she could be heard a great way away, and she could not restrain herself from doing so.

Then she was astonished how our Lady might suffer or endure to see his precious body being scourged and hanged on the cross. It also came into her mind how people had said to her before that our Lady, Christ's own mother, did not cry as she did, and that caused her to say in her crying, 'Lord, I am not your mother. Take away this pain from me, for I cannot bear it. Your Passion will kill me.'

So a worthy cleric came past her, a doctor of divinity, and said, 'It would be preferable to me than having twenty pounds, if I could have such a sorrow for our Lord's Passion.'

Then the said doctor sent for her to come and speak with him where he was, and she very willingly went to him in his chamber, weeping tears. That worthy and estimable cleric made her have a drink and was very welcoming to her. Afterwards he led her to an altar, and asked what was the reason that she cried and wept so bitterly. Then she told him many great causes of her weeping, and yet she told him of no revelation.[3] And he said she was much obliged to love our Lord for the tokens of love that he showed her in various ways.

Afterwards there came a parson who had taken a degree, and who would preach both morning and afternoon. And as he preached most holily and devoutly, the said creature was moved by devotion during his sermon, and at last she burst out with a cry, and people began to grumble about her crying, for this was in the time that the good friar preached against her, as is written before, and also before our Lord took her crying from her. (For although that matter is written before this, nevertheless it happened after this.)

Then the parson stopped for a little while from his preaching and said to the people, 'Friends, be quiet, and do not complain about this woman, for each of you may sin mortally in her, and she is not the cause, but rather your own judgement. For, though this manner of proceeding may seem both good and bad, yet you ought to judge for the best in your hearts – and I do not doubt that it is a very good thing. I also dare say it is a most gracious gift of God, blessed may he be.'

Then the people blessed him for his good words, and were all the more moved to believe in his holy deeds. Afterwards, when the sermon was ended, a good friend of the said creature met the friar who had preached so keenly against her, and asked him what he thought of her. The friar, answering back sharply, said, 'She has a devil within her,' not at all shifted from his opinion, but instead defending his error.

Chapter 68

Soon afterwards, the Chapter of the Preaching Friars was held at Lynn, and to that there came many worthy clerics of that holy order, one of whom was to preach a sermon in the parish church.

And amongst others who had come to the said Chapter was a worthy doctor called Master Custawns,[1] and he had known the said creature many years before. When this creature heard tell that he had come there, she went to him and showed him why she cried and wept so bitterly, in order to learn if he could find any fault in her crying or in her weeping.

The worthy doctor said to her, 'Margery, I have read of a holy woman[2] to whom God had given great grace of weeping and crying as he has done to you. In the church where she lived was a priest who had no favourable opinion of her weeping, and caused her through his prompting to go out of the church. When she was in the churchyard, she prayed God that the priest might have some feeling of the grace that she felt, just as surely as it did not lie in her power to cry out or weep except when God willed. And so, suddenly, our Lord sent him such devotion during his mass, that he could not control himself, and then, after that, he no longer wished to despise her but rather to comfort her.'

Thus the said doctor, confirming her crying and her weeping, said it was a gracious and a special gift of God, and God was highly to be magnified for his gift.

And then the same doctor went to another doctor of divinity, who was assigned to preach in the parish church before all the people, asking him that, if the said creature cried out or wept at his sermon, he would bear with it meekly, and not be at all dismayed by it, nor speak against it. So afterwards, when the worthy doctor was going to preach, and was brought fittingly to the pulpit, he began to preach most holily and devoutly of our Lady's Assumption, and the said creature – lifted up in her mind by high sweetness and devotion – burst out with a loud voice and cried very loudly, and wept very bitterly. The worthy doctor stood still, and bore with it meekly until it stopped, and afterwards he preached his sermon through to the end.

In the afternoon he sent for the same creature to the place where he was, and made her very welcome. Then she thanked him for his meekness and his charity, which he showed in putting up with her crying and her weeping in the morning at his sermon. The worthy doctor replied to her, 'Margery, I would not have spoken against you, though you had cried until evening. If you will come to Norwich, you will be very welcome and have such hospitality as I can offer you.'

Thus God sent her an excellent patron in this worthy doctor, to strengthen her against her detractors, worshipped be his name.

Afterwards, in Lent, a good clerk, an Augustinian Friar, preached in his own house at Lynn and had a very large audience, the said creature being present at that time. And God, of his goodness, inspired the friar to preach a great deal about his Passion, so compassionately and so devoutly that she could not bear it. Then she fell down weeping and crying so violently that many people were astonished at her, and cursed her most vehemently, supposing that she could have left off her crying if she had wished, inasmuch as the good friar had so preached against it, as is written before. And then this good man who now preached at this time said to the people, 'Friends, be quiet – you know very little what she is feeling.'

And so the people stopped and were still, and heard out the sermon in quietness and rest of body and soul.

Chapter 69

Also, on a Good Friday at St Margaret's Church, the Prior[1] of the same place and the same town of Lynn was going to preach. And he took as his theme 'Jesus is dead'. Then the said creature, all wounded with pity and compassion, cried and wept as if she had seen our Lord dead with her bodily eyes. The worthy Prior and doctor of divinity bore with her most meekly and held nothing against her.

Another time, Bishop Wakeryng,[2] Bishop of Norwich, preached at Lynn in the said Church of St Margaret, and this creature cried and wept most violently during his sermon, and he put up with it most meekly and patiently, and so did many a worthy clerk, both regular and secular, for there was never any clerk who preached openly against her crying except the Grey Friar, as is written before.

So our Lord of his mercy, just as he had promised the said creature that he would ever provide for her, stirring the spirits of two good clerics[3] who had for many long years known her conversings and all her search for perfection, made them strong and bold to speak for his part in excusing the said creature, both in the pulpit and outside it, wherever they heard anything moved against her, strengthening their arguments sufficiently with authorities from holy scripture. Of these clerks, one was a White Friar, a doctor of divinity; the other was a bachelor of canon law, a man who had laboured much on the scriptures.

And then some envious persons complained to the Provincial of the White Friars[4] that the said doctor was associating too much with the said creature, forasmuch as he supported her in her weeping and in her crying, and also informed her in questions of scripture, when she would ask him any. Then he was admonished, by virtue of obedience, that he should no longer speak with her nor inform her about any texts of scripture, and that was most painful to him, for, as he said to some people, he would rather have lost a hundred pounds, if he had had it, than her conversation – it was so spiritual and fruitful.

When her confessor perceived how the worthy doctor was charged by obedience that he should not speak with her, then he, to exclude all opportunity and occasion, also warned her by virtue of obedience that she should not go any more to the friars, nor speak with the said doctor, nor ask him any questions, as she had done before.

And then her thoughts were very sorrowful and gloomy, for she was excluded from much spiritual comfort. She would rather have lost any earthly good than his conversation, for it was to her a great increasing of virtue.

Then long afterwards, she happened as she went along the street to meet the said doctor, and neither of them spoke one word to the other, and then she had a great cry, with many tears. Afterwards, when she came to her meditation, she said in her mind to our Lord Jesus Christ, 'Alas, Lord, why may I have no comfort from this worthy clerk, who has known me so many years and often strengthened me in your love? Now you have, Lord, taken from me the anchorite – I trust to your mercy – the most special and singular comfort that I ever had on earth, for he always loved me for your love and would never forsake me while he lived for anything that anyone could say or do. And now Master Aleyn is barred from seeing me, and I from him. Sir Thomas Andrew and Sir John Amy[5] have got benefices and are out of town. Master Robert scarcely dares speak to me. Now I have in a way no comfort from either man or child.'

Our merciful Lord Christ Jesus, answering in her mind, said, 'Daughter, I am more worthy of your soul than ever was the anchorite and all the others you have mentioned, or than all the world may be, and I shall comfort you myself, for I would speak to you more often than you will let me. And, daughter, I want you to know that you will speak to Master Aleyn again, as you have done before.'

And then our Lord sent, through the provision of the Prior of Lynn, a priest to be the keeper of a chapel of our Lady, called the Gesine, within the church of St Margaret, and this priest[6] many times heard her confession in the absence of her principal confessor. And to this priest she confided her whole life, as near as she could, from her young age, both her sins, her troubles, her trials, her contemplations, and also her revelations, and such grace as God worked in her through his mercy, and so that priest well believed that God performed very great grace in her.

Chapter 70

At one time God visited the said doctor, Master Aleyn, with great sickness so that no man who saw him would promise him life. And so the said creature was told of his sickness. Then she grieved for him, especially because she had had it by revelation that she should speak with him again as she had done before and, if he had died of this illness, her feeling would not have been true.

Therefore she ran into the choir at St Margaret's Church, kneeling down before the sacrament and saying in this way: 'Ah, Lord, I pray you, for all the goodness that you have shown me, and as surely as you love me, let this worthy cleric never die until I may speak with him, as you have promised me that I should do. And you, glorious Queen of Mercy, remember what he used to say about you in his sermons: he used to say, Lady, that he was indeed blessed who had you for his friend, for, when you prayed, all the company of heaven prayed with you. Now, for the blissful love that you had for your son, let him live until such time as he has leave to speak with me, and I with him, for now we are separated by obedience.'

Then she was answered in her soul that he should not die before the time that she had permission to speak with him, and he with her, as they had done years before.

And, as our Lord willed, a short time afterwards the worthy cleric recovered and went about hale and healthy, and had leave from his Provincial [1] to speak with the said creature. And she had leave from her confessor to speak with him.

It so happened that the said doctor was to dine in town with a worthy woman who had taken the mantle and the ring, and he sent for the said creature to come and speak with him. She, much surprised at this, got permission and went to him. When she came into the place where he was, she could not speak for weeping and for joy that she had in our Lord, inasmuch as she found her feeling true and not deceptive, in that he had leave to speak to her, and she to him.

Then the worthy doctor said to her, 'Margery, you are welcome to me, for I have long been kept from you, and now our Lord has sent you here so that I may speak with you, blessed may he be.'

There was a dinner of great joy and gladness, much more spiritual than bodily, for it was sauced and savoured with tales from holy scripture. And then he gave the said creature a pair of knives, in token that he would stand with her in God's cause, as he had done before.

Chapter 71

One day there came a priest to the said creature who had great faith in her feelings and in her revelations – but desired to test them at various times – and asked her to pray to our Lord that she might have some understanding whether the Prior of Lynn, who was a good patron of the said priest, should be removed or not. Just as she felt, she was to give him a true account. She prayed for the said matter and, when she had an answer to it, she told the priest that the Prior of Lynn, his master, should be called home to Norwich, and another of his brethren should be sent to Lynn in his stead.[1] And so it was indeed. But he that was sent to Lynn only stayed there a little while before he was called home to Norwich again, and he that had been Prior of Lynn before was sent to Lynn again, and stayed there about four years until he died.

And in the meantime, the said creature often had a feeling that he who was last called home to Norwich, and only stayed a little while at Lynn, should yet be Prior of Lynn again. She would give no credence to this, inasmuch as he had already been there, and was within a little while called home again.

Then as she once walked up and down in the White Friars' church at Lynn, she felt a wonderfully sweet and heavenly savour, so that she thought she might have lived by means of it, without food or drink, if it would have continued. And in that moment our Lord said to her, 'Daughter, by this sweet smell you may know that there shall in a short time be a new Prior in Lynn, and that shall be he who was last removed from there.'

And soon after the old Prior died, and then our Lord said to her as she lay in her bed, 'Daughter, loath as you are to believe my stirrings, you shall yet see him, of whom I told you before, Prior of Lynn before the week is out.'

And so our Lord repeated this matter to her each day for a week, until she saw it was so indeed, and then she was very glad and joyful that her feeling was true.

Afterwards, when this worthy man had come to Lynn and had lived there only a little while – he was a most respected clerk, a doctor of divinity – he was appointed to go over the sea to the King in France, together with other clerks as well, among the worthiest in England.

Then a priest who had an office under the said Prior came to the said creature and begged her to bear this matter in mind, when God should minister his holy dalliance to her soul, and discover in this matter whether the Prior should go over the sea or not. And so she prayed to have some understanding in this matter, and she was answered that he would not go. Nevertheless, he himself expected to have gone, and was all provided for it, and had with great grief taken leave of his friends, supposing never to have come back, for he was a very weak man and had a feeble constitution. And in the meantime the King died, and the Prior stayed at home.[2] And so her feeling was true, without deception.

It was also voiced about that the Bishop of Winchester was

dead,[3] and, notwithstanding that, she had a feeling that he was alive – and so it was in truth. And so she had feelings about many more than can be written, which our Lord, of his mercy, revealed to her understanding, though she were unworthy by her own merits.

Chapter 72

So by process of time her mind and her thoughts were so joined to God that she never forgot him, but had him in mind continually, and beheld him in all creatures. And the more that she ever increased in love and in devotion, the more she increased in sorrow and in contrition, in lowness, in meekness, and in holy dread of our Lord, and in knowledge of her own frailty, so that, if she saw a creature being punished or sharply chastised, she would think that she was more worthy to be chastised than that creature, for her unkindness towards God. Then she would cry, weep and sob for her own sin, and for compassion of the creature that she saw being so punished and sharply chastised.

If she saw a prince, a prelate, or a worthy man of state and degree, whom men worshipped and reverenced with lowness and meekness, her mind was immediately refreshed in our Lord, thinking what joy, what bliss, what worship and reverence he had in heaven among his blessed saints, since a mortal man had such great honours on earth.

And most of all, when she saw the precious sacrament borne about the town with lights and reverence, the people kneeling on their knees, then she had many holy thoughts and meditations, and then she would often cry and roar, as though she would have burst, for the faith and the trust that she had in the precious sacrament.

The said creature was also desired by many people to be with them at their dying and to pray for them, for, although they had no love for her weeping or her crying during their lifetimes, they desired that she should both weep and cry when they were dying, and so she did. When she saw people anointed, she had many holy thoughts, many holy meditations, and – if she saw them dying – she thought she saw our Lord dying, and sometimes our Lady, as our God would illumine her spiritual sight with understanding. Then she would cry, weep, and sob amazingly, as if she had beheld our Lord in his dying, or our Lady in her dying. And she thought in her mind that God took many out of this world who would have very gladly lived, 'and I, Lord,' she thought, 'would very gladly come to you, and for me you have no yearning,' and such thoughts increased her weeping and her sobbing.

On one occasion, a worthy lady sent for her to talk with her, and as they were in conversation, the lady paid her a kind of respect and praise, and it was great pain to her to have any praise. Nevertheless she immediately offered it up to our Lord – for she desired no praise but his alone – with a great cry and many devout tears.

So there was neither honour nor praise, love nor detraction, shame nor contempt, that might draw her love from God, but, after the saying of St Paul, 'To them that love God, all things turn into goodness,'[1] and so it happened with her. Whatever she saw or heard, her love and her spiritual affection always increased towards our Lord – blessed may he be – who worked such grace in her for many men's profit.

Another time she was sent for by another worthy lady who had a large retinue about her, and great honour and great reverence was shown her. When the said creature saw all her retinue about her and the great reverence and honour that was shown her, she fell to much weeping and cried out at it most sorrowfully. There was a priest who heard how she cried and wept – and he was a man not savouring spiritual things – and he cursed her, saying to her, 'What the devil's wrong with you? Why do you weep so? God give you sorrow!'

She sat still, and answered not a word. Then the lady took her into a garden by themselves alone, and asked her to tell her why she cried so grievously. And then she, supposing it was fitting to do so, told her in part of the cause. Then the lady was displeased with her priest, who had so spoken against her, and had great love for her, desiring and asking her still to remain with her. Then she excused herself, and said she could not agree with the manner of dress and behaviour that she saw among her household.

Chapter 73

On Holy Thursday, as the said creature went in procession with other people, she saw in her soul our Lady, St Mary Magdalene, and the twelve apostles. And then she beheld with her spiritual eye how our Lady took her leave of her blessed son, Jesus, how he kissed her and all his apostles, and also his true lover, Mary Magdalene. Then she thought it was a sorrowful parting, and also a joyful parting. When she beheld this sight in her soul, she fell down in the field among the people.[1] She cried, she roared, she wept as though she would have burst. She could not control herself or master herself, but cried and roared so that many people were astonished at her. But she took no notice of what anyone said or did, for her mind was occupied with our Lord.

She felt many a holy thought at that time which she could never know afterwards. She had forgotten all earthly things and only attended to spiritual things. She thought that all her joy was gone. She saw her Lord ascend up into heaven, yet she could not do without him on earth. Therefore she desired to go with him, for all her joy and all her bliss was in him, and she well knew that she would never have joy or bliss until she came to him. Such holy thoughts and holy desires caused her to weep, and people did not know what was wrong with her.

Another time, the said creature beheld how our Lady was – as she thought – dying, and all the apostles kneeling before her and asking for grace. Then she cried and wept grievously. The apostles commanded her to stop, and be quiet. The creature answered the apostles, 'Would you have it that I should see the mother of God dying and not weep? It may not be, for I am so full of sorrow that I may not withstand it. I simply must cry and weep.'

And then she said in her soul to our Lady, 'Ah, blessed Lady, pray for me to your son, that I may come to you, and no longer be delayed from you; for, Lady, this is all too great a sorrow, to be both at your son's death, and at your death, and not die with you, but still live on alone and have no comfort with me.'

Then our gracious Lady answered to her soul, promising her to pray for her to her son, and said, 'Daughter, all these sorrows that you have had for me and for my blessed son shall turn for you to great joy and bliss in heaven without end. And do not doubt, daughter, that you shall come to us indeed, and be most welcome when you come. But you may not come yet, for you shall come in very good time. And daughter, be assured that you will find me a true mother to you, to help you and succour you as a mother ought to her daughter, and obtain for you grace and virtue. And the same pardon that was granted you before was confirmed on St Nicholas's Day [2] – that is to say, plenary remission – and it is not only granted to you, but also to all those who believe, and to all those who shall believe until the world's end, that God loves you, and will thank God for you. If they will forsake their sin, and fully intend to turn to it no more, but are sorry and grieved for what they have done and will do due penance for it, then they shall have the same pardon that is granted to yourself, and that is all the pardon that is in Jerusalem, as was granted to you when you were at Ramleh,' – as is written before.

Chapter 74

The said creature one day hearing her mass, and turning over in her mind the time of her death, grievously sighing and sorrowing because it was so long delayed, said in this way: 'Alas, Lord, how long shall I thus weep and mourn for your love and for desire of your presence?'

Our Lord answered in her soul, and said, 'All these fifteen years.'

Then said she, 'Ah, Lord, I shall think it many thousand years.'

Our Lord answered to her, 'Daughter, you must think to yourself of my blessed mother, who lived on after me on earth for fifteen years;[1] also St John the Evangelist, and Mary Magdalene,[2] who loved me most highly.'

'Ah, blissful Lord,' said she, 'I wish I were as worthy to be assured of your love as Mary Magdalene was.'

Then our Lord said, 'Truly, daughter, I love you as well, and the same peace that I gave to her, the same peace I give to you. For, daughter, no saint in heaven is displeased, though I love a creature on earth as much as I do them. Therefore they do not wish otherwise than as I wish.'

Thus our merciful Lord Christ Jesus drew this creature to his love and to recollection of his Passion, so that she could not endure to look at a leper or any other sick man, especially if he had any wounds showing on him. Then she cried so and wept, as if she had seen our Lord Jesus Christ with his wounds bleeding. And so she did in the sight of her soul, for through the beholding of the sick man her mind was all taken into our Lord Jesus Christ.

Then she felt great mourning and sorrow because she might not kiss the lepers, for the love of Jesus, when she saw them or met with them in the streets. Now she began to love what she had most hated before, for there was nothing more loathsome or abominable to her while she was in her years of worldly prosperity than to see a leper, whom now, through our Lord's mercy, she desired to embrace and kiss for the love of Jesus, when she had time and a convenient place.[3]

Then she told her confessor how great a desire she had to kiss lepers, and he warned her that she should kiss no men, but, if she would kiss anyhow, she should kiss women. Then she was glad, because she had permission to kiss the sick women, and went to a place where sick women lived who were very full of the disease, and fell down on her knees before them, begging them that she might kiss their mouths for the love of Jesus. And so she there kissed two sick women, with many a holy thought and many a devout tear and, when she had kissed them, she spoke very many good words to them, and stirred them to meekness and patience, that they should not resent their illness, but thank God highly for it, and they should have great bliss in heaven through the mercy of our Lord Jesus Christ.

Then one woman had so many temptations that she did not know how best to behave. She was so troubled by her spiritual enemy that she did not dare to bless herself, nor offer any worship to God, for fear that the devil would slay her. And she was tormented with many foul and horrible thoughts, many more than she could tell. And, as she said, she was a virgin.[4] Therefore the said creature went to her many times to comfort her, and prayed for her, most especially that God should strengthen her against her enemy. And it is to be believed that he did so, blessed may he be.

Chapter 75

As the said creature was in a church of St Margaret to say her devotions, there came a man and knelt behind her back, wringing his hands and showing signs of great distress. She, perceiving his distress, asked what was troubling him. He said things were very difficult for him, because his wife had just had a baby, and she was out of her mind.[1]

'And, lady,' he said, 'she doesn't know me, or any of her neighbours. She roars and cries, so that she scares folk badly. She'll both hit out and bite, and so she's manacled on her wrists.'

Then she asked the man if he would like her to go with him and see her, and he said, 'Yes, lady, for God's love.' So she went off with him to see the woman. And when she came into the house, as soon as that sick woman who had lost her reason saw her, she spoke to her seriously and kindly, and said she was most welcome to her. And she was very glad she had come, and greatly comforted by her presence. 'For you are,' she said, 'a very good woman, and I behold many fair angels round about you, and therefore, I pray you, don't leave me, for I am greatly comforted by you.'

And when other people came to her, she cried and gaped as if she would have eaten them, and said that she saw many devils around them. She would not willingly allow them to touch her. She roared and cried so, for the most part of both day and night, that people would not allow her to live amongst them, she was so tiresome to them. Then she was taken to a room at the furthest end of the town, so that people should not hear her crying. And there she was bound hand and foot with chains of iron, so that she should not strike anybody.

And the said creature went to her each day, once or twice at least; and while she was with her she was meek enough, and heard her talk and chat willingly, and without any roaring or crying. And the said creature prayed for this woman every day that God should, if it were his will, restore her to her wits again. And our Lord answered in her soul and said she should get on very well. Then she was bolder to pray for her recovery than she was before, and each day, weeping and sorrowing, prayed for her recovery until God gave her her wits and her mind again. And then she was brought to church and purified as other women are, blessed may God be.

It was, as they thought who knew about it, a very great miracle, for he who wrote this book had never before that time seen any man or woman, as he thought, so far out of herself as this woman was, nor so hard to control, and afterwards he saw her serious and sober enough – worship and praise be to our Lord without end for his high mercy and his goodness, who ever helps at time of need.

Chapter 76

It happened one time that the husband of the said creature – a man of great age, over sixty years old – would have come down from his chamber bare-foot and bare-legged, and he slithered, or else missed his footing, and fell to the ground from the stairs, with his head twisted underneath him, seriously broken and bruised, so much so that he had five linen plugs in the wounds in his head[1] for many days while his head was healing.

And, as God willed, it was known to some of his neighbours how he had fallen down the stairs, perhaps through the din and the rushing of his falling. And so they came in to him and found him lying with his head twisted under himself, half alive, all streaked with blood, and never likely to have spoken with priest nor clerk, except through high grace and miracle.

Then the said creature, his wife, was sent for, and so she came to him. Then he was taken up and his head was sewn, and he was ill for a long time after, so that people thought he would die. And then people said, if he died, his wife deserved to be hanged for his death, for as much as she could have looked after him and did not. They did not live together, nor did they sleep together, for – as it is written before – they both with one assent and with the free will of each other had made a vow to live chaste. And therefore, to avoid all risks, they lived in different places, where no suspicion could be had of their lack of chastity. For, at first, they lived together after they had made their vow, and then people slandered them, and said they enjoyed their lust and their pleasure as they did before the making of their vow. And when they went out on pilgrimage, or to see and speak with other spiritually-minded creatures, many evil folk whose tongues were their own hurt, lacking the fear and love of our Lord Jesus Christ, believed and said that they went rather to woods, groves or valleys, to enjoy the lust of their bodies, where people should not espy it or know it.

Knowing how prone people were to believe evil of them, and desiring to avoid all occasion as far as they properly could, by mutual good will and consent, they parted from each other as regards their board and lodging, and went to board in different places. And this was the reason that she was not with him, and also so that she should not be hindered from her contemplation. And therefore, when he had fallen and was seriously hurt, as is said before, people said, if he died, it was proper that she should answer for his death. Then she prayed to our Lord that her husband might live a year, and she be delivered from slander, if it were his pleasure.

Our Lord said to her mind, 'Daughter, you shall have your boon, for he shall live, and I have performed a great miracle for you that he was not dead. And I bid you take him home, and look after him for my love.'

She said, 'No, good Lord, for I shall then not attend to you as I do now.'

'Yes, daughter,' said our Lord, 'you shall have as much reward for looking after him and helping him in his need at home, as if you were in church to say your prayers. And you have said many times that you would gladly look after me. I pray you now, look after him for love of me, for he has sometime fulfilled both your will and my will, and he has made your body freely available to me, so that you should serve me and live chaste and clean, and therefore I wish you to be available to help him in his need, in my name.'

'Ah, Lord,' said she, 'for your mercy, grant me grace to obey your will, and fulfil your will, and never let my spiritual enemies have any power to hinder me from fulfilling your will.'

Then she took her husband home with her and looked after him for years afterwards, as long as he lived. She had very much trouble with him, for in his last days he turned childish and lacked reason, so that he could not go to a stool to relieve himself, or else he would not, but like a child discharged his excrement into his linen clothes as he sat there by the fire or at the table – wherever it was, he would spare no place. And therefore her labour was all the greater, in washing and wringing, and so were her expenses for keeping a fire going. All this hindered her a very great deal from her contemplation, so that many times she would have disliked her work, except that she thought to herself how she in her young days had had very many delectable thoughts, physical lust, and inordinate love for his body. And therefore she was glad to be punished by means of the same body, and took it much the more easily, and served him and helped him, she thought, as she would have done Christ himself.

Chapter 77

When the said creature first had her astonishing cries, and was once in spiritual dalliance with her sovereign Lord Christ Jesus, she said, 'Lord, why will you give me such crying that people wonder at me because of it? And they say I am in great peril, for, as they say, I am the cause that many men sin over me. And you know, Lord, that I would give no man cause nor occasion for sin if I could, for I would rather, Lord, be in a prison ten fathoms deep, there to cry and weep all my lifetime for my sins and for all men's sins, and specially for your love, than I would give people occasion to sin wilfully because of me.

'Lord, the world may not allow me to do your will, nor to follow your directing, and therefore I pray you, if it be your will, take from me these cryings during sermons, so that I do not cry at your holy preaching, and let me have them alone by myself, so that I be not barred from hearing your holy preaching and your holy words; for greater pain may I not suffer in this world than to be debarred from hearing your holy word. And if I were in prison, my greatest pain would be to forgo your holy words and your holy sermons. And, good Lord, if you wish in any case that I cry, I pray you, give me it alone in my chamber as much as you will, and spare me when among people, if you please.'

Our merciful Lord Christ Jesus, answering to her mind, said, 'Daughter, do not pray for this; you shall not have your desire in this, though my mother and all the saints in heaven pray for you, for I shall make you obedient to my will, so that you shall cry when I will, and where I will, both loudly and quietly; for I told you, daughter, you are mine and I am yours, and so shall you be without end.[1]

'Daughter, you see how the planets are obedient to my will, and that sometimes there come great thunderclaps and make people terribly afraid. And sometimes, daughter, you see how I send great flashes of lightning that burn churches and houses. You also sometimes see that I send great winds that blow steeples and houses down, and trees out of the earth, and do much harm in many places, and yet the wind may not be seen, but it may well be felt.

'And just so, daughter, I proceed with the might of my Godhead; it may not be seen with man's eye, and yet it may well be felt in a simple soul where it pleases me to work grace, as I do in your soul. And as suddenly as the lightning comes from heaven, so suddenly I come into your soul, and illumine it with the light of grace and of understanding, and set it all on fire with love, and make the fire of love to burn there inside, and purge it clean from all earthly filth. And sometimes, daughter, I cause earthquakes to frighten people so that they should fear me.

'And so, daughter, spiritually speaking, have I done with you, and with other chosen souls that shall be saved, for I turn the earth of their hearts upside down and make them so intensely afraid that they dread that vengeance will fall on them for their sins. And so did you, daughter, when you first turned to me, and it is needful that young beginners do so; but now, daughter, you have great cause to love me well, for the perfect charity that I give you dispels all fear from you. And though other people set little value on you, I set the more value on you. As sure as you are of the sun, when you see it shining brightly, just as sure are you of the love of God at all times.

'You also well know, daughter, that I sometimes send many great rains and sharp showers, and sometimes only small and gentle drops. And just so I proceed with you, daughter, when it pleases me to speak in your soul. I sometimes give you slight weeping and soft tears, as a token that I love you. And sometimes I give you great cries and roarings, to make people afraid at the grace that I put into you, in token that I wish that my mother's sorrow be known through you, so that men and women might have the more compassion of her sorrow that she suffered for me.

'And the third token is this, daughter: that whatever creatures will feel as much sorrow for my Passion as you have done many times, and will cease from their sins, then they shall have the bliss of heaven without end.

'The fourth token is this: that any creature on earth, though he have been ever so horrible a sinner, he need never fall into despair if he will take example from your way of living and act somewhat like it, as he is able to.

'Also, daughter, the fifth token is: that I wish you to know in yourself, by the great pain that you feel in your heart when you cry so intensely for my love, that it shall be the cause why you shall feel no pain when you have come out of this world, and also that you shall have the less pain in your dying, for you have so great compassion for my flesh that I must needs have compassion on your flesh.

'And therefore, daughter, allow the people to say what they will about your crying, for you are in no way cause of their sin. Daughter, people sinned over me, and yet I was not the cause of their sin.'

Then she said, 'Ah, Lord, blessed may you be, for I think you do yourself all that you bid me do. In Holy Writ, Lord, you bid me love my enemies,[2] and I well know that in all this world was never so great an enemy to me, as I have been to you. Therefore, Lord, if I were slain a hundred times in a day, if it were possible, for your love, yet I could never repay you the goodness that you have shown me.'

Then our Lord answered her and said, 'I pray you, daughter, give me nothing else but love. You may never please me better than to have me always in your love, nor shall you ever, in any penance that you may do on earth, please me so much as by loving me. And, daughter, if you will be high in heaven with me, keep me always in your mind as much as you can, and do not forget me at your meals, but always think that I sit in your heart and know every thought that is inside, both good and ill, and that I perceive the least thinking and twinkling of your eye.'

She replied to our Lord, 'Now, truly, Lord, I wish I could love you as much as you might make me love you. If it were possible, I would love you as well as all the saints in heaven love you, and as well as all the creatures on earth might love you. And I would, Lord, for your love, be laid naked on a hurdle for all men to wonder at me for your love – so long as it were no danger to their souls – and they to throw mud and slime at me, and to be drawn from town to town every day of my life, if you were pleased by this and no man's soul hindered – your will be fulfilled and not mine.'

Chapter 78

For many years on Palm Sunday,[1] as this creature was at the procession with other good people in the churchyard, and saw how the priests kept their observances, how they knelt to the sacrament, and the people too, it seemed to her spiritual sight as though she had been at that time in Jerusalem, and seen our Lord in his manhood received by the people as he was while he went about here on earth.

Then she had so much sweetness and devotion that she could not bear it, but cried, wept, and sobbed very violently. She had many a holy thought of our Lord's Passion, and beheld him in her spiritual sight as truly as if he had been before her in her bodily sight. Therefore she could not resist weeping and sobbing, but she simply had to weep, cry and sob, when she saw her Saviour suffer such great pains for her love.

Then she would pray for all the people living on earth, that they might do our Lord due worship and reverence at that time and all times, and that they might be worthy to hear and understand the holy words and laws of God, and meekly obey and truly fulfil them according to their power.

And it was the custom in the place where she was dwelling to have a sermon on that day, and then, as a worthy doctor of divinity was in the pulpit and preached the sermon, he often repeated these words: 'Our Lord Jesus languishes for love.' Those words so worked in her mind, when she heard speak of the perfect love that our Lord Jesus Christ had for mankind, and how dearly he bought us with his bitter Passion, shedding his heart's blood for our redemption, and suffered so shameful a death for our salvation, that she could no longer keep the fire of love enclosed within her breast, but, whether she would or no, what was enclosed within would insist on appearing outwardly.

And so she cried very loudly and wept and sobbed very bitterly, as though she would have burst for the pity and compassion that she had for our Lord's Passion. And sometimes she was all of a sweat with the effort of the crying, it was so loud and violent, and many people wondered at her and cursed her roundly, supposing that she had pretended to cry.

And soon after our Lord said to her, 'Daughter, this is very pleasing to me, for the more shame and more contempt that you endure for my love, the more joy shall you have with me in heaven, and it is just that it should be so.'

Sometimes she heard great sounds and great melodies with her bodily ears, and then she thought it was very merry in heaven, and had very great languishing and very great longing for heaven, with much silent mourning.

And then many times our Lord Jesus Christ would say to her, 'Daughter, here today are some fair people, and yet many of them shall be dead before this day twelve-month,' and told her beforehand when plague should occur. And she found it to be indeed as she had felt before, and that much strengthened her in the love of God.

Our Lord would also say, 'Daughter, those who will not believe the goodness and the grace that I show you in this life, I shall make them know the truth when they are dead, and out of this world. Daughter, you show a good zeal in charity, in that you wish all men were saved, and so do I. And they say that they wish so themselves, but you may well observe that they do not want themselves to be saved, for they will all sometimes hear the word of God, but they will not always act according to it, and they will not sorrow for their sins themselves, nor will they allow others to suffer for them.

'Nevertheless, daughter, I have ordained you to be a mirror amongst them, to have great sorrow, so that they should take example from you to have some little sorrow in their hearts for their sins, so that they might through that be saved; yet they have no love to hear of sorrow or of contrition. But, good daughter, do your duty and pray for them while you are in this world, and you shall have the same reward in heaven, as if all the world were saved by your good will and your prayer. Daughter, I have many times said to you that many thousand souls shall be saved through your prayers, and some that lie at the point of death shall have grace through your merits and your prayers, for your tears and your prayers are very sweet and acceptable to me.'

Then she said in her mind to our Lord Jesus Christ, 'Ah, Jesus, blessed may you be without end, for I have many a great cause to thank you and love you with all my heart, for it seems to me, Lord, that you are all charity, to the profit and health of man's soul. Ah, Lord, I believe that he shall be very wicked, that shall be parted from you without end. He shall neither wish for good, nor do good, nor desire good. And therefore, Lord, I thank you for all the goodness that you have shown me, most unworthy wretch.'

And then, on the same Sunday, when the priest took the staff of the cross and smote on the church door, the door was opened to him; and then the priest entered with the sacrament, while all the people followed into the church. Then she thought that our Lord spoke to the devil and opened hell's gates, confounding him and all his host – and what grace and goodness he showed to those souls, delivering them from everlasting prison, in spite of the devil and all that were his!

She had many a holy thought and many a holy desire which she could never tell or repeat, nor could her tongue ever express the abundance of grace that she felt, blessed be our Lord for all his gifts.

When they had come into church, she saw the priests kneeling before the crucifix, and as they sang, the priest who was conducting the service that day drew up a cloth in front of the crucifix three times, each time higher than the other, so that the people should see the crucifix. Then her mind was wholly taken out of all earthly things and set entirely upon spiritual things, praying and desiring that she might at the last have a full sight of him in heaven, who is both God and man in one Person.

And then afterwards, for the duration of the mass, she would weep and sob most abundantly, and sometimes, in the middle of all this, cry out most fervently, for she thought that she saw our Lord Christ Jesus as truly in her soul with her spiritual eye, as she had seen the crucifix before with her bodily eye.

Chapter 79

Then she beheld, in the sight of her soul, our blissful Lord Christ Jesus coming towards his Passion, and before he went, he knelt down and received his mother's blessing. Then she saw his mother falling down in a swoon before her son, saying to him, 'Alas, my dear son, how shall I suffer this sorrow, and have no joy in all this world but you alone? Ah, dear son, if you will die at any event, let me die before you, and let me never suffer this day of sorrow, for I may never bear this sorrow that I shall have for your death. I wish, son, that I might suffer death for you, so that you should not die – if man's soul might so be saved. Now, dear son, if you have no pity for yourself, have pity on your mother, for you very well know that no man can comfort me in all this world but you alone.'

Then our Lord took up his mother in his arms and kissed her very sweetly, and said to her, 'Ah, blessed mother, be cheered and comforted, for I have very often told you that I must needs suffer death, or else no man would be saved, or ever come to bliss. And mother, it is my father's will that it be so, and therefore, I pray you, let it be your will also, for my death shall turn for me to great worship, and to great joy and profit for you and all mankind who shall trust in my Passion, and act in accordance with it.

'And therefore, blessed mother, you must remain here after me, for in you shall rest all the faith of Holy Church, and by your faith Holy Church shall increase in her faith. And therefore I pray you, beloved mother, cease from your sorrowing, for I will not leave you comfortless. I shall leave John, my cousin, here with you to comfort you instead of me; I shall send my holy angels to comfort you on earth; and I shall comfort you in your soul myself, for mother, you well know I have promised you the bliss of heaven, and that you are sure of.

'Ah, beloved mother, what would you wish for better than, where I am king, you to be queen, and all angels and saints shall be obedient to your will. And whatever grace you ask of me, I shall not deny your desire. I shall give you power over the devils, so that they shall be afraid of you, and you not of them. And also, my blessed mother, I have said to you before that I shall come for you myself, when you shall pass out of this world, with all my angels and all my saints who are in heaven, and bring you before my father with all manner of music, melody and joy. And there I shall set you in great peace and rest without end. And there you shall be crowned as queen of heaven, as lady of all the world, and as empress of hell.

'And therefore, my beloved mother, I pray you, bless me and let me go to do my father's will, because for that I came into this world, and took flesh and blood of you.'

When the said creature beheld this glorious sight in her soul, and saw how he blessed his mother, and his mother him, and then his blessed mother could not speak one more word to him, but fell down to the ground, and so they parted from each other, his mother lying still, as though she were dead – then the said creature thought she took our Lord Jesus Christ by the clothes, and fell down at his feet, praying him to bless her, and with that she cried very loudly and wept very bitterly, saying in her mind, 'Ah, Lord, what shall become of me? I had much rather that you would slay me than let me remain in the world without you, for without you I may not stay here, Lord.'

Then our Lord answered to her, 'Be still, daughter, and rest with my mother here, and comfort yourself in her, for she that is my own mother must suffer this sorrow. But I shall come again, daughter, to my mother, and comfort both her and you, and turn all your sorrow into joy.'

And then she thought our Lord went forth on his way, and she went to our Lady and said, 'Ah, blessed lady, rise up and let us follow your blessed son as long as we may see him, so that I may look upon him enough before he dies. Ah, dear lady, how can your heart last, and see your blissful son see all this woe? Lady, I may not endure it, and yet I am not his mother.'

Then our Lady answered and said, 'Daughter, you have heard that it will not be otherwise, and therefore I simply must suffer it for my son's love.'

And then she thought that they followed on after our Lord, and saw how he made his prayers to his father on the Mount of Olivet, and heard the beautiful answer that came from his father, and the beautiful answer that he gave his father.

Then she saw how our Lord went to his disciples and ordered them to wake up – his enemies were near. And then came a great multitude of people with many lights, and many of them armed with staves, swords and pole-axes, to seek out our Lord Jesus Christ – our merciful Lord, meek as a lamb, saying to them, 'Whom do you seek?'

They answered in rough mood, 'Jesus of Nazareth.'

Our Lord replied, *'Ego sum.'*

And then she saw the Jews fall down to the ground – they could not stand for fear – but immediately they got up again, and searched as they had done before. And our Lord asked, 'Whom do you seek?'

And they said again, 'Jesus of Nazareth.'

Our Lord answered, 'I am he.'

And then she immediately saw Judas come and kiss our Lord, and the Jews laid hands upon him most violently. Then our Lady and she had much sorrow and great pain to see the Lamb of Innocence so contemptuously handled and dragged about by his own people, to whom he was especially sent. And very soon the said creature beheld with her spiritual eye the Jews putting a cloth before our Lord's eyes, beating him and buffeting him on the head, and striking him on his sweet mouth, shouting very cruelly at him, 'Tell us now, who hit you?'

They did not spare to spit in his face in the most shameful way that they could. And then our Lady and she, her unworthy handmaid for the time, wept and sighed keenly because the Jews so foully and so venomously treated her blissful Lord. And they would not spare to lug his blessed ears, and pull the hair of his beard.

And soon after, she saw them pull off his clothes and strip him all naked, and then drag him before them as if he had been the greatest malefactor in the world. And he went on very meekly before them, as naked as he was born, towards a pillar of stone, and spoke no word back to them, but let them do and say what they wished. And there they bound him to the pillar as tightly as they could, and beat him on his fair white body with rods, with whips, and with scourges.

And then she thought our Lady wept wonderfully sorely, and therefore the said creature had to weep and cry, when she saw such spiritual sights in her soul as freshly and veritably as if they had been done in her bodily sight, and she thought that our Lady and she were always together to see our Lord's pains. Such spiritual sights she had every Palm Sunday and every Good Friday, and in many other ways as well, many years together. And therefore she cried and wept very bitterly, and suffered much contempt and rebuke in many places.

And then our Lord said to her soul, 'Daughter, these sorrows, and many more, I suffered for your love, and divers pains, more than any man on earth can tell. Therefore, daughter, you have great cause to love me very well, for I have bought your love most dearly.'

Chapter 80

Another time she saw in her contemplation our Lord Jesus Christ bound to a pillar, and his hands were bound above his head.[1] And then she saw sixteen men with sixteen scourges, and each scourge had eight tips of lead on the end, and each tip was full of sharp prickles, as if it had been the rowel of a spur. And those men with the scourges made a covenant that each of them should give our Lord forty strokes.[2]

When she saw this piteous sight, she wept and cried very loudly, as if she would have burst for sorrow and pain. And when our Lord was severely beaten and scourged, the Jews loosed him from the pillar, and gave him his cross to bear on his shoulder. And then she thought that our Lady and she went by another way to meet with him, and when they met with him, they saw him carrying the heavy cross with great pain, it was so heavy and so huge that he could scarcely bear it.[3]

And then our Lady said to him, 'Ah, my sweet son, let me help to carry that heavy cross.'[4]

And she was so weak that she could not, but fell down and swooned, and lay as still as if she had been a dead woman. Then the creature saw our Lord fall down by his mother, and comfort her as he could with many sweet words. When she heard the words and saw the compassion that the mother had for the son, and the son for the mother, then she wept, sobbed and cried as though she would have died, for the pity and compassion that she had for that piteous sight, and the holy thoughts that she had in the meantime, which were so subtle and heavenly that she could never describe them afterwards, as she had them in feeling.

Later she went forth in contemplation, through the mercy of our Lord Jesus Christ, to the place where he was nailed to the cross. And then she saw the Jews with great violence tear off of our Lord's precious body a cloth of silk, which had stuck and hardened so firmly and tightly to our Lord's body with his precious blood, that it pulled away with it all the skin from his blessed body and renewed his precious wounds, and made the blood to run down all around on every side. Then that precious body appeared to her sight as raw as something that was newly flayed out of its skin, most pitiful to behold. And so she had a new sorrow, so that she wept and cried very bitterly.

And soon after, she beheld how the cruel Jews laid his precious body on the cross, and then took a long nail, all rough and coarse, and set it on one hand, and with great violence and cruelty they drove it through his hand. His blessed mother beholding – and this creature – how his precious body shrank and drew together with all the sinews and veins in that precious body for the pain that it suffered and felt, they sorrowed and mourned and sighed very grievously.

Then she saw, with her spiritual eye, how the Jews fastened ropes on to the other hand – for the sinews and veins were so shrunken with pain that it would not reach to the hole that they had drilled for it [5] – and they pulled on it to make it reach the hole. And so her pain and her sorrow ever increased. And later they pulled his blessed feet in the same way.

And then she thought, in her soul, she heard our Lady say to the Jews, 'Alas, you cruel Jews, why do you treat my sweet son like this, and he never did you any harm? You fill my heart full of sorrow.'

And then she thought the Jews spoke back roughly to our Lady, and moved her away from her son.

Then the said creature thought that she cried out at the Jews, and said, 'You accursed Jews, why are you killing my Lord Jesus Christ? Kill me instead, and let him go.'

And then she wept and cried surpassingly bitterly, so that many people in the church were astonished. She straightaway saw them take up the cross with our Lord's body hanging on it, and make a great noise and cry; and they lifted it up from the earth a certain distance, and then let the cross fall down into the mortise. [6] And then our Lord's body shook and shuddered, and all the joints of that blissful body burst and broke apart, and his precious wounds ran down with rivers of blood on every side, and so she had ever more reason for more weeping and sorrowing.

And then she heard our Lord, hanging on the cross, say these words to his mother, 'Woman, see your son, St John the Evangelist.'

Then she thought our Lady fell down and swooned, and St John took her up in his arms and comforted her with sweet words, as well as he could. This creature then said to our Lord, as it seemed to her, 'Alas, Lord, you are leaving here a mother full of care. What shall we do now, and how shall we bear this great sorrow that we shall have for your love?'

And then she heard the two thieves speaking to our Lord, and our Lord said to the one thief, 'This day you shall be with me in paradise.'

Then she was glad of that answer, and prayed our Lord, for his mercy, that he would be as gracious to her soul when she should pass out of this world as he was to the thief – for she was worse, she thought, than any thief.

And then she thought our Lord commended his spirit into his father's hands, and with that he died. Then she thought she saw our Lady swoon and fall down and lie still, as if she had been dead. Then this creature thought that she ran all round the place like a mad woman, crying and roaring. And later she came to our Lady, and fell down on her knees before her, saying to her, 'I pray you, Lady, cease from your sorrowing, for your son is dead and out of pain, and I think you have sorrowed enough. And Lady, I will sorrow for you, for your sorrow is my sorrow.'

Then she thought she saw Joseph of Arimathea take down our Lord's body from the cross, and lay it before our Lady on a marble stone.[7] Our Lady had a kind of joy when her dear son was taken down from the cross and laid on the stone before her. And then our blessed Lady bowed down to her son's body and kissed his mouth, and wept so plentifully over his blessed face, that she washed away the blood from his face with the tears of her eyes.

And then this creature thought she heard Mary Magdalene say to our Lady, 'I pray you, Lady, give me leave to handle and kiss his feet, for at these I get grace.'

At once our Lady gave leave to her and all those who were there, to offer what worship and reverence they wished to that precious body. And Mary Magdalene soon took our Lord's feet, and our Lady's sisters took his hands, the one sister one hand and the other sister the other hand, and wept very bitterly in kissing those hands and those precious feet. And the said creature thought that she continually ran to and fro, as if she were a woman without reason, greatly desiring to have had the precious body by herself alone, so that she might have wept enough in the presence of that precious body, for she thought she would have died with weeping and mourning for his death, for love that she had for him.

And at once she saw St John the Evangelist, Joseph of

Arimathea, and other friends of our Lord, come and want to bury our Lord's body, and they asked our Lady that she would allow them to bury that precious body. Our sorrowful Lady said to them, 'Sirs, would you take away from me my son's body? I might never look upon him enough while he lived. I pray you, let me have him now he is dead, and do not part my son and me from each other. And if you will bury him in any case, I pray you, bury me with him, for I may not live without him.'

And then this creature thought that they asked our Lady so beautifully, until at last our Lady let them bury her dear son with great worship and great reverence, as was fitting for them to do.

Chapter 81

When our Lord was buried, our Lady fell down in a swoon as she would have come from the grave, and St John took her up in his arms, and Mary Magdalene went on the other side, to support and comfort our Lady as much as they could. Then the said creature, desiring to remain still by the grave of our Lord, mourned, wept, and sorrowed with loud crying for the tenderness and compassion that she had of our Lord's death, and the many mournful desires that God put into her mind at that time. Because of this, people wondered at her, marvelling at what was the matter with her, for they little knew the cause. She thought she would never have departed from there, but desired to have died there and been buried with our Lord. Later the creature thought she saw our Lady going homewards again, and, as she went, many good women came to her and said, 'Lady, we are very sorry that your son is dead, and that our people have done him so much shame.'

And then our Lady, bowing down her head, thanked them very meekly by her looks and expression, for she could not speak, her heart was so full of grief.

Then this creature thought, when our Lady had come home and was laid down on a bed, that she made for our Lady a good hot drink of gruel and spiced wine,[1] and brought it to her to comfort her, and then our Lady said to her, 'Take it away, daughter. Give me no food but my own child.'

The creature replied, 'Ah, blessed Lady, you must comfort yourself, and cease from your sorrowing.'

'Ah, daughter, where should I go, or where should I live without sorrow? I tell you, there was certainly never any woman on earth who had such great cause to sorrow as I have, for there was never woman in this world who bore a better child, nor a meeker to his mother, than my son was to me.'

And she thought she soon heard our Lady cry with a lamentable voice and say, 'John, where is my son, Jesus Christ?'

And St John answered and said, 'Dear Lady, you well know that he is dead.'

'Ah, John,' she said, 'that is a very sorrowful counsel for me.'

The creature heard this answer as clearly, in the understanding of her soul, as she would understand one man speaking to another. And soon the creature heard St Peter knocking at the door,[2] and St John asked who was there. Peter answered, 'I, sinful Peter, who have forsaken my Lord Jesus Christ.' St John would have made him come in, and Peter would not, until our Lady told him to come in. And then Peter said, 'Lady, I am not worthy to come in to you,' and was still outside the door.

Then St John went to our Lady and told her that Peter was so abashed that he dared not come in. Our Lady told St John to go back quickly to St Peter and bid him come in to her. And then this creature, in her spiritual sight, beheld St Peter come before our Lady and fall down on his knees, with great weeping and sobbing, and say, 'Lady, I beg your forgiveness, for I have forsaken your beloved son and my sweet master, who loved me so well, and therefore, Lady, I am never worthy to look upon him, or you either, except by your great mercy.'

'Ah, Peter,' said our Lady, 'don't be afraid, for, though you have forsaken my sweet son, he never forsook you, Peter, and he shall come again and comfort us all indeed; for he promised me, Peter, that he would come again on the third day and comfort me. Ah, Peter,' said our Lady, 'I shall think it a very long time, until that day comes that I may see his blessed face.'

Then our Lady lay still on her bed, and heard how the friends of Jesus made their lament for the sorrow that they had. And always our Lady lay still, mourning and weeping with sorrowful expression, and at last, Mary Magdalene and our Lady's sisters took their leave of our Lady, in order to go and buy ointment, so that they might anoint our Lord's body with it.

Then this creature was left alone with our Lady and thought it a thousand years until the third day came; and that day she was with our Lady in a chapel where our Lord Jesus Christ appeared to her [3] and said, *'Salve, sancta parens.'* [4]

And then this creature thought in her soul that our Lady said. 'Are you my sweet son, Jesus?'

And he said, 'Yes, my blessed mother, I am your son, Jesus.'

Then he took up his blessed mother and kissed her very sweetly.

And then this creature thought that she saw our Lady feeling and searching all over our Lord's body, and his hands and his feet, to see if there were any soreness or any pain. And she heard our Lord say to his mother, 'Dear mother, my pain is all gone, and now I shall live for ever more. And mother, so shall your pain and your sorrow be turned into very great joy. Mother, ask what you will, and I shall tell you.'

And when he had allowed his mother to ask what she wished and had answered her questions, then he said, 'Mother, by your leave, I must go and speak with Mary Magdalene.'

Our Lady said, 'That is well done, for, son, she has very great sorrow over your absence. And, I pray you, do not be long from me.'

These spiritual sights and understandings caused the creature to weep, to sob and to cry very loudly, so that she could not control or restrain herself on Easter Day and other days when our Lord would visit her with his grace – blessed and worshipped may he be.

And soon after, this creature was – in her contemplation – with Mary Magdalene, mourning and seeking our Lord at the grave, and heard and saw how our Lord Jesus Christ appeared to her in the likeness of a gardener, saying, 'Woman, why are you weeping?'

Mary, not knowing who he was, all enflamed with the fire of love, replied to him, 'Sir, if you have taken away my Lord, tell me, and I shall take him back again.'

Then our merciful Lord, having pity and compassion on her, said, 'Mary.'

And with that word she – knowing our Lord – fell down at his feet, and would have kissed his feet, saying, 'Master.'

Our Lord said to her, 'Touch me not.'

Then this creature thought that Mary Magdalene said to our Lord, 'Ah, Lord, I see you don't want me to be as homely with you as I have been before,' and looked very miserable.

'Yes, Mary,' said our Lord, 'I will never forsake you, but I shall always be with you, without end.'

And then our Lord said to Mary Magdalene, 'Go, tell my brethren and Peter that I have risen.'

And then this creature thought that Mary went with great joy, and it was a great marvel to her that Mary rejoiced for, if our Lord had spoken to her as he did to Mary, she thought she could never have been happy. That was when she would have kissed his feet, and he said, 'Touch me not.' This creature had such great grief and sorrow at those words that, whenever she heard them in any sermon, as she did many times, she wept, sorrowed and cried as though she would have died, for the love and desire that she had to be with our Lord.

Chapter 82

On the Purification Day – otherwise Candlemas Day – when the said creature saw people with their candles in church, her mind was ravished into beholding our Lady offering her blessed son, our Saviour, to the priest Simeon in the Temple, as veritably to her spiritual understanding as if she had been there in her bodily presence to offer with our Lady herself.[1] Then she was so comforted by the contemplation in her soul which she had in beholding our Lord Jesus Christ, his blessed mother, Simeon the priest, Joseph, and other people who were there when our Lady was purified, and the heavenly songs that she thought she heard when our blissful Lord was offered up to Simeon, that she could scarcely carry up her own candle to the priest, as people did at the time of the offering, but went reeling about on all sides as if she were a drunk woman, weeping and sobbing so intensely that she could hardly stand on her feet, for the fervour of love and devotion that God put into her soul through high contemplation. And sometimes she could not stand, but fell down amongst people and cried very loudly, so that many men wondered at her, and marvelled at what was the matter with her, for the fervour of the spirit was so great that the body failed, and could not endure it.

She had such holy thoughts and meditations many times when she saw women being purified after childbirth. She thought in her soul that she saw our Lady being purified, and had high contemplation in beholding the women who came to make offerings together with the women that were being purified. Her mind was wholly drawn from earthly thoughts and earthly sights, and set altogether upon spiritual sights, which were so delectable and so devout, that she could not in the time of fervour withstand her weeping, her sobbing, nor her crying, and therefore she endured much wondering at herself, many a jibe, and much scorn.

Also, when she saw weddings – men and women being joined together according to the law of Holy Church – at once she had in meditation how our Lady was joined to Joseph, and of the spiritual joining of man's soul to Jesus Christ, praying to our Lord that her love and her affection might be joined to him alone without end, and that she might have grace to obey him, love and dread him, worship and praise him, and love nothing but what he loved, nor want anything but what he wanted, and ever to be ready to fulfil his will both night and day without resentment or sadness, with all gladness of spirit; and many more holy thoughts than she could ever repeat, for she did not get them from her own study nor her own wit, but of his gift, whose wisdom is incomprehensible to all creatures, except to those alone whom he chooses and illumines more or less as he will his own self, for his will may not be constrained – it is in his own free disposition.

She had these thoughts and these desires with profound tears, sighings and sobbings, and sometimes with great violent cryings, as God would send them, and sometimes soft and secret tears without any violence. She could neither weep loudly nor quietly except when God would send it her, for she was sometimes so barren of tears for a day or sometimes half a day, and had such great pain for the desire that she had of them, that she would have given all this world, if it had been hers, for a few tears, or have suffered very great bodily pain to have got them with.

And then, when she was barren in this way, she could find no joy or comfort in food or drink, or chat, but was always glum of face and manner until God would send tears to her again, and then she was happy enough. And although it happened that our Lord sometimes withdrew from her the abundance of her tears, yet he did not withdraw from her for years together her holy thoughts and desires, for her mind and her desire was ever upon our Lord. But she thought there was no savour nor sweetness, except when she might weep, for then she thought that she could pray.

Chapter 83

Two priests who had great faith in her manner of crying and weeping were, nevertheless, sometimes in great doubt whether it were deceptive or not. Because she cried and wept in people's sight, they had an idea to themselves, unbeknown to her, that they would test whether she cried so that people should hear her or not. One day, the priests came to her and asked if she would go two miles from where she lived, on pilgrimage to a church that stood out in the country, a good distance from any other house, which was dedicated in honour of God and St Michael the Archangel.[1] And she said she would very willingly go with them.

They took with them a child or two, and went to the said place in a company. When they had said their prayers for a while, the said creature had so much sweetness and devotion, that she could not keep it secret, but burst out in violent weeping and sobbing, and cried as loud, or else louder, than she did when she was amongst people at home, and she could not restrain herself from this, no other people being present there than the two priests, and a child or two with them.

And then, as they came homewards again, they met women with children in their arms, and the said creature asked if there were any male child among them, and the women said no. Then her mind was so ravished into the childhood of Christ, for desire that she had to see him, that she could not bear it, but fell down and wept and cried so intensely that it was marvellous to hear it. Then the priests had the more faith that all was indeed well with her, when they heard her cry in out-of-the-way places as well as public places, and in the fields as in the town.

There were also nuns who desired to have some knowledge of this creature, in order that they should be the more stirred to devotion. She was in their church at midnight to hear their matins, and our Lord sent her such high devotion and such high meditation, and such spiritual comforts, that she was all enflamed with the fire of love, which increased so intensely that it burst out with loud voice and great crying, so that our Lord's name was the more magnified among his servants, those who were good, meek and simple souls and would believe the goodness of our Lord Jesus Christ, who gives his grace to whom he will.

And especially to those who do not doubt or mistrust in their asking, her crying greatly profited to the increase of merit and of virtue. To those who little trusted and little believed, there was perhaps little increase of virtue and of merit. But whether people believed in her crying or not, her grace was never the less, but ever increased. Our Lord visited her with equal kindness by night as by day, when he would, and how he would, and where he would, for she lacked no grace except when she doubted or mistrusted the goodness of God, supposing or dreading that it was the guile of her spiritual enemy to inform her or teach her otherwise than was to her spiritual health.

When she supposed this, or consented to any such thoughts through the prompting of any man or through any evil spirit in her mind – which would many a time have caused her to leave her good purpose, had the mightly hand of our Lord's mercy not withstood his great malice – then she lacked grace and devotion, and all good thoughts and all good memories, until she was, through the mercy of our Lord Jesus Christ, compelled to believe steadfastly, without any doubting, that it was God who spoke in her, and would be magnified in her for his own goodness and her profit, and the profit of many others.

And when she believed it was God and no evil spirit that gave her so much grace of devotion, contrition, and holy contemplation, then she had so many holy thoughts, holy speeches and conversation in her soul, teaching her how she should love God, how she should worship him and serve him, that she could never repeat but a few of them. They were so holy and so high that she was abashed to tell them to any creature, and they were also so high above her bodily wits that she could never express them with her bodily tongue just as she felt them. She understood them better in her soul than she could utter them.

If one of her confessors came to her when she rose up newly

from her contemplation or meditation, she could have told him many things of the converse that our Lord communicated to her soul, and within a short time afterwards she had forgotten the most part of it, and nearly everything.

Chapter 84

The Abbess of Denny,[1] a house of nuns, often sent for the said creature, that she should come to speak with her and with her sisters. This creature thought she would not go until another year, for she could ill endure the effort. Then, as she was in her meditation, and had great sweetness and devotion, our Lord commanded her to go to Denny and comfort the ladies who desired to converse with her, saying in this way to her soul, 'Daughter, set off for the house of Denny in the name of Jesus, for I wish you to comfort them.'

She was loath to go, for it was a time of pestilence, and she thought she might, for no advantage, have died there. Our Lord said to her mind again, 'Daughter, you shall go safely, and come safely back.'

She then went to a worthy burgess's wife, who loved and trusted her very much, and whose husband lay very ill, and told the worthy wife that she would be going to Denny. The worthy woman did not want her to go, and said, 'I would not for forty shillings,' she said, 'that my husband died while you were away.'

And she replied, 'If you gave me a hundred pounds, I would not remain at home.'

For when she was commanded in her soul to go, she would in no way withstand it, but in spite of anything she would set off, whatever happened. And when she was commanded to be at home, she would not go out for anything.

And then our Lord told her that the said burgess would not die, and she went back to the worthy wife and told her to be comforted, for her husband would live and get on well, and he would not die yet. The good wife was very glad and replied to her, 'Now Gospel may it be in your mouth.'

Then this creature would have hurried off, as she was commanded, but when she came to the waterside, all the boats had already left in the direction of Cambridge before she got there. Then she had great distress as to how she would fulfil our Lord's bidding. And at once she was bidden in her soul that she should not be sorry or miserable, because she would be provided for well enough, and she should go safely and come safely back. And so it happened indeed.

Then our Lord in a way thanked her, because she in contemplation and in meditation had been his mother's handmaid, and helped to look after him in his childhood and so forth, until the time of his death, and said to her, 'Daughter, you shall have as great reward with me in heaven for your good service, and the good deeds that you have done in your mind and meditation, as if you had done those same deeds with your bodily senses outwardly. And also, daughter, when you do any service to yourself and your husband, in meals or drink or any other thing that is needful for you, for your confessors, or for any others that you receive in my name, you shall have the same reward in heaven as though you did it to my own person or to my blessed mother, and I shall thank you for it.

'Daughter, you say that it is a good name for me to be called All Good, and you shall find that name is all good to you. And also, daughter, you say it is very fitting that I be called All Love, and you shall find indeed that I am all love to you, for I know every thought of your heart. And I well know, daughter, that you have many times thought, if you had many churches full of money, you would have given it in my name. And also you have thought that you would, if you had had enough money, have founded many abbeys for my love, for religious men and women to live in, and given each of them a hundred pounds a year to be my servants. And you have also in your mind desired to have many priests in the town of Lynn, who might sing and read night and day to serve me, worship me, praise and thank me for the goodness that I have done to you on earth.

'And therefore, daughter, I promised you that you shall have the same reward in heaven for this good will and these good desires, as if you had done them indeed. Daughter, I know all the thoughts of your heart that you have for all kinds of men and women, for all lepers, for all prisoners; and as much money as you would give them in a year to serve me with, I take it as if it were done indeed. And daughter, I thank you for the charity that you have towards all lecherous men and women, for you pray for them and weep many a tear for them, desiring that I should deliver them from sin, and be as gracious to them as I was to Mary Magdalene, and that they might have as great a love towards me as Mary Magdalene had. And, with this condition, you would like every one of them to have twenty pounds a year to love and praise me.

'And daughter, this great charity that you have towards them in your prayer very much pleases me. And also, daughter, I thank you for the charity that you have in your prayer when you pray for all Jews and Saracens, and all heathen people, that they should come to Christian faith, so that my name might be magnified in them; and for the holy tears and weeping that you have wept for them, praying and desiring that if any prayer might bring them to grace or Christian belief, that I should hear your prayer for them, if it were my will.

'Furthermore, daughter, I thank you for the general charity that you have towards all people now living in this world, and all those that are to come until the end of the world: that you would be chopped up as small as meat for the pot for their love, so that I would, by your death, save them all from damnation if it pleased me. For you often say in your thoughts that there are enough in hell, and you wish that no more men should ever deserve to go there.

'And therefore, daughter, for all these good wills and desires, you shall have most high reward in heaven. Believe it well, and never doubt it at all, for all these graces are my graces, and I work them in you myself, so that you should have the more reward in heaven. And I tell you truly, daughter, every good thought and every good desire that you have in your soul is the speech of God, even if you do not hear me speaking to you sometimes, as I sometimes do to your clear understanding.

'And therefore, daughter, I am like a hidden God in your soul, and I sometimes withdraw your tears and your devotion, so that you should think in yourself that you have no goodness of yourself, but all goodness comes from me; and also, so that you should truly know what pain it is to be without me, and how sweet it is to feel me, and that you should be the more busy to seek me again; also, daughter, so that you should know what pain other men have, who wish to feel me and may not. For there is many a man on earth who, if he had for only one day in his whole lifetime what you have many days, he would always love me better, and thank me because of that one day. And you may not, daughter, do without me for one day without great pain. Therefore, daughter, you have great cause to love me well, for it is not because of any anger, daughter, that I sometimes withdraw from you the feeling of grace and the fervour of devotion, but so that you should know for sure that you cannot be a hypocrite for any weeping, for any crying, for any sweetness, for any devotion, for any thought of my Passion, or for any other spiritual grace that I give or send to you. For these are not the devil's gifts, but they are my graces and my gifts, and these are my own special gifts that I give to my own chosen souls, whom I knew without beginning should come to grace and dwell with me without end.

'For in all other things you may be a hypocrite if you wish, that is to say, in understanding, in praying many beads, in great fasting, in doing of great penance outwardly, so that people may see it, or in doing great deeds of charity with your hands, or in speaking good words with your mouth. In all these, daughter, you may be a hypocrite if you wish, and you may also do them well and holily, if you wish to yourself.

'See, daughter, I have given you such a love that you shall be no hypocrite in it. And daughter, you will never be losing time while you are so occupied, for whoever is thinking well may not sin during that time. And the devil does not know your holy thoughts that I give you, nor does any man on earth know how well and holily you are occupied with me, nor can you describe yourself the great grace and goodness that you feel in me. And therefore, daughter, you beguile both the devil and the world with your holy thoughts, and it is very great folly for worldly people to judge your heart, which no man may know, but God alone.

'And therefore, daughter, I tell you truly, you have as great cause to rejoice and be merry in your soul as any lady or maiden in this world. So great is my love towards you, that I may not withdraw it from you, for, daughter, no heart may think, nor tongue tell, the great love that I have to you, and for that I take witness of my blessed mother, of my holy angels, and of all the saints in heaven, for they all worship me, for your love, in heaven. And so I shall be worshipped on earth for your love, daughter, for I will have the grace I have shown you on earth known to the world, so that people may wonder at my goodness that I have shown to you who have been sinful. And because I have been so gracious and merciful to you, they who are in the world shall not despair, be they never so sinful, for they may have mercy and grace, if they will, themselves.'

Chapter 85

One time, as the said creature was kneeling before an altar of the Cross and saying a prayer, her eyelids kept closing together, as though she would have slept. And in the end she couldn't choose; she fell into a little slumber, and at once there appeared truly to her sight an angel, all clothed in white as if he were a little child, bearing a huge book before him. Then this creature said to the child, or else to the angel, 'Ah,' she said, 'this is the Book of Life.'

And she saw in the book the Trinity, and all in gold. Then she said to the child, 'Where is my name?'

The child answered and said, 'Here is your name, written at the Trinity's foot,' and with that he was gone, she didn't know where.

And soon afterwards, our Lord Jesus Christ spoke to her and said, 'Daughter, see that you are now true and steadfast, and have a good faith, for your name is written in heaven in the Book of Life, and this was an angel who gave you comfort. And therefore, daughter, you must be very merry, for I am very busy both morning and afternoon to draw your heart into my heart, for you should keep your mind altogether upon me, and you shall much increase your love towards God. For, daughter, if you will follow after God's counsel, you may not do amiss, for God's counsel is to be meek, patient in charity and in chastity.'

Another time, as this creature lay in her contemplation in a chapel of our Lady, her mind was occupied in the Passion of our Lord Jesus Christ, and she thought truly that she saw our Lord appear to her spiritual sight in his manhood, with his wounds bleeding as freshly as though he had been scourged before her. And then she wept and cried with all the strength of her body, for, if her sorrow were great before this spiritual sight, it was yet greater afterwards than it was before, and her love was more increased towards our Lord. And then she felt great wonder that our Lord would become man, and suffer such grievous pain for her, who was so unkind a creature to him.

Another time, as she was in a church of St Margaret, in the choir, being in great sweetness and devotion, with great abundance of tears, she asked our Lord Jesus Christ how she might best please him. And he answered her soul, saying, 'Daughter, have mind of your wickedness, and think of my goodness.'

Then she prayed these words many times and often, 'Lord, for your great goodness, have mercy on all my wickedness, as surely as I was never so wicked as you are good, nor ever may be, even if

I would, for you are so good that you may be no better. And therefore it is a great marvel that any man should ever be parted from you without end.'

Then as she lay still in the choir, weeping and mourning for her sins, she was suddenly in a kind of sleep. And at once she saw, with her spiritual eye, our Lord's body lying before her, and his head, as she thought, close by her, with his blessed face turned upwards, the handsomest man that ever might be seen or imagined. And then, as she looked, there came someone with a dagger and cut that precious body all along the breast. And then she wept amazingly bitterly, having more thought, pity and compassion of the Passion of our Lord Jesus Christ than she had before. And so every day her thoughts and her love for our Lord increased, blessed may he be, and the more that her love increased, the more was her sorrow for the sins of the people.

Another time, the said creature being in a chapel of our Lady, weeping bitterly at the memory of our Lord's Passion, and such other graces and goodness as our Lord ministered to her mind, suddenly – she knew not how soon – she was in a kind of sleep.

And at once, in the sight of her soul, she saw our Lord standing right up over her, so near that she thought she took his toes in her hand and felt them, and to her feeling it was as if they had been really flesh and bones. And then she thanked God for everything, for through these spiritual sights her affection was entirely drawn into the manhood of Christ and into the memory of his Passion, until that time that it pleased our Lord to give her understanding of his incomprehensible Godhead.

As is written before, these kinds of visions and feelings she had soon after her conversion, when she was all set and fully intending to serve God with all her heart and strength, and had completely left the world, and stayed in church both morning and afternoon, and most especially in the time of Lent, when she with great insistence and much prayer had her husband's permission to live chaste and clean, and did great bodily penance before she went to Jerusalem.

But afterwards, when her husband and she with one assent had made a vow of chastity, as is written before, and she had been to Rome and Jerusalem, and suffered much contempt and reproof for her weeping and her crying, our Lord, of his mercy, drew her affection into his Godhead, and that was more fervent in love and desire, and more subtle in understanding, than was the manhood. And nevertheless, the fire of love increased in her, and her understanding was more enlightened and her devotion more fervent than it was before, while she had her meditation and her contemplation only in his manhood. Yet she did not have that manner of proceeding with crying as she had before, but it was more subtle and more soft, and easier for her spirit to bear, and as plentiful in tears, as it ever was before.

Another time, while this creature was in a house of the Preaching Friars, in a chapel of our Lady, standing at her prayers, her eyelids went a little together in a kind of sleep, and suddenly she saw, she thought, our Lady in the fairest vision that she ever saw, holding a fair white kerchief in her hand and saying to her, 'Daughter, would you like to see my son?'

And with that she saw forthwith our Lady hold her blessed son in her hand, and swathe him very lightly in the white kerchief, so that she could see how she did it. This creature then had a new spiritual joy and a new spiritual comfort, which was so marvellous that she could never tell of it as she felt it.

Chapter 86

On one occasion our Lord spoke to the said creature, when it pleased him, saying to her spiritual understanding, 'Daughter, for as many times as you have received the blessed sacrament of the altar with many more holy thoughts than you can repeat, for as many times you shall be rewarded in heaven with new joys and new comforts. And daughter, in heaven it shall be known to you how many days you have had of high contemplation through my gift on earth, and although they are my gifts and graces which I have given you, yet you shall have the same grace and reward in heaven as if they were of your own merits, for I have freely given them to you.

'But I thank you highly, daughter, that you have allowed me to work my will in you, and that you would let me be so homely with you. For in nothing, daughter, that you might do on earth might you any better please me than allow me to speak to you in your soul, for at that time you understand my will and I understand your will. And also, daughter, you call my mother to come into your soul, and take me in her arms, and lay me to her breasts and give me suck.[1]

'Also, daughter, I know the holy thoughts and the good desires that you have when you receive me, and the good charity that you have towards me in the time that you receive my precious body into your soul, and also how you call Mary Magdalene into your soul to welcome me, for, daughter, I know well enough what you are thinking. You think that she is worthiest, in your soul, and you trust most in her prayers, next to my mother, and so you may indeed, daughter, for she is a very great mediator to me for you in the bliss of heaven. And sometimes, daughter, you think your soul so large and so wide that you call all the court of heaven into your soul to welcome me. I know very well, daughter, what you say: "Come, all twelve apostles, who were so well beloved of God on earth, and receive your Lord in my soul."

'You also pray Katherine, Margaret, and all holy virgins to welcome me in your soul. And then you pray my blessed mother, Mary Magdalene, all apostles, martyrs, confessors, Katherine, Margaret, and all holy virgins, that they should decorate the chamber of your soul with many fair flowers and with many sweet spices, so that I might rest there within.

'Furthermore, you sometimes imagine, daughter, that you have a cushion of gold, another of red velvet, the third of white silk, in your soul. And you think that my Father sits on the cushion of gold, for with him lies might and power. And you think that I, the

Second Person of the Trinity, your love and your joy, sit on the red cushion of velvet, for upon me is all your thought, because I bought you so dearly, and you think that you can never requite me the love that I have shown you, though you were slain a thousand times a day, if it were possible, for my love. Thus you think, daughter, in your soul, that I am worthy to sit on a red cushion, in remembrance of the red blood that I shed for you. Moreover, you think that the Holy Ghost sits on a white cushion, for you think that he is full of love and purity, and therefore it is fitting for him to sit on a white cushion, for he is a giver of all holy thoughts and chastity.

'And yet I know well enough, daughter, that you think you may not worship the Father unless you worship the Son, and that you may not worship the Son unless you worship the Holy Ghost. And you also think sometimes, daughter, that the Father is almighty and all-knowing, and all grace and goodness, and you think the same of the Son, that he is almighty and all-knowing and all grace and goodness. And you think that the Holy Ghost has the same properties, equal with the Father and the Son, and proceeding from them both.

'You also think that each of the three Persons in the Trinity has what the other has in their Godhead, and so you truly believe, daughter, in your soul, that there are three divers Persons and one God in substance, and that each knows what the others know, and each may do what the others may, and each wills what the others will. And, daughter, this is a true faith and a right faith, and this faith you have only of my gift.

'And therefore, daughter, if you will consider thoroughly, you have great cause to love me very well, and to give me your heart completely, so that I may fully rest within it, as I wish to myself. For if you allow me, daughter, to rest in your soul on earth, believe it indeed that you shall rest with me in heaven without end.

'And therefore, daughter, don't be surprised if you weep bitterly when you are given communion, and receive my blessed body in form of bread, for you pray to me before you receive communion, saying to me in your mind, "As surely, Lord, as you love me, make me clean from all sin, and give me grace to receive your precious body worthily, with all manner of worship and reverence."

'And, daughter, rest assured that I hear your prayer, for you may not say anything to please me better than "as surely as I love you", for then I fulfil my grace in you, and give you many a holy thought – it is impossible to tell them all.

'And because of the great homeliness that I show towards you at that time, you are much bolder to ask for grace for yourself, for your husband, for your children; and you make every Christian man and woman your child in your soul for the time, and would have as much grace for them as for your own children. You also ask for mercy for your husband, and you think you are much beholden to me, that I have given you the sort of man who would let you live chaste, he being alive and in good physical health. In truth, daughter, you think most truly, and therefore you have great cause to love me very well.

'Daughter, if you knew how many wives there are in this world, who would love me and serve me well and duly, if they might be as free from their husbands as you are from yours, you would say that you were very much beholden to me. And yet they are thwarted from their will and suffer very great pain, and therefore they shall have great reward in heaven, for I receive every good will as a deed.

'Sometimes, daughter, I make you have great sorrow for your confessor's sins especially, so that he should have as full forgiveness for his sins as you would have for yours. And sometimes, when you receive the precious sacrament, I make you pray for your confessor in this way – that as many men and women might be turned by his preaching, as you wish were turned by the tears of your eyes, and that my holy words might settle as keenly in their hearts, as you wish they would settle in your heart. And you also ask the same grace for all good men who preach my word on earth, that they might bring profit to all reasonable creatures.

'And often, on the day that you receive my precious body, you ask for grace and mercy for all your friends, and for all your enemies who ever caused you shame or rebuke, either scorned you or jibed at you for the grace that I work in you, and for all this world, both young and old, bitterly weeping many tears and sobbing. You have suffered much shame and much reproof, and therefore you shall have very much bliss in heaven.

'Daughter, do not be ashamed to receive my grace when I will give it you, for I shall not be ashamed of you, so that you shall be received into the bliss of heaven – there to be rewarded for every good thought, for every good word, and for every good deed, and for every day of contemplation, and for all good desires that you have had here in this world – with me everlastingly as my beloved darling, as my blessed spouse, and as my holy wife.

'And therefore, do not be afraid, daughter, though people wonder why you weep so bitterly when you receive me, for, if they knew what grace I place in you at that time, they should rather wonder that your heart does not burst asunder. And so it should, if I did not control that grace myself; but you see for yourself, daughter, that when you have received me into your soul, you are in peace and quiet, and sob no longer. And at this people are greatly amazed, but it need be no surprise to you, for you know that I proceed like a husband who would wed a wife. At the time he weds her, he thinks he is sure enough of her, and that no man shall part them, for then, daughter, they may go to bed together without any shame or fear of other people, and sleep in rest and peace if they will. And things are like this between you and me, daughter, for you have every week, especially on Sunday, great fear and dread in your soul how you may best be sure of my love, and, with great reverence and holy dread, how you may best receive me to the salvation of your soul, with all manner of meekness, humility and charity, as any lady in this world is busy to receive her husband, when he comes home and has been long away from her.

'My beloved daughter, I thank you highly for all people whom you have looked after when ill in my name, and for all kindness and service that you have done them in any degree, for you shall have the same reward with me in heaven, as though you had looked after my own self, while I was here on earth. Also, daughter, I thank you for as many times as you have bathed me, in your soul, at home in your chamber, as though I had been present there in my manhood, for I well know, daughter, all the holy thoughts that you have shown me in your mind. And also, daughter, I thank you for all the times that you have harboured me and my blessed mother in your bed.

'For these, and all other good thoughts and good deeds that you have thought in my name, and performed for my love, you shall have with me and with my mother, with my holy angels, with my apostles, with my martyrs, confessors and virgins, and with all my holy saints, all manner of joy and bliss, lasting without end.'

Chapter 87

The said creature lay very still in the church, hearing and understanding this sweet dalliance in her soul as clearly as if one friend was speaking to another. And when she heard the great promises that our Lord promised her, then she thanked him with much weeping and sobbing, and with many holy and reverent thoughts, saying in her mind, 'Lord Jesus, blessed may you be, for I never deserved this of you, but I wish I were in that place where I should never displease you from this time forward.'

With such manner of thoughts, and many more than I could ever write, she worshipped and magnified our Lord Jesus Christ for his holy visitation and his comfort. And in such kinds of visitations and holy contemplations as are written before, though much more subtle and higher without comparison than are written, the said creature had continued her life, through the preserving of our Saviour Jesus Christ, for more than twenty-five years when this treatise was written, week by week, day by day, unless she were occupied with sick folk, or else prevented by some other needful occupation which was necessary to her or to her fellow Christians. Then it was withdrawn sometimes, for it can only be had in great quietness of soul through long exercise.

By this manner of speech and converse she was made mighty and strong in the love of our Lord, and greatly stabilized in her faith, and increased in meekness and charity with other good virtues. And she firmly and steadfastly believed that it was God that spoke in her soul, and no evil spirit, for in his speech she had most strength and most comfort and most increase of virtue – blessed be God.

Various times, when this creature was so ill that she expected to die, and other people thought the same, it was answered in her soul that she should not die, but she should live and be well, and so she did. Sometimes our Lady spoke to her, and comforted her in her sickness. Sometimes St Peter, or St Paul, sometimes St Mary Magdalene, St Katherine, St Margaret, or whichever saint in heaven that she could think of, through the will and sufferance of God, spoke to the understanding of her soul, and informed her how she should love God and how she should best please him, and answered to whatever she would ask them, and she could understand by their manner of speaking which of them it was that spoke to her and comforted her.

Our Lord, of his mercy, visited her so much and so plentifully with his holy speeches and his holy dalliance, that many times she did not know how the day went. She sometimes supposed that periods of five or six hours had not been the space of an hour. It was so sweet and so devout that it was as if she had been in heaven. She never thought it was a long time, and she was never irked by it – the time went past, she knew not how. She would rather have served God, if she could have lived so long, for a hundred years in this manner of life, than one day as she first began.

And she often said to our Lord Jesus, 'Ah, Lord Jesus, since it is so sweet to weep for your love on earth, I well know it will be truly joyful to be with you in heaven. Therefore, Lord, I pray you, let me never have other joy on earth but mourning and weeping for your love. For I think, Lord, though I were in hell, if I might weep there and mourn for your love as I do here, hell would not annoy me, but it would be a kind of heaven, for your love sets aside every sort of fear of our spiritual enemy, and I had rather be there as long as you wished, and please you, than be in this world and displease you. Therefore, Lord, as you will, so may it be.'

Chapter 88

When this book was first being written the said creature was more at home in her chamber with the man doing the writing, and said fewer beads than she had done for years before, in order to speed the writing. And when she came to church to hear mass, intending to say her matins and such other devotions as she had performed before, her heart was drawn away from recitation and much set upon meditation. She being afraid of the displeasure of our Lord, he said to her soul, 'Do not be afraid, daughter, for as many beads as you would like to say, I accept them as though you said them; and your concentration on getting written down the grace that I have shown you pleases me greatly, and he who is doing the writing as well. For though you were in church and both wept together as bitterly as you ever did, you still would not please me more than you do with your writing, for, daughter, by this book many a man shall be turned to me and believe.

'Daughter, where is a better prayer, by your own reason, than to pray to me with your heart or your thought? Daughter, when you pray by thought, you yourself understand what you ask of me, and you also understand what I say to you, and you understand what I promise to you and yours, and to all your confessors. And as for Master Robert, your confessor, I have granted you what you desired, that he should have half your tears and half the good works that I have worked in you.[1] Therefore he shall truly be rewarded for your weeping, as though he had wept himself. And believe indeed, daughter, that you shall be very merry in heaven together at the last, and shall bless the time that you ever knew each other.

'And, daughter, you shall bless me without end that I ever gave you so true a confessor, for, though he has been sharp with you sometimes, it has been greatly to your advantage, for otherwise you would have had too great an affection for him personally. And when he was sharp to you, then you ran with all your mind to me, saying, "Lord, there is no trust but in you alone." And then you cried to me with all your heart, "Lord, for your smarting wounds, draw all my love into your heart." And, daughter, so I have done.

'You often think that I have done very much for you, and you think that it is a great miracle that I have drawn all your affection to me, for sometimes you were so fond of some particular person, that you thought at the time that it would have been in a way impossible to have withdrawn your affection from him. And later you have desired, if it pleased me, that this same person should have forsaken you for my love, for, if he had not supported you, few men would have set any value on you, as it seemed. And you thought, if he had abandoned you, it would have been the greatest rebuke that ever befell you in people's eyes; and therefore you would willingly have endured that reproof for my love, if it had pleased me.

'And so, with such doleful thoughts you increased your love towards me, and therefore, daughter, I receive your desires as if they were done indeed. And I well know that you have very true love for that same person, and I have often said to you that he would be very glad to love you, and that he would believe it is God that speaks in you, and no devil. Also, daughter, that person has very well pleased me, because he has often in his sermons excused your weeping and your crying, and so has Master Aleyn done as well, and therefore they shall have very great reward in heaven. Daughter, I have told you many times that I should maintain your weeping and your crying by sermons and preaching.

'Also, daughter, I tell you that Master Robert, your confessor, pleases me very much when he tells you to believe that I love you. And I know that you have great faith in his words, and so you may, for he will not flatter you. And also, daughter, I am highly pleased with him, because he tells you that you should sit still and give your heart to meditation, and think such holy thoughts as God will put into your mind. I have often told you so myself, and yet you will not do so except with much grumbling.

'And yet I am not displeased with you, daughter, for I have often said to you that whether you pray with your mouth, or think with your heart, whether you read or hear things read, I will be pleased with you. And yet, daughter, I tell you, if you would believe me, that thinking is best for you and will most increase your love towards me; and the more homely that you allow me to be in your soul on earth, it is worthy and right that I be the more homely with your soul in heaven. And therefore, daughter, if you will not follow my advice, follow the advice of your confessor, for he bids you do the same as I bid you do.

'Daughter, when your confessor says to you that you displease God, you believe him, and then you feel much sorrow and great misery and weep copiously until you have gained grace again. And then I often come to you myself and comfort you, for, daughter, I cannot allow you to have pain for any time without having to remedy it. And therefore, daughter, I come to you and make you sure of my love, and tell you with my own mouth that you are as sure of my love as God is God, and that nothing on earth that you may see with your bodily eye is so secure to you. And therefore, blessed daughter, love him that loves you, and do not forget me, daughter, for I do not forget you, for my merciful eye is ever upon you. And my merciful mother knows that very well, daughter, for she has often told you so, and many other saints as well.

'And therefore, daughter, you have great cause to love me well, and to give me your whole heart with all your affections, for that I desire, and nothing else, from you. And I shall give you in return my whole heart. And if you will be obedient to my will, I shall be obedient to your will, daughter – believe it indeed.'

Chapter 89

Also, while the said creature was occupied with the writing of this treatise, she had many holy tears and much weeping, and often there came a flame of fire about her breast, very hot and delectable; and also, he that was writing for her could sometimes not keep himself from weeping.

And often in the meantime, when this creature was in church, our Lord Jesus Christ with his glorious mother, and many saints as well, came into her soul and thanked her, saying that they were well pleased with the writing of this book. And she also heard many times a voice of a sweet bird singing in her ear, and often she heard sweet sounds and melodies that surpassed her wit to tell of them. And she was many times ill while this treatise was being written, and, as soon as she would set about the writing of this treatise, then in a sudden way she was hale and healthy. And often she was commanded to make herself ready in all haste.

On one occasion, as she lay at her prayers in the church during the time of Advent before Christmas, she thought in her heart that she wished that God, of his goodness, would make Master Aleyn to preach a sermon as well as he could. And as soon as she had thought in this way, she heard our Sovereign Lord Christ Jesus saying in her soul, 'Daughter, I know very well what you are thinking now about Master Aleyn, and I tell you truly that he shall preach a very holy sermon. And see that you believe steadfastly the words that he shall preach, as though I preached them myself, for they shall be words of great solace and comfort to you, for I shall speak in him.'

When she had heard this answer, she went and told it to her confessor and two other priests whom she greatly trusted. And when she had told them her feeling, she was sorry, for fear as to whether he would speak as well as she had felt or not – for revelations are hard sometimes to understand.

And sometimes those that people think were revelations are deceits and illusions, and therefore it is not appropriate to give credence too readily to every stirring, but wait steadfastly and prove if they be sent from God. Nevertheless, as for this feeling of this creature, it was very truth, shown in experience, and her fear and her heaviness of heart turned into great spiritual comfort and gladness.

Sometimes she was greatly depressed about her feelings – when she did not know how they should be understood for many days together, because of the dread that she had of deceptions and delusions – so that she thought she wished her head had been struck from her body until God, of his goodness, explained them to her mind.

For sometimes, what she understood physically was to be understood spiritually, and the fear that she had of her feelings was the greatest scourge that she had on earth; and especially when she had her first feelings; and that fear made her most meek, for she had no joy in the feeling until she knew by experience whether it was true or not.

But ever blessed may God be, for he made her always more mighty and more strong in his love and in his fear, and gave her increase of virtue, with perseverance.

Here ends this treatise, for God took him to his mercy who wrote the first copy of this book. And though he did not write clearly or openly to our manner of speaking, he in his own way of writing and spelling made true sense, which – through the help of God, and of herself who experienced all this treatise in feeling and acting – is now truly drawn out of that copy into this little book.

BOOK II

*

Chapter 1

After our Sovereign Saviour had taken to his manifold mercy the person who first wrote the said treatise, and the priest, of whom is written before, had copied the same treatise according to his simple knowledge, he held it appropriate to the honour of the blissful Trinity[1] that God's holy works should be notified and declared to the people, when it pleased him, to the worship of his holy name.

And then he began to write in the year of our Lord 1438, on the feast of St Vitalis, Martyr,[2] of such grace as our Lord worked in his simple creature during the years that she lived afterwards; not all, but some of it, as she told him with her own tongue.

And first, here is a notable matter which is not written in the preceding treatise. It happened soon after the creature previously written about had forsaken the occupations of the world and was joined in her mind to God, as much as frailty would allow.

The said creature had a son, a tall young man, living with a worthy burgess in Lynn, involved in business as a merchant and sailing overseas, whom she desired to draw away from the perils of this wretched and unstable world, if her power could attain to it. She did as much as was in her, and whenever she could meet with him at leisure she many times counselled him to leave the world and follow Christ – so much so, that he fled her company, and would not gladly meet her.

So, on one occasion, it happened that the mother met with her son, although it was against his will and his intention at that time. And as she had done before, so now she spoke to him again, that he should flee the perils of this world, and not set all his study and business so much upon it as he did. He not agreeing, but answering back sharply, and she, somewhat moved herself with sharpness of spirit, said, 'Now, since you will not leave the world at my advice, I charge you – at my blessing – at least to keep your body clean from women's company until you take a wife according to the law of the Church. And if you do not, I pray God chastise you and punish you for it.'

They parted, and soon afterwards the same young man went overseas on business, and then, what with the evil enticing of other people, and what with his own folly, he fell into the sin of lechery. Soon after, his colour changed, and his face grew full of pimples and pustules, like a leper's.

Then he came home again to Lynn to his master, with whom he had been living previously. His master put him out of his service, not for any fault he found with him, but perhaps supposing he had been a leper, as it seemed by his face.

The young man told where he pleased how his mother had cursed him, because of which, as he supposed, God so grievously punished him. Some people, knowing of his lament and pitying his distress, came to see his mother, saying she had acted very badly, for through her prayer God had taken vengeance on her own child. Taking little notice of their words, she let it pass as if she didn't care, until he would come and pray for grace himself. So at last, when he saw no other remedy, he came to his mother, telling her of his misconduct, promising he would be obedient to God and to her, and amend his fault through the help of God, avoiding all misbehaviour from that time forwards, according to his power.

He prayed his mother for her blessing, and he especially prayed her to pray for him that our Lord, of his high mercy, would forgive him that he had trespassed, and take away that great sickness because of which people fled from his company as if he were a leper. For he supposed by her prayers our Lord sent him that punishment, and therefore he trusted by her prayers to be delivered of it, if she would, of her charity, pray for him. Then she, trusting in his amending and having compassion for his infirmity, with sharp words of correction, promised to fulfil his intent, if God would grant it.

When she came to her meditation, not forgetting the fruit of her womb, she asked forgiveness for his sins and release from the illness that our Lord had given him, if it were his pleasure, and profit to his soul. She prayed so long, that he was completely freed from the illness and lived many years after, and had a wife and a child, blessed may God be, for he wedded his wife in Prussia, in Germany.

When news came to his mother from overseas that her son had married, she was very pleased, and thanked God with all her heart, supposing and trusting that he would live clean and chaste, as the law of matrimony requires. Later, when God willed, his wife had a child, a beautiful girl. Then he sent news to his mother in England how graciously God had treated him and his wife. His mother being in a chapel of our Lady, thanking God for the grace and goodness that he showed to her son, and desiring to see him if she might, it was answered to her mind that she should see them all before she died.

She marvelled at this feeling, how it could be as she felt, inasmuch as they were beyond the sea, and she on this side of the sea, never intending to cross the sea while she lived. Nevertheless, she well knew that to God nothing was impossible. Therefore she trusted it should be as she had feeling, when God willed.

Chapter 2

A few years after this young man had married, he came home to England to his father and his mother, all changed in his clothes and his disposition. For before his clothes were all fashionably slashed, and his conversation all vanity; now he wore no slashes, and his talk was full of virtue.

His mother, amazed at this sudden change, said to him, 'Blessings on us, son, how is it that you are so changed?'

'Mother,' he said, 'I believe that through your prayers our Lord has drawn me to him, and I intend by the grace of God to follow your advice more than I have done before.'

Then his mother, seeing this marvellous power in our Lord to draw souls to him, thanked God as she could, paying close attention to her son's behaviour for fear of dissimulation. The longer she watched his behaviour, the steadier she thought he was, and the more reverent towards our Lord. When she knew it was the pull of our Lord's mercy, then she was very joyful, thanking God very many times for his grace and his goodness.

Later, so that he should be the more diligent and the more busy to follow as our Lord would draw him, she opened her heart to him, showing and informing him how our Lord had drawn her through his mercy and by what means, and also how much grace he had shown for her, which he said he was unworthy to hear.

Then he went on many pilgrimages to Rome and to many other holy places to gain pardon, returning again to his wife and child as he was bound to do. He told his wife all about his mother, so much so that she wanted to leave her father and mother, and her own country, to come to England to see his mother. He was very glad of this, and sent word to his mother in England to let her know of his wife's desire, and to find out whether his mother would advise him to come by land or water, for he trusted a great deal in his mother's advice, believing it was of the Holy Ghost.

His mother, when she had had a letter from him, and knew his desire, went to pray to know our Lord's counsel and our Lord's will. And as she prayed about the said matter, she was answered in her soul, that whether her son came by land or water, he should come in safety. Then she wrote letters to him, saying that whether he came by land or by water, he should come in safety, by the grace of God.

When he was informed of his mother's advice, he inquired when ships would come to England, and hired a ship, or else part of a ship, in which he put his goods, his wife, his child, and himself, all proposing to come to England together.

When they were in the ship, such storms arose that they did not dare put to sea, and so they came on land again, both he and his wife, and their child. They left their child in Prussia with their friends, and he and his wife came to his father and mother in England by the overland route. When they had come, his mother greatly rejoiced in our Lord that her feeling was true, for she had a feeling in her soul, as is written before, that whether they came by land or by water they should come in safety. And so it was indeed – blessed may God be.

They came home on the Saturday in good health, and on the next day, that was the Sunday, while they were having a meal at noon with other good friends, he fell very ill, so that he rose from the table and laid himself down on a bed – which sickness and infirmity occupied him for about a month, and then, in good life and right belief, he passed to the mercy of our Lord. So, spiritually and bodily, it might well be verified – 'he shall come home in safety' – not only into this mortal land, but also into the land of living men, where death shall never appear.

A short time after, the father of the said person followed the son the way which every man must go.

Then there lived still the mother of the said person – of whom this treatise specially makes mention – and she who was his wife, a German woman, living with his mother for eighteen months, until her friends in Germany, desiring to have her home, wrote letters and urged her to return to her own country. And so she, desiring the kindness of her friends, told her idea to her mother-in-law, telling her of the desire of her friends, asking her for her love and her leave, that she might return to her own country.

And so, with her mother-in-law's consent, she prepared to go as soon as any ships went to that country. They inquired for a ship from that same country, in which her own countrymen should sail there, for they thought it was best for her to sail with them in their ship rather than with other people.

Then she went to her confessor to be shriven, and while she was being confessed, the said creature, her mother-in-law, went up and down in the choir, thinking in her mind, 'Lord, if it were your will, I would take leave of my confessor and go with her over the sea.'

Our Lord answered to her thought, saying, 'Daughter, I well know, if I bade you go, you would go very readily. Therefore I do not wish you to speak a word to him about this matter.'

Then she was very glad and happy, believing she should not go over the sea, for she had been in great peril on the sea in the past, and intended never to go on it any more by her own will.

When her daughter-in-law was shriven, the good man who was confessor to them both at that time came to her and said, 'Who will go with your daughter-in-law to the coast until she come to her ship? It is not proper that she should go so far alone with a young man in a strange country where neither of them is known,' for a foreigner had come to fetch her, and both of them were only little known in this area, for which reason her confessor had the more compassion for her.

Then the said creature replied, 'Sir, if you will bid me go, I will go with her myself until she gets to Ipswich, where lies the ship and her own countrymen that will take her over the sea.'

Her confessor said, 'How should you go? You only recently hurt your foot, and you are not yet completely better – and also you are an old woman. You can't go.'

'Sir,' she said, 'God, as I trust, shall help me very well.'

Then he asked who should go with her and bring her home again.

And she said, 'Sir, there is a hermit belonging to this church, a young man. I hope that he will for our Lord's love go and come back with me, if you will give me leave.'

So she had permission to take her daughter-in-law to Ipswich, and then come back to Lynn. Thus they set off on their journey in time of Lent, and, when they were five or six miles from Lynn, they passed a church, and so they turned in to hear mass. And while they were in the church, the said creature, desiring tears of devotion, could gain none at that time, but was continually commanded in her soul to go over the sea with her daughter-in-law. She would have put it out of her mind, and it always came back again so fast that she could have no rest or quiet in her mind, but was continually tormented and commanded to go over the sea. She thought it was hard on her to take such trouble upon herself, and excused herself to our Lord in her mind, saying, 'Lord, you know I have no leave from my confessor, and I am bound to obedience. Therefore I may not do so without his will and his consent.'

She was answered in her thought, 'I bid you go in my name, Jesus, for I am above your confessor, and I shall excuse you, and lead you, and bring you home again in safety.'

She would still have excused herself if she could in any way, and therefore she said, 'I am not sufficiently provided with gold or silver to go with, as I ought to be, and even though I were, and wanted to go, I know my daughter-in-law would rather I were at home, and perhaps the ship's master would not allow me on the ship to go with them.'

Our Lord replied, 'If I be with you, who shall be against you? I shall provide for you, and get you friends to help you. Do as I bid you, and no man on the ship shall say no to you.'

This creature saw there was no other help for it, but that she must set forth at the commanding of God. She thought that she would first go to Walsingham[1] and offer in worship of our Lady, and as she was on the way there, she heard tell that a friar would preach a sermon in a little village a little out of her way. She turned in to the church where the friar preached the sermon, a famous man, who had a great audience at his sermon. And many times he said these words, 'If God be with us, who shall be against us?'[2] – through which words she was the more stirred to obey the will of God and perform her intention.

So she went on to Walsingham, and then to Norwich, with her daughter-in-law, and the hermit with them. When they came to Norwich, she met a Grey Friar, a worthy clerk, a doctor of divinity, who had heard of her life and her feelings before. The doctor welcomed her warmly and chatted with her as he had done before. She, sighing many times, was gloomy in face and manner. The doctor asked her what was the matter.

'Sir,' she said, 'when I came away from Lynn with the permission of my confessor, I intended to escort my daughter-in-law to Ipswich, where there is a ship in which she, by the grace of God, shall sail to Germany; and I was then to return home again to Lynn as soon as I properly could, with a hermit who came with me with that same intent to escort me home again. And he fully expected that I should do so. And, sir, when I was about six miles out of Lynn, in a church to say my prayers, I was commanded in my soul that I should go over the sea with my daughter-in-law, and I well know she would rather I were at home, and so would I, if I dared. Thus was I moved in my soul, and could have no rest in my spirit, or devotion, until I consented to do as I was moved in my spirit, and this is for me a great fear and grief.'

The worthy clerk said to her, 'You shall obey the will of God, for I believe it is the Holy Ghost that is speaking in you, and therefore follow the moving of your spirit in the name of Jesus.'

She was much comforted by his words and took her leave, going on to the coast with her companions. When they arrived there, the ship was ready to sail. Then she asked the master that she might sail with them to Germany, and he kindly received her, and those who were in the ship did not once say no. There was no one so much against her as was her daughter-in-law, who ought to have been most on her side.

Then she took her leave of the hermit who had come there with her, rewarding him somewhat for his labour, and praying him to excuse her to her confessor and her other friends when he got home to Lynn, for it was not her intention when she parted from them to have ever crossed the sea again in her life, 'But,' she said, 'I must obey the will of God.'

The hermit parted from her with a sorrowful face and came home again to Lynn, excusing her to her confessor and to other friends, telling them of her sudden and astonishing departure, and how he was not to know that they should be so suddenly separated.

People that heard of it were much amazed, and said what they wanted to. Some said it was a woman's wit, and great folly for the love of her daughter-in-law, to put herself, a woman of great age, to all the perils of the sea, and to go into a strange country where she had not been before, nor knew how she should come back. Some held it to be a very charitable deed, inasmuch as her daughter-in-law had previously left her friends and her country, and came with her husband to visit her in this country, and she would now help her daughter-in-law return to the country she came from. Others, who knew more of this creature's life, supposed and trusted that it was the will and the working of Almighty God, to the magnifying of his own name.

Chapter 3

The said creature and her companions entered their ship on the Thursday in Passion Week,[1] and God sent them fair wind and weather that day and on the Friday. But on the Saturday, and Palm Sunday also, our Lord – turning his hand as he liked, trying their faith and their patience – sent them on those two nights such storms and tempests that they all thought they would perish. The storms were so severe and terrible that they could not control their ship. They knew no better expedient than to commend themselves and their ship to the guidance of our Lord; they abandoned their skill and their cunning, and let our Lord drive them where he would. The said creature had sorrow and care enough; she thought she never had so much before. She cried to our Lord for mercy and for the preserving of her and all her company. And she thought in her mind, 'Ah, Lord, for your love I came here, and you have often promised me that I should never perish on land or on water or through storms. People have many times cursed me for the grace that you have worked in me, desiring that I should die in misfortune and great distress; and now, Lord, it is likely that their cursing is coming into effect, and I, unworthy wretch, am deceived and cheated of the promise that you have many times made to me, who have always trusted in your mercy and your goodness, unless you soon withdraw these storms and show us mercy. Now may my enemies rejoice and I may sorrow, if they have their intent and I be deceived. Now, blissful Jesus, remember your manifold mercy, and fulfil your promises that you have promised me. Show you are truly God, and no evil spirit, that has brought me here into the perils of the sea, whose counsel I have trusted and followed for many years, and shall do, through your mercy, if you deliver us from out of these grievous perils. Help us and succour us, Lord, before we perish or despair, for we may not long endure this sorrow that we are in without your mercy and succour.'

Our merciful Lord, speaking in her mind, blamed her for her fear, saying, 'Why do you fear? Why are you so afraid? I am as mighty here on the sea as on the land. Why will you mistrust me? All that I have promised you I shall truly fulfil, and I shall never deceive you. Suffer patiently for a while, and trust in my mercy. Do not waver in your faith, for without faith you may not please me. If you would truly trust me and doubt nothing, you may have great comfort within yourself, and might comfort all your companions, whereas you are all now in great fear and grief.'

With such manner of converse, and much more high and holy than I could ever write, our Lord comforted his creature, blessed may he be. Holy saints that she prayed to conversed with her soul with our Lord's permission, giving her words of great comfort. At last our Lady came and said, 'Daughter, be comforted. You have always found true what I have told you, and therefore don't be afraid any longer, for I tell you truly, these winds and storms shall soon cease, and you will have fair weather.'

And so, blessed may God be, a short time afterwards her ship was driven towards the Norwegian coast, and there they landed on Good Friday, and remained there Easter Eve, Easter Day and the Monday after Easter. And on that Monday all who belonged to the ship received communion on the ship.

On Easter Day, the master of the ship and the said creature, and the most part of the company, went on land and heard the service at the church. After the custom of the country, the cross was raised at about noon,[2] and she had her meditation and her devotion with weeping and sobbing as well as if she had been at home. God did not withdraw his grace from her either in church, on the ship, on the sea, or in any other place that she went to, for she always had him in her soul.

When they had received the sacrament on Easter Monday, as is written before, our Lord sent them a fair wind that brought them away from that country and blew them home to Germany as they desired. The said creature found such grace in the master of the ship that he provided her with food and drink and everything that she needed as long as she was on the ship, and he was as gentle with her as if she had been his mother. He covered her while on board ship with his own clothes, for otherwise she might have died of cold, as she was not prepared like the others were. She went at the bidding of our Lord, and therefore her Master, who bade her go, provided for her so that she managed as well as any of her company – worship and praise be to our Lord for it.

Chapter 4

The said creature remained in Danzig in Germany for about five or six weeks, and was warmly welcomed by many people for our Lord's love. There was no one so much against her as was her daughter-in-law, who was most obliged and beholden to have comforted her, if she had been kind.

Then this creature rejoiced in our Lord that she was so kindly received for his love, and intended to stay there longer. Our Lord, speaking to her thought, commanded her to leave that country. She was then in great distress and doubt as to how she should do the bidding of God, which she would in no way withstand, and yet had neither man nor woman to accompany her. She would not travel by sea, because she had been so frightened at sea on her way there; and she could not travel easily by land, because there was a war going on in the country she would pass by.[1] So for one reason and another she was in great distress, not knowing how things would improve for her. She went into a church and prayed that our Lord, since he commanded her to go, should send her help, and company with whom she could travel.

And suddenly, a man came to her and asked if she would like to go on pilgrimage to a place far distant from there called Wilsnack,[2] where the precious blood of our Lord Jesus Christ is venerated, which came by a miracle from three Hosts, the sacrament of the altar. These three Hosts and precious blood are held in great veneration there to this day, and visited by pilgrims from many countries.

She happily said she would go there if she had good company, and if she knew of any honest man who might afterwards take her to England. And he promised her that he would go on pilgrimage with her to the said place at his own expense, and afterwards, if she would completely pay his expenses to England, he would come with her until she was on the coast of England, where she could find companions from her own country.

He obtained a small ship in which they should sail towards the holy place, but then she could not get permission to leave that country because she was an Englishwoman,[3] and so she had great trouble and much hindrance before she could get permission from one of the Teutonic Knights to leave there. At last, through the direction of our Lord, a merchant from Lynn heard tell of it, and he came and comforted her, promising her that he would help her to get away from there, either secretly or openly. And this man with great effort got her permission to go where she wished.

Then she took ship, with the man who had provided for her, and God sent them calm wind, which pleased her very well, for there rose not a wave on the water. Her company thought they were making no progress, and were gloomy and grumbling. She prayed to our Lord, and he sent them enough wind that they sailed on a great way and the waves rose. Her companions were glad and cheerful, and she was miserable and sorrowful for fear of the waves. When she looked at them she was always frightened. Our Lord, speaking to her spirit, ordered her to lay her head down, so that she would not see the waves, and she did so. But she was always frightened, and she was often criticized for that. And so they sailed on to a place which is called Stralsund.[4] (If the names of the places are not correctly written, let no one be surprised, for she concentrated more on contemplation than the names of the places, and he who wrote them never saw them, and therefore do excuse him!)

Chapter 5

When they had come to Stralsund they landed, and so the said creature, with the previously mentioned man, went towards Wilsnack in great fear, and passed many dangers. The man who was her guide was always afraid, and would continually have liked to abandon her. Many times she spoke as nicely to him as she could, that he should not abandon her in those unfamiliar parts and in the midst of her enemies, for there was open war between the English and those countries. Therefore her fear was much the greater, and in the midst of it our Lord always spoke in her mind, 'Why are you afraid? No man shall harm you or anyone that you travel with. Therefore comfort your man, and tell him no man shall hurt him or harm him while he is in your company. Daughter, you well know that a woman who has a handsome man for her husband, if she love him, will go with him wherever he wants. And daughter, there is no one so handsome or so good as I. Therefore, if you love me, you shall not fear to go with me wherever I will have you. Daughter, I brought you here, and I shall bring you home again to England in safety. Do not doubt it, but well believe it.'

Such holy dalliance and speeches in her soul caused her to sob very violently, and weep most abundantly. The more she wept, the more her man was irked by her company, and busied himself to go from her and leave her alone. He went so fast that she could not keep up without great effort and distress. He said that he was afraid of enemies and of thieves; that they would take her away from him perhaps, and beat him and rob him as well. She comforted him as well as she could, and said she dared undertake that no man should beat them or rob them, or say a bad word to them.

And soon after she had said this, a man came out of a wood, a tall man with good weapons, and well-armed to fight, as it seemed to them.

Then her man, being in great fear, said to her, 'Look, what do you say now?'

She said, 'Trust in our Lord God, and fear no man.'

The man came by them, and did not say a bad word to them, and so they passed on towards Wilsnack with great effort. She could not endure such long day's journeys as the man could, and he had no pity on her and would not wait for her. And therefore she struggled on for as long as she could, until she fell ill and could go no further. It was a great marvel and miracle that a woman unaccustomed to walking, and also about sixty years of age,[1] could manage each day to keep pace on her journey with a vigorous man.

On Corpus Christi Eve,[2] they happened to come to a little hostelry far from any town, and there they could get no bedding but a little straw. And the said creature rested upon it that night and the next day until it was evening again. Our Lord sent thunder and lightning, and rain nearly all the time, so that they did not dare do anything outdoors. She was very glad of this, for she was very ill and she well knew that, if the weather had been fine, the man who travelled with her would not have waited for her, he would have left her. Therefore she thanked God who gave him occasion to wait, although it was against his will.

In the meantime, because of her illness, a wagon was provided, and so she was carried on to the Holy Blood of Wilsnack, with great distress and discomfort. The women of the district as they went along, having compassion on her, said many times to this man that he deserved great blame because he tormented her so dreadfully. Desiring to be rid of her, he took no notice of what they said, and never spared her any more because of it. In this way, through thick and thin, through the help of our Lord, she was brought to Wilsnack and saw that precious blood, which by a miracle came out of the blessed sacrament of the altar.

Chapter 6

They did not stay long in the said place, but within a short time began to make their way towards Aachen, riding in wagons until they came to a river where there was a great gathering of people, some going towards Aachen and some to other places, among whom was a monk, a very negligent and misdirected man, and in his company were some young men who were merchants.

The monk and the merchants knew the man well who was the said creature's guide, and called him by his name, and were very friendly to him. When they had crossed the water and were travelling on land (the monk with the merchants, and the said creature with her man, altogether in a party in wagons), they came past a house of Friars Minor, and were very thirsty. They told the said creature to go in to the friars and get them some wine. She said, 'Sirs, you will excuse me, for if it were a house of nuns I would very gladly go, but because they are men, I shall not go, by your leave.'

So one of the merchants went to fetch them a measure of wine. Then the friars came to them and asked them to come and see the blessed sacrament in their church, for it was within the Octave[1] of Corpus Christi, and it stood open in a crystal container, so that people could see it if they wished.

The monk and the men went with the friars to see the precious sacrament. The said creature thought she would see it as well as them, and followed after, as though it were against her will. And when she beheld the precious sacrament, our Lord gave her so

much sweetness and devotion that she wept and sobbed amazingly bitterly and could not restrain herself from doing so. The
monk and all her party were angry because she wept so bitterly,
and when they had come back to their wagons they scolded her
and rebuked her, calling her a hypocrite, and said many a wicked
word to her. She, to excuse herself, quoted scripture against them,
verses of the Psalter, *'Qui seminant in lacrimis'* etc., *'euntes ibant et
flebant'* etc.,[2] and such others. Then they were even angrier, and
said that she should no longer travel in their company, and
persuaded her man to abandon her.

She meekly and gently begged them that they would, for God's
love, allow her to travel on in their company, and not leave her
alone where she knew nobody and nobody knew her, wherever
she went. With great prayer and urging she did travel on with
them until they came to a fine town, in the Octave of Corpus
Christi. And there they said absolutely that she should not for
anything go with them any longer. He who was her guide and
had promised to take her to England abandoned her, giving her
back such gold and other things of hers that he had in safekeeping,
and promised to lend her more money if she had wanted. She said
to him, 'John, I did not want your money; I would rather have
had your company in these strange countries than all the money
you have, and I believe you would please God more to go with me
as you promised me in Danzig, than if you went to Rome on foot.'

Thus they ejected her from their company and let her go where
she wished. She said then to him who had been her guide, 'John,
you abandon me for no other reason than that I weep when I see
the sacrament, and when I think of our Lord's Passion. And since
I am forsaken for God's cause, I believe that God shall provide for
me and bring me forth as he would himself, for he never deceived
me, blessed may he be.'

So they went on their way and left her there still. Night fell
around her, and she was very miserable, for she was alone. She
did not know whom she could rest with that night, nor with whom
she could travel the next day. Priests of that country came to her
where she was lodged. They called her an Englishwoman with a

tail,[3] and spoke many filthy words to her, giving her indecent looks, and offering to lead her about if she liked. She had great fear for her chastity and was very wretched.

Then she went to the good wife of the house, asking her to have some of her maids who could sleep with her that night. The good woman let her have two maids, who were with her all that night, yet she did not dare sleep for fear of being violated. She stayed awake and prayed nearly all that night that she might be preserved from all uncleanness and meet with some respectable companions who might help her on her way to Aachen. Suddenly, she was commanded in her soul to go to church early on the next day, and there she would meet with companions.

Early the next day, she paid for her lodging, inquiring of her hosts if they knew of any party travelling towards Aachen. They said 'no'. Taking her leave of them, she went to the church to find and prove if her feeling were true or not. When she came there, she saw a company of poor folk. Then she went up to one of them, inquiring where they were intending to go. He said, 'To Aachen.' She asked him to allow her to travel in their company.

'Why, lady,' he said, 'don't you have any man to go with you?'

'No,' she said, 'my man has left me.'

So she was received into a company of poor people, and when they came to any town, she bought her food and her companions went about begging. When they were outside the towns, her companions took off their clothes, and, sitting about naked, picked themselves for vermin. Need compelled her to wait for them and prolong her journey, and be put to much more expense than she would otherwise have been.

This creature was afraid to take off her clothes as her fellows did, and therefore, through mixing with them, she caught some of their vermin and was dreadfully bitten and stung both day and night, until God sent her other companions. She remained in their company with great anguish and discomfort, and much delay, until the time that they reached Aachen.

Chapter 7

When they reached Aachen, the said creature met a monk from England on his way to Rome. Then she was much comforted, because she had someone that she could understand. And so they remained together ten or twelve days, in order to see our Lady's smock and other holy relics which were shown on St Margaret's Day.[1]

And while they remained there, it happened that a worthy woman came from London, a widow with a large retinue with her, to see and worship the holy relics. The said creature came to this worthy woman, complaining that she had no companions to go with her home to England. The worthy woman granted her all her desire, and made her eat and drink with her, and was very friendly to her.

When St Margaret's Day was come and gone, and they had seen the holy relics, the worthy woman sped quickly out of Aachen with all her retinue. The said creature, thinking to have gone with her and thus cheated of her purpose, was in great distress. She took her leave of the monk who was on his way to Rome, as is written before, and afterwards got herself a wagon with other pilgrims, and followed after the said worthy woman as fast as she could, to see if she could overtake her, but it was not to be.

Then she happened to meet two Londoners going back to London. She asked to travel in their company. They said, if she could bear to go as quickly as them, she would be welcome, but they could have no great delaying; nevertheless, they would willingly help her on with her journey. So she followed after them with great effort, until they came to a fine town where they met English pilgrims, who had come from the court of Rome and were going home again to England. She prayed them that she might go with them, and they said shortly that they would not hamper their travelling for her, for they had been robbed and had little money to get themselves home, because of which they must make good time on their journey. And therefore, if she could bear to go as quickly as them she would be welcome, and otherwise not.

She saw no other help for it but to remain with them as long as she could, and so she left the other two men and stayed with these men. Then they went to their meal and enjoyed themselves. The said creature looked a little to one side, and saw a man lying and resting himself on a bench's end. She inquired what man that was. They said he was a friar, one of their party.

'Why doesn't he eat with you?'

'Because we were robbed as well as he, and therefore each man must help himself as well as he can.'

'Well,' said she, 'he shall have part of such money as God sends me.'

She trusted that our Lord would provide what was needful for them both. She made him eat and drink, and comforted him a great deal. Afterwards they all went on together. The said creature soon fell behind; she was too aged and weak to keep pace with them. She ran and jumped as fast as she could until her strength failed.

Then she spoke to the poor friar whom she had cheered before, offering to pay his expenses until he got to Calais, if he would stay with her and let her travel with him until they got there, and still give him a reward besides for his trouble. He was well content and agreed to her wish. So they let their companions go on ahead, and the two of them followed at a gentle pace, as they could manage.

The friar, being very thirsty, said to this creature, 'I know these parts well enough, for I have often gone thus to Rome, and I know there is a place for refreshments a little way from here. Let us go there and have a drink.'

She was well pleased, and followed him. When they got there, the good wife of the house, having compassion for this creature's difficulties, advised that she should take a wagon with other pilgrims and not travel so with a man alone. She said that she had intended and fully trusted to have travelled with a worthy woman of London, and she was deceived. By the time they had rested a while and chatted with the good wife of the house, a wagon came past with pilgrims. The good wife, having knowledge of the pilgrims in the wagon, called them back when they had passed her house, beseeching them that this creature might ride with them in their wagon to speed her journey. They, kindly consenting, received her into their wagon, riding altogether until they came to a good town where the said creature noticed the worthy woman of London, previously mentioned.

Then she asked the pilgrims in the wagon to excuse her, and let her pay for the time that she had been with them as they pleased, for she would go to a worthy woman of her own nation who she noticed was in the town, and with whom she had agreed while she was at Aachen to travel home to England. She took a fond leave, and parted from them.

They rode on, and she went to the worthy woman, thinking to have been very kindly received. It was just the opposite: she was received in a very short manner and with very sharp words, the worthy woman saying to her, 'What! do you think to go with me? No, I'll have you know that I'll not get involved with you.'

This creature was so rebuked that she did not know what to do. She did not know anybody there, and nobody knew her. She did not know where to go. She did not know where the friar was, who should have been her guide, nor whether he would come that way, or not. She was in great uncertainty and grief, the greatest, she thought, that she had suffered since she left England.

Nevertheless, she trusted in our Lord's promise and remained still in the town until God would send her some comfort. And when it was nearly evening, she saw the friar coming into the town. She hurried to speak to him, complaining how she was deceived and rejected by the good woman in whom she had trusted so much. The friar said they would do as well as God would give them grace, and comforted her as much as was in his power. But he said he would not stay in that town that night, for he knew very well that they were dangerous people.

Then they went on together out of the town again in the evening in great fear and grief, mourning along the way as to where they should find lodging that night. They happened to come along the side of a wood, busily looking if they could spy any place where they could rest. And, as our Lord willed, they noticed one or two buildings, and they went hastily to where a good man was living with his wife and two children. But they did not lodge travellers, and would not receive guests in their home.

The said creature saw a heap of bracken in an outhouse, and with great insistence she obtained leave to rest herself on the bracken that night. The friar, after much asking, was laid in a barn, and they thought they were well off that they had a roof over them. The next day they settled up for their lodging, taking the way towards Calais, and going very wearying and tiresome ways through deep sands, hills and valleys for two days before they came there. They suffered great thirst and discomfort, for there were few towns along the way that they went and very poor lodgings.

And at nights she was often most afraid, and perhaps this was because of her spiritual enemy, because she was always afraid of being raped or violated. She dared trust no man; whether she had reason or not, she was always afraid. She scarcely dared sleep any night, because she believed men would have raped her. Therefore she did not gladly go to bed any night, unless she had a woman or two with her. For that grace God sent her, that wherever she went, for the most part, young girls would cheerfully lie beside her, and that was a great comfort to her. She was so weary and so overcome with exertion on the way to Calais that she thought her spirit would have departed from her body as she went along the way.

Thus with great effort she came to Calais, and the good friar with her, who had been most kindly and decently behaved towards her during the time that they travelled together. And therefore she gave him such reward as she could manage, so that he was well pleased and content, and so they parted from each other.

Chapter 8

In Calais this creature was made welcome by various people, both men and women, who had never seen her before. There was a good woman who had her home to her house, and washed her clean and put a new smock on her, and comforted her greatly. Other good people had her for meals and drinks. While she was there three or four days waiting for a ship she met various people who had known her before, and who spoke handsomely to her and gave her kind words. They did not give her anything else, these people who were waiting like her for a ship.

She wanted to sail with them to Dover, but they would not help her at all, nor let her know which ship they proposed to sail in. She inquired and watched out as diligently as she could, and she always had knowledge of their intentions one way or another, until she had arranged the same ship as them. And when she had carried her things into the ship where they were – supposing they should have sailed in haste, she did not know how soon – they got themselves another ship ready to sail. What the cause was, she never knew.

Through grace, she, having knowledge of their purpose and of how ready they were to sail, left all her things in the vessel that she was in, and went to the ship that they were in, and through our Lord's help she was received into the ship. And the worthy woman from London was there who had refused her, as is written before. And so they all sailed together to Dover.

The said creature, perceiving from their faces and expressions that they had little affection for her, prayed to our Lord that he would grant her grace to hold her head up, and preserve her from bringing up vomit in their presence, so that she should cause them no abhorrence. Her desire was fulfilled, so that, while others in the ship were throwing up very violently and foully, she was able – to the amazement of them all – to help them and do what she wished. And the woman from London especially had the worst of that sickness, and this creature was most busy to help her and comfort her for our Lord's love and charity – she had no other reason.

So they sailed on until they came to Dover, and then each of that party got company to travel with, if he wanted, except only her, for she could get no companion to help her. Therefore she set off for Canterbury by herself alone, sorrowful and grieving that she had no company and that she did not know the way. She was up early in the morning and came to a poor man's house, knocking at the door. The good poor man, pulling on his clothes, which were unfastened and unbuttoned, came to the door to learn her will. She prayed him, if he had any horse, that he would help her get to Canterbury, and she would reward him for his trouble. He, desiring to do her pleasure in our Lord's name, fulfilled her desire and took her to Canterbury.

She had great joy in our Lord, who sent her help and succour in every need, and thanked him with many a devout tear, with much sobbing and weeping, in nearly every place that she came to, so that it cannot all be written, as much as on the other side of the sea as on this side, on water as on land – blessed may God be.

Chapter 9

From there she went on to London, clad in a canvas cloth, a kind of sacking garment, just as she had gone overseas. When she came into London, many people knew her well enough. Because she was not dressed as she would like to have been for lack of money, and wishing to go about unrecognized until she could arrange a loan, she held a handkerchief in front of her face. Notwithstanding that she did so, some dissolute persons, supposing it was Mar. Kempe[1] of Lynn, said – so that she might easily hear – these words of reproof, 'Ah, you false flesh, you shall eat no good meat!'

She, not answering, passed by as if she had not heard. The said words were never of her speaking, neither of God nor of any good man, even though it was charged against her, and she many times and in many places had great rebuke because of it. They were invented by the devil, father of lies, favoured, maintained and born from his members, false envious people, who were indignant at her virtuous living and had no power to hinder her except through their false tongues.

There was never man or woman that might ever prove that she said such words, but they always made other liars their authorities, saying to excuse themselves that other men told them so. In this way were these false words invented through the devil's suggestion.

Some person, or else more than one person, deceived by their spiritual enemy, contrived this tale not long after the conversion of the said creature, saying that she – sitting down to a meal on a fish day at a good man's table, served with various fish, such as red herring and good pike and others such – was supposed to have said, as they reported it, 'Ah, false flesh, you would now eat red herring, but you shall not have your will.'

And with that she set aside the red herring and ate the good pike.[2] And other things of this kind she was supposed to have said, as they said, and thus it sprang up into a kind of proverb against her, so that some people said, 'False flesh, you shall eat no herring.' And some said the words that are written before, and all were false, but still they were not forgotten; they were repeated in many a place where she was never known.

She went on to a worthy widow's house in London, where she was kindly received and made welcome for our Lord's love; and in many places in London she was highly encouraged in our Lord's name, God reward them all. There was one worthy woman especially who showed her high charity, both in food and drink and in giving other benefits. On one occasion she was at dinner at her house with various other people of various conditions, she being unknown to them and they to her, of whom some were from the Cardinal's house[3] (as she was told by other people), and they had a great feast and a good time.

And when they were in their mirth, some repeated the words before written, or others like them, that is to say: 'You false flesh, you shall eat none of this good meat.'

She sat still, and suffered a good while. Each of them joked to each other, having great sport with the imperfection of the person that these words were said of. When they had thoroughly amused themselves with these words, she asked them if they had any knowledge of the person who was supposed to have said these words.

They said, 'No, indeed. But we have heard tell that there is such a false, pretending hypocrite in Lynn who says such words and, leaving coarse meats, she then eats the most delicious and delectable meats that are placed on the table.'

'Look, sirs,' she said, 'you ought to say no worse than you know, and yet not as bad as you know. Nevertheless, you are here saying worse than you know. God forgive it you, for I am that same person to whom these words are imputed, and I often suffer great shame and reproof, and I am not guilty in this matter, I take God as witness.'

When they saw her unmoved in this matter, not reproving them at all, desiring their correction in a spirit of charity, they were rebuked by their own decency, humbling themselves to make amends.

She spoke boldly and strongly wherever she went in London against swearers, cursers, liars and other such vicious people, and against the pompous fashions of both men and women. She did not spare them, she did not flatter them, neither for their gifts, nor for their food and drink. Her speaking profited many people very much. Therefore, when she came into church to her contemplation, our Lord sent her most high devotion, thanking her that she was not afraid to reprove sin in his name, and because she suffered scorn and reproofs for his sake, promising her very much grace in this life and, after this life, to have joy and bliss without end.

She was so comforted in the sweet communications of our Lord that she could not control herself nor govern her spirit according to her own will or the discretion of other men, but according to how our Lord would lead it and control it himself, in sobbing very violently and weeping most abundantly, for which she suffered very great slander and reproof, especially from the curates and priests of the churches in London. They would not allow her to remain in their churches, and therefore she went from one church to another so that she should not be tiresome to them. Many of the common people glorified God in her, having firm belief that it was the goodness of God which performed that high grace in her soul.

Chapter 10

From London she went to Sheen, three days before Lammas Day,[1] to obtain her pardon through the mercy of our Lord. And when she was in church at Sheen,[2] she had great devotion and very high contemplation. She had abundant tears of compunction and of compassion, in recollection of the bitter pains and passions which our merciful Lord Jesus Christ suffered in his blessed manhood. Those who saw her weep and heard her sob so violently were seized with marvelling and wonder as to what was pre-occupying her soul.

A young man who watched her face and manner, moved by tne Holy Ghost, went to her when he properly could, alone by himself, with a fervent desire to have some understanding of what might be the cause of her weeping. He said to her, 'Mother, if you please, I pray you tell me the reason for your weeping, for I have not seen a person so abundant in tears as you are, and especially, I have not heard before any person so violent in sobbing as you are. And, mother, though I am young, my desire is to please my Lord Jesus Christ, and so to follow him as I can and may. And I intend by the grace of God to take the habit of this holy order, and therefore I beg you not to be distant with me. Be so motherly and kind as to tell me your opinion, as I trust in you.'

She, benignly and meekly, with gladness of spirit, as she thought proper, commended him in his intention, and partly revealed to him that the cause of her weeping and sobbing was her great unkindness towards her maker, through which she had many times offended against his goodness. And also the great abomination that she had of her sins caused her to sob and weep. The great, excellent charity of her Redeemer too, by which, through the virtue of his suffering of the Passion and his shedding of his precious blood, she was redeemed from everlasting pain, trusting to be an heir of joy and bliss, moved her to sob and weep, and this was no cause for surprise. She spoke many good words of spiritual comfort to him, through which he was stirred to great virtue, and afterwards he ate and drank with her during the time that she was there, and was very glad to be in her company.

Lammas Day was the principal day of pardon, and, as the said creature entered the church at Sheen, she caught sight of the hermit who escorted her from Lynn when she went to the coast with her daughter-in-law, as is written before. At once, with great joy of spirit, she went over to him, welcoming him from her heart and saying to him, 'Ah, Reynald, you are welcome! I believe our Lord sent you here, for I hope that, just as you escorted me out of Lynn, so now you shall bring me home again to Lynn.'

The hermit gave her a short look and frowned heavily, neither wishing nor intending to bring her home to Lynn as she desired. Answering very shortly, he said, 'I'll have you know that your confessor has given you up, because you went overseas and wouldn't tell him a word about it. You took leave to bring your daughter to the coast; you asked no leave for any further. None of your friends knew what was in your mind, and therefore I suppose you will find but little friendship when you get home. I pray you, get yourself travelling companions where you can, because I got the blame for your fault when I escorted you last. I don't want any more of it.'

She spoke nicely to him, and prayed for God's love that he

would not be annoyed, because those who loved her for God before she left, would love her for God when she came home. She offered to pay his expenses on the way home. So at last he consented, and brought her back to London and then home to Lynn, to the high worship of God and to the great merit of both their souls.

When she came home to Lynn, she humbled herself obediently to her confessor. He gave her some very sharp words, because she was under his obedience and had taken such a journey upon her without his knowing. Therefore he was all the angrier with her, but our Lord helped her so that she had as good love from him and other friends afterwards as she had before – God be worshipped. Amen.

This creature, who has been written about in the preceding treatise, used for many years to begin her prayers in this manner. First, when she came to church, kneeling before the sacrament in worship of the Blessed Trinity (Father, Son, and Holy Ghost, one God and three Persons), of that glorious Virgin, Queen of Mercy, our Lady St Mary, and of the twelve apostles, she said this holy hymn, *Veni creator spiritus*, with all the verses belonging to it, that God should illumine her soul, as he did his apostles on Pentecost Day, and endue her with the gifts of the Holy Ghost, that she might have grace to understand his will and put it into action, and that she might have grace to withstand the temptations of her spiritual enemies, and eschew all manner of sin and wickedness.

When she had said *Veni creator spiritus*, with the verses, she said in this way: 'The Holy Ghost I take to witness, our Lady, St Mary, the mother of God, all the holy court of heaven, and all my confessors here on earth, that, even though it were possible that I might have all knowledge and understanding of the secrets of God through the telling of any devil of hell, I would not have it.

'And as surely as I would not know, hear, see, feel, nor understand in my soul in this life more than is the will of God that I should know, as surely God may help me in all my works, in all my thoughts, and in all my speeches, eating and drinking, sleeping and waking.

'As surely as it is not my will nor my intention to worship any false devil for my God, nor any false faith, nor to have any false belief, as surely I defy the devil and all his false counsel, and all that I have ever done, said or thought according to the counsel of the devil, thinking it had been the counsel of God and the inspiration of the Holy Ghost.

'If it has not been so, God, who sees and knows the secrets of all men's hearts, have mercy on me because of it, and grant me in this life a well of tears springing plenteously, with which I may wash away my sins through your mercy and your goodness.

'And, Lord, for your high mercy, all the tears that may increase my love towards you, and increase my merit in heaven, and help and profit my fellow Christian souls alive or dead, visit me with here on earth.

'Good Lord, do not spare the eyes in my head any more than you did the blood in your body, which you shed plentifully for sinful man's soul, and grant me so much pain and sorrow in this world that I be not hindered from your bliss and the beholding of your glorious face when I shall pass hence.

'As for my crying, my sobbing, and my weeping, Lord God Almighty, as surely as you know what scorn, what shame, what contempt, and what reproofs I have had because of them, and as surely as it is not in my power to weep loudly or quietly for devotion or sweetness, but only through the gift of the Holy Ghost, so surely, Lord, justify me so that all this world knows and trusts that it is your work and your gift, for the magnifying of your name, and for increasing of other men's love for you, Jesus.

'And I pray you, Sovereign Lord Christ Jesus, that as many men may be turned by my crying and weeping as have scorned me for it or shall scorn until the world's end, and many more, if it be your will. And as regards any earthly man's love, as surely as I would have no love but God to love above all things, and love all other creatures for God and in God, so surely quench in me all fleshly lust, and in all those that I have beheld your blissful body in. And give us your holy dread in our hearts, for your painful wounds.

'Lord, make my confessors fear you in me and love you in me, and make all the world have more sorrow for their own sins, for the sorrow that you have given me for other men's sins. Good Jesus, make my will your will, and your will my will, that I have no will but your will alone.

'Now, good Lord Christ Jesus, I cry you mercy for all the states that are in Holy Church, for the Pope and all his cardinals, for all archbishops and bishops, and for the whole order of priesthood, for all men and women of religion, and especially for those that are busy to save and defend the faith of Holy Church. Lord, for your mercy, bless them and grant them the victory over all their enemies, and speed them in all that they go about to do to your worship; for all that are in grace at this time, God send them perseverance until the end of their lives, and make me worthy to be partaker of their prayers, and them of mine, and each of us of the other's.

'I cry you mercy, blissful Lord, for the King of England, and for all Christian kings, and for all lords and ladies that are in this world. God establish them in such authority that they may most please you, and be lords and ladies in heaven without end. I cry you mercy, Lord, for the rich men in this world who have your goods in their control; give them grace to spend them to your pleasure. I cry you mercy, Lord, for Jews and Saracens, and all heathen people. Good Lord, remember that there is many a saint in heaven who once was a heathen upon earth, and so you have spread your mercy to those who are on earth.

'Lord, you say yourself that no man shall come to you without you, nor shall any man be drawn to you unless you draw him. And therefore, Lord, if there be any man who is not drawn, I pray you, draw him to you.

'You have drawn me, Lord, and I never deserved to be drawn, but according to your great mercy you have drawn me. If all this world knew my wickedness as you do, they would marvel and wonder at the great goodness that you have shown me. I would that all this world were worthy to thank you for me, and, as you have made unworthy creatures worthy, so make all this world worthy to thank and praise you.

'I cry you mercy, Lord, for all false heretics and for all misbelievers, for all false tithe-payers, thieves, adulterers and all common women, and for all wicked livers. Lord, for your mercy, have mercy upon them, if it be your will, and bring them out of their misconduct the sooner for my prayers.

'I cry you mercy, Lord, for all those who are tempted and troubled with their spiritual enemies, that you of your mercy give them grace to withstand their temptations, and deliver them from them when it is your greatest pleasure.

'I cry you mercy, Lord, for all my confessors, that you vouchsafe to spread as much grace in their souls as I would that you did in mine.

'I cry you mercy, Lord, for all my children, spiritual and bodily, and for all the people in this world, that you make their sins to me, by true contrition, as it were my own sins, and forgive them as I would that you forgave me.

'I cry you mercy, Lord, for all my friends and for all my enemies, for all that are sick especially, for all lepers, for all bedridden men and women, for all who are in prison, for all creatures who in this world have spoken of me either good or ill, or shall do until the world's end. Have mercy upon them, and be as gracious to their souls as I would that you were to mine.

And those who have said anything evil about me, for your high mercy, forgive it them; and those who have spoken well, I pray you, Lord, reward them, for that is through their charity and not through my merits; for, although you allowed all this world to avenge you on me and to hate me because I have displeased you, you would do me no wrong.

'I cry you mercy, Lord, for all the souls that are in the pains of purgatory, there awaiting your mercy and the prayers of Holy Church as surely, Lord, as they are your own chosen souls. Be as gracious to them as I would that you were to my soul if it were in the same pain that they are in.

'Lord Christ Jesus, I thank you for all health and all wealth, for all riches and all poverty, for sickness and all scorn, for all humiliations and all wrongs, and for all divers tribulations that have befallen or shall befall me as long as I live. Highly I thank you, that you would let me suffer any pain in this world in remission of my sins and increasing of my merit in heaven.

'As surely as I have great cause to thank you, hear my prayers. For though I had as many hearts and souls enclosed in my soul as God knew from without beginning how many should dwell in heaven without end, and as there are drops of water, fresh and salt, chips of gravel, stones small and great, grasses growing in all the earth, kernels of corn, fish, fowl, beasts, and leaves on trees when there is greatest abundance, feather of fowl or hair of beast, seeds that grow in plant, or in weed, in flower, on land, or in water when most grow, and as many as have been on earth, are, or shall and might be in your might, and as there are stars and angels in your sight, or other kinds of good that grow upon earth, and each were a soul as holy as ever was our Lady St Mary who bore Jesus our Saviour, and if it were possible that each could think and speak as great reverence and worship as ever did our Lady St Mary here on earth and now does in heaven and shall do without end, I may well think in my heart and speak it with my mouth at this time in worship of the Trinity and of all the court of heaven, to the great shame and ignominy of Satan, who fell from God's face, and of all his wicked spirits, so that all these hearts and souls could never thank God nor fully praise him, fully bless him nor fully worship him, fully love him nor fully give praise, laud and reverence to him as he were worthy to have for the great mercy that he has shown to me on earth. That I cannot do nor may not do.

'I pray my Lady, who is alone the Mother of God, the well of grace, flower and fairest of all women that God ever made on earth, the worthiest of all to be seen and heard by God, and the highest that has deserved it in this life, benign Lady, meek Lady, charitable Lady, with all the reverence that is in heaven, and with all your holy saints, I pray you, Lady, offer thanks and praise to the blissful Trinity for love of me, asking mercy and grace for me and for all my confessors, and perseverance until our life's end in that life we may most please God in.

'I bless my God in my soul, and all you that are in heaven. Blessed may God be in you all, and you in God. Blessed be you, Lord, for all your mercies that you have shown to all that are in heaven and on earth. And especially, I bless you, Lord, for Mary Magdalene, for Mary of Egypt, for St Paul, and for St Augustine. And as you have shown mercy to them, so show your mercy to me and to all that ask you mercy of heart. The peace and the rest that you have bequeathed to your disciples and to your lovers, may you bequeath the same peace and rest to me on earth and in heaven without end.

'Remember, Lord, the woman who was taken in adultery and brought before you, and as you drove away all her enemies from her as she stood alone by you, so truly you may drive away all my enemies from me, both bodily and spiritual, so that I may stand alone by you, and make my soul dead to all the joys of this world, and alive and greedy for high contemplation in God.

'Remember, Lord, Lazarus who lay four days dead in his grave, and as I have been in that holy place where your body was alive and dead and crucified for man's sin, and where Lazarus was raised from death to life, as surely Lord, if any man or woman be dead in this hour through mortal sin, if any prayer may help them, hear my prayers for them and make them live without end.

'I thank you, Lord, for all those sins that you have kept me from, which I have not done, and I thank you, Lord, for all the sorrow that you have given me for those that I have done, for these graces, and for all other graces that are needful to me and to all creatures on earth.

'And for all those who have faith and trust, or shall have faith and trust, in my prayers until the world's end, such grace as they desire, spiritual or bodily, to the profit of their souls, I pray you, Lord, grant them, for the abundance of your mercy. Amen.'

Notes

Introduction

1. The MS was edited by S. B. Meech and H. E. Allen in *The Book of Margery Kempe* (Early English Text Society, O.S. 212, 1940), and modernized by W. Butler-Bowdon in *The Book of Margery Kempe* (London, 1936). The MS – which is an early copy, but not the original dictated by Margery – was acquired by the British Library in 1980, and is now B.L. Add. MS 61823.

2. See James Hogg, 'Mount Grace Charterhouse and Late Medieval English Spirituality', *Analecta Cartusiana*, 82 (1980), 1–53; M. Sargent, 'The Transmission by the English Carthusians of Some Late Medieval Spiritual Writings', *Journal of Ecclesiastical History*, 27 (1976), 225–40; E. M. Thompson, *The Carthusian Order in England* (London, 1930).

3. See further, J. A. F. Thomson, *The Later Lollards 1414–1520* (Oxford, 1965); N. P. Tanner (ed.), *Heresy Trials in the Diocese of Norwich 1428–31* (London, 1977); Anne Hudson (ed.), *Selections from English Wycliffite Writings* (Cambridge, 1978); M. D. Lambert, *Medieval Heresy* (London, 1977).

4. See E. Colledge and J. Walsh (eds.), *A Book of Showings to the Anchoress Julian of Norwich* (Toronto, 1978), Introduction, pp. 33–8.

5. For the background, see J. Sumption, *Pilgrimage: An Image of Medieval Religion* (London, 1975); R. C. Finucane, *Miracles and Pilgrims: Popular Beliefs in Medieval England* (London, 1977); C. K. Zacher, *Curiosity and Pilgrimage* (Baltimore, 1976); D. R. Howard, *Writers and Pilgrims: Medieval Pilgrimage Narratives and their Posterity* (Berkeley, 1980).

6. See Felix Fabri, *Book of the Wanderings of Felix Fabri*, tr. A. Stewart (Palestine Pilgrims' Text Society, 1892); John Poloner, *Description of the Holy Land*, tr. A. Stewart (Palestine Pilgrims' Text Society, 1894); *Pilgrimage of Arnold von Harff*, tr. M. Letts (Hakluyt Society, 1946); William Wey, *Itineraries to Jerusalem*, 1458 (Roxburghe Club, 1857); Seigneur d'Anglure, *Le Saint Voyage de Jherusalem*, 1395, ed. F. Bonnardot and A. Longnon (S.A.T.F., Paris, 1878); *Le voyatge d'oultremer en Jherusalem de Nompar, seigneur de Caumont*, ed. P. S. Noble (Medium Aevum Monographs, N.S. vii, Oxford, 1975).

7. See E. Underhill (ed.), *The Scale of Perfection* (London, 1923), and J. E.

Milosh, *The Scale of Perfection and the English Mystical Tradition* (Madison, 1966).

8. See M. Deanesly (ed.), *The Incendium Amoris of Richard Rolle of Hampole* (Manchester, 1915); C. Wolters (tr.), *The Fire of Love* (Penguin, 1972); H. E. Allen, *Writings Ascribed to Richard Rolle Hermit of Hampole and Materials for His Biography* (New York, 1927).

9. See P. Hodgson (ed.), *The Cloud of Unknowing and Related Treatises* (Salzburg, 1982).

10. See H. E. Allen (ed.), *English Writings of Richard Rolle* (Oxford, 1931).

11. See *Meditations on the Life of Christ: An Illustrated Manuscript of the Fourteenth Century* (*MS. Ital. 115, Paris Bibl. Nat.*), ed. and tr. I. Ragusa and R. B. Green (Princeton, 1961); also E. Salter, 'Nicholas Love's *Myrrour of the Blessed Lyf of Jesu Christ*', *Analecta Cartusiana*, 10 (1974).

12. See C. Kirchberger (ed.), *The Goad of Love* (London, 1952), and H. Kane (ed.), *The Prickynge of Love* (Salzburg, 1983).

13. Such works of Blessed Jan van Ruysbroeck (1293–1381) as *Die Geestelike Bruloht* ('The Spiritual Espousals') and *Van den Blinckenden Steen* were available in England. See J. Bazire and E. Colledge (eds.), *The Chastising of God's Children and The Treatise of Perfection of the Sons of God* (Oxford, 1957); Suso's *Horologium Sapientiae* was translated, cf. C. Horstmann (ed.), '*Orologium Sapientiae* or *The Seven Poyntes of Trewe Wisdom*, aus MS Douce 114', *Anglia* 10 (1888), 323–89; see also R. Lovatt, 'The Imitation of Christ in Late Medieval England', *Transactions of the Royal Historical Society*, 5th ser., 18 (1968), 97ff.

14. See a Middle English version, W. P. Cumming (ed.), *The Revelations of St Birgitta* (E.E.T.S., O.S. 178, 1929); also, J. Jorgensen, *Saint Bridget of Sweden*, 2 vols. (London, 1954).

15. See Jacques de Vitry's *Vita Maria Oigniacensis*, in *Acta Sanctorum*, 25 (1867), 542–72.

16. See further B. M. Bolton, 'Mulieres sanctae', in *Studies in Church History*, 10 (1973), 77–95, and '*Vitae Matrum*: A Further Aspect of the *Frauenfrage*', in *Medieval Women*, ed. D. Baker (Oxford, 1978), pp. 253–73. See also E. W. McDonnell, *The Beguines and Beghards in Medieval Culture* (New Brunswick, 1954); M. Goodich, 'Contours of Female Piety in Later Medieval Hagiography', *Church History*, 50 (1981), 20–32.

17. See C. Horstmann (ed.), 'Prosalegenden: Die Legenden des ms. Douce

114', *Anglia*, 8 (1885), 102–96; cf. also P. S. Jolliffe, 'Two Middle English Tracts on the Contemplative Life', *Medieval Studies*, 37 (1975), 85–121.

18. Her *Dialogo della divina provvidenza* exists in a fifteenth-century English version; see P. Hodgson and G. M. Liegey (eds.), *The Orcherd of Syon* (E.E.T.S., O.S. 258, 1966). See also P. Hodgson, The Orcherd of Syon *and the English Mystical Tradition* (London, 1964).

19. St Mechthild of Hackeborn, *The Booke of Gostlye Grace*, ed. T. A. Halligan (Toronto, 1979); cf. C. W. Bynum, *Jesus as Mother: Studies in the Spirituality of the High Middle Ages* (Berkeley, 1982).

20. See M. Doiron (ed.), 'Margarete Porete, *The Mirror of Simple Souls*, A Middle English Translation; with an Appendix: The Glosses by "M.N." and Richard Methley to the "Mirror" by E. Colledge and R. Guarnieri', *Archivio italiano per la storia della pietà*, 5 (1968). See also R. E. Lerner, *The Heresy of the Free Spirit in the Later Middle Ages* (Berkeley, 1972).

21. See P. Doncoeur (ed.), *Le livre de la Bienheureuse Angèle de Foligno* (Paris, 1926).

22. See H. Westpfahl (ed.), *Vita Dorothea Montoviensis Magistri Johannis Marienwerder* (Cologne, 1964); also the article by H. Westpfahl in the *Dictionnaire de Spiritualité*, Vol. 3, cols. 1664–8 (Paris, 1957). Dorothea was canonized in 1976.

23. R. Pascal, *Design and Truth in Autobiography* (Cambridge, Mass., 1960); Mary G. Mason, 'The Other Voice: Autobiographies of Women Writers', in *Autobiography: Essays Theoretical and Critical*, ed. J. Olney (Princeton, 1980), pp. 207–35.

24. In S. Medcalf (ed.), *The Later Middle Ages* (London, 1981), a modern diagnosis of Margery by Dr Anthony Ryle is recorded (pp. 114–15), and is here reproduced by kind permission:

As is so often the case, she revealed a great deal of herself in her opening statement; partly in giving the account of her puerperal breakdown following her first child, which seems to have been psychotic in nature; but more so by revealing her discontent with those who had attempted to help her at this time, and this became recurrent throughout her account.

Prior to her puerperal breakdown, she was already preoccupied with some secret guilt, and it seems certain, from the evidence later in the story, that this guilt was sexual in nature; thus, she is continually preoccupied with the bad thoughts of others, and even in her sixties, when travelling, was worried that she might be the victim of rape; and, on one occasion, fairly late in life, seems to have had a brief recurrence of a psychotic period lasting a week or two, in which she was deluded and possibly hallucinated about the sexuality of the males surrounding her. Given, therefore, that this preoccupation was probably persistent, whether conscious or unconscious, a great deal of her subsequent behaviour can be seen as some form of defence against this. The defence she has chosen is one which, within the culture, was clearly the most powerful one, namely the assumption of a direct and special link with God. I feel this was a spurious claim, because her main concern, despite the attempts at visionary writing, would seem to be with the view others held of her as a person of particular religious capacity.

Her claims to the special relationship were made manifest through conspicuous activities, like dressing in white, weeping copiously and persistently, howling, grovelling on the floor, etc. Those around her, in general, are unimpressed by these various behaviours but, in her own system, their failure to acknowledge her claim was one more proof of its rightness because she could convert their rejection to a persecution, which she bore for Christ's sake. This system seems to have been, therefore, coherent and largely impenetrable, and she received enough reward from it to maintain her in a reasonable equilibrium but, I imagine, at considerable cost to those around her for most of her life.

I don't think that there is any evidence of a continuing psychotic process at work here. The most satisfactory description would be of a hysterical personality organization; her behaviours served as a constant source of attention and, in her own terms, of confirmation from others around her.

The Proem

1. Margery consistently refers to herself in the third person throughout her *Book*.
2. Literally 'how homely our Lord was in her soul'; also a frequent idea in Julian of Norwich: cf. 'in us is his homeliest home' (*Revelations of Divine Love*, tr. C. Wolters, Penguin, 1966, chapter 67).

3. Margery's word is 'Dewchlond', an inclusive term for the German-speaking lands, and usually including the Low Countries.

The Preface

1. The Carmelite, Alan of Lynn; see chapter 9.
2. i.e. 23 July.

Book I
Chapter 1

1. In Book II, chapter 5, which probably records events in 1433, Margery describes herself as about sixty years of age, which suggests she was born c. 1373 and married c. 1393. Margery begins abruptly at marriage and first childbirth and passes over her childhood, unlike many biographies of saintly women that Margery would have known, where the saint evinces signs of exceptional devotion from an early age.
2. Square brackets indicate additions by medieval annotators of the Mount Grace MS. Margery at first seems to conceal the identity of her home town and indicates it by the letter 'N'. Later, the town is openly named.
3. The nature of this unconfessed sin is never revealed by Margery. Some past sexual sin has been suggested, or some connection with William Sawtre, the first Lollard to be burnt for his beliefs in 1401, who was a priest in Lynn for some time before 1399.
4. i.e. confessed. Auricular confession was deemed essential.
5. In her *Mystic and Pilgrim: The Book and the World of Margery Kempe* (Cornell, 1983), p. 209, Clarissa W. Atkinson suggests Margery is here suffering from 'postpartum psychosis', a much more severe condition than common post-natal depression and sometimes involving delirium.

Chapter 2

1. Probably referring to the *crespine*, fashionable female head-dress of gold wire and mesh, sometimes shaped into the elaborate 'horns' frequently attacked by contemporary preachers. In head-dress and clothes Margery follows latest fashion.
2. i.e. her madness.

Chapter 3

1. Melody is a traditional accompaniment of mystical experience; see Richard Rolle, *The Fire of Love*, tr. C. Wolters (Penguin, 1972), chapters 33, 34.
2. Margery here acquires three persistent features of her subsequent life: her weeping, her continual thinking and irrepressible talking of heaven, and her wish for chastity.
3. i.e. the right of both parties to sexual intercourse within marriage under medieval canon law.
4. Excessive bodily penance – more common among continental mystics – was discouraged by such influential English guides as the author of the *Ancrene Riwle*, Richard Rolle, and Walter Hilton.
5. Frequent confession was recommended to the devout and noted in the lives of such female visionaries familiar to Margery as St Bridget of Sweden and Mary of Oignies.
6. cf. chapter 4: three years of temptation followed two years of quiet. As the Proem warns: 'This book is not written in order . . .'

Chapter 4

1. St Margaret of Antioch, a legendary virgin martyr (supposedly martyred in the persecution of Diocletian) whose cult was very popular in later medieval England. Olybrius, governor of Antioch, tried to marry or seduce her, but she declared herself a Christian and rebuffed him. She was subjected to torture, and was swallowed by a dragon, which exploded into pieces when she made the sign of the cross. She was eventually beheaded. Her feast day was 20 July.
2. i.e. the church of St Margaret which still survives in King's Lynn, although the nave was rebuilt after a spire fell causing damage in 1741. The church belonged to the Benedictine priory of Lynn, which was itself a cell of Norwich Cathedral monastery.

Chapter 5

1. Advent was traditionally a season for thoughts of penance and of the Last Judgement.
2. A repeated conviction in Margery: see chapters 8, 15, 22, 29, 36, 57.

3. cf. the inscription on Margery's wedding ring to Jesus in chapter 31, and God's words in chapter 65.

4. At her audience with Archbishop Arundel (chapter 16), Margery gains permission to receive communion every Sunday, and this is later confirmed so that she may receive communion as often as required (chapter 57). Such frequency of communion was most exceptional at the time, although St Bridget of Sweden and her daughter St Catherine were allowed weekly communion, as was Blessed Dorothea of Montau.

5. i.e. cod-fish cured and dried; a commodity in medieval Lynn.

6. i.e. a recluse attached to the Dominican house at Lynn; he is later (chapter 15) described as a doctor of divinity, and as Margery's principal confessor (chapter 18), as well as being credited with a 'spirit of prophecy', which suggests he was himself inclined to mysticism. He is consistently loyal to Margery (chapters 18, 19), but evidently dies before she returns from Jerusalem (chapter 58).

7. cf. 'The human mother will suckle her child with her milk, but our beloved Mother, Jesus, feeds us with himself' (Julian of Norwich, *Revelations of Divine Love*, tr. C. Wolters, Penguin, 1966, chapter 60).

Chapter 8

1. Margery evidently lay on the ground during her devotions (see chapters 6, 22, 23, 38, 87).

2. Presumably the Master Robert Spryngolde named as her confessor in chapter 57. God again alludes to his role as 'executor' in chapters 63 and 88.

Chapter 9

1. The words in brackets are added by an annotator in the MS margin. But in chapter 11 Margery reminds her husband that she told him he would be suddenly slain, and so she perhaps did believe that John Kempe would have been struck dead by God if he had not refrained from intercourse with her. Such married women mystics as St Bridget of Sweden and Blessed Dorothea of Montau were eventually able to live chaste by their husbands' consent, while Mary of Oignies and St Catherine of Sweden managed to remain virgin wives.

2. Probably 26 April 1413, i.e. two months before Margery's argument with John Kempe in chapter 11 (datable to 23 June 1413), when he is said to have gone without sex for eight weeks.
3. John Wyrham, a mercer, is mentioned in the medieval records of Lynn, and was a member of the Guild of St Giles and St Julian.
4. This Carmelite friar, Alan of Lynn (born c. 1348), was a Cambridge doctor of divinity and, among his writings, is recorded as having made indexes of the revelations and prophecies of St Bridget of Sweden, and of the pseudo-Bonaventuran *Stimulus Amoris*. A native of Lynn, he was to prove a good friend to Margery.

Chapter 10

1. cf. John xiv, 20; xv, 4–5; xvii, 23; vi, 57; also I John iv, 1, 6, 12, 13. God repeats this assurance to Margery in chapters 34 and 35.

Chapter 11

1. Probably 23 June 1413. After seeing Philip Repyngdon (who became Bishop of Lincoln in 1405) about her vows of chastity (chapter 15), Margery later visits Archbishop Arundel (chapter 16), who died in February 1414. Moreover, Margery – married c. 1393 – records that she bore her husband fourteen children (chapter 48). Between 1405 and 1414 Midsummer's Eve fell upon a Friday only in 1413. As Corpus Christi Day in 1413 fell on 22 June, it is likely that Margery and her husband had seen the Mystery Plays performed at York.
2. Surviving Lynn records refer to Margery's father, John Brunham, as alive but in ill health on 19 December 1412, and on 16 October 1413 as deceased. Inheritance of a legacy may have helped Margery to strike this bargain with her husband.

Chapter 12

1. Even the Franciscans in the Holy Land have heard that God speaks to Margery (chapter 29). After her trials for heresy she later becomes more cautious (e.g. chapters 46, 55, 63).
2. cf. Chaucer's portrait of the Monk in the General Prologue: '. . . a monk, whan he is reccheles, / Is likned til a fissh that is waterlees – / This is to seyn, a monk out of his cloystre . . .' (179–81).

Chapter 13

1. Probably John Kynton (d. 1416), formerly chancellor to Queen Joanna, wife of Henry IV, before becoming a monk of Christ Church, Canterbury, in 1408.
2. Possibly enclosure as an anchoress, but perhaps imprisonment.
3. i.e. a heretic with opinions derived from John Wyclif or his followers. Among their other beliefs, Lollards were held to question the authority of the priesthood and the institution of religious orders, and to maintain that every Christian could discover for him or herself the true sense of the Bible and live by it.
4. A note here in the MS margin comments that Richard Methley 'was wont so to say'. Methley (b. 1451), a Carthusian mystic of Mount Grace, translated into Latin *The Cloud of Unknowing* and *The Mirror of Simple Souls*, with a preface on pseudo-Dionysian mysticism. Of himself he wrote: 'My life consists of love, langour, sweetness, heat and melody . . .'
5. The MS margin here contains a drawing of a pillar. Some medieval German women mystics also thought of themselves as chosen in this way.

Chapter 14

1. cf. Isaiah xlix, 16: 'Behold, I have graven thee upon the palms of my hands . . .'
2. cf. Isaiah xlv, 15: 'Verily thou art a God that hidest thyself.' Hilton, *Scale of Perfection*, I, chapter 49, also citing this verse, comments: 'Jesus is treasure hid in thy soul.'
3. Margery is assured of the importance of the gift of tears by Julian of Norwich (chapter 18), and by her Dominican anchorite (chapter 19); they are later seen as a most important token of love (chapter 64), a gift of God (chapters 61, 67, 68).
4. Mark iii, 35.

Chapter 15

1. i.e. probably in 1411, as Margery apparently left for the Holy Land in 1413, and visited the shrine of St James at Santiago de Compostela in north-west Spain in 1417.

2. White clothes would be taken as a claim to special virtue (chapter 33) or virginity (chapter 52).

3. Philip Repyngdon, Bishop of Lincoln 1405–19. Margery visited him sometime after 23 June 1413 (probably because the Bishop of Norwich had died in April 1413, and his successor died without having visited his diocese in 1415). Repyngdon had long ago abjured his earlier support for Wyclif at Oxford, where he had defended Wycliffite doctrine on the sacrament 'but had won universal esteem for his moderate and kindly bearing' (DNB). Archbishop Arundel later regarded him as a most orthodox bishop, who energetically pursued Lollards. Repyngdon seems to have heard of Margery before.

4. For Margery as prophet, see chapters 17, 23, 24, 71; for contemporary religious as prophets, see R. M. Clay, *The Hermits and Anchorites of England* (London, 1914), 155ff.

5. The mantle and the ring would indicate the taking of a vow of chastity before a bishop.

6. Those in heaven are clothed in white; cf. Revelation iii, 4; iv, 4; Matthew xxviii, 3.

7. Repyngdon 'was described in his lifetime as a "powerful and God-fearing man, a lover of truth and hater of avarice" . . . He does not appear to have possessed any great force of character, and his promotion was perhaps chiefly due to his friendship with Henry IV' (DNB).

8. Thomas Arundel (1353–1414), third son of Richard Fitz Alan, fourth Earl of Arundel. Enthroned as Archbishop of Canterbury in 1397, he was banished in the same year by Richard II, returning to England with Henry IV, when he was restored to the archbishopric. A vigorous opponent of the Lollards, he presided at the trials of the heretics William Sawtre, John Badby, and Sir John Oldcastle. See M. Aston, *Thomas Arundel* (Oxford, 1967).

Chapter 16

1. The first of many rebukes that Margery's book records her as giving to those who sin by swearing. Oaths by aspects of the Passion and Christ's body were felt to torture our Lord all over again, as Chaucer's Parson says in his tale: 'For Cristes sake, ne swereth nat so synfully

in dismembrynge of Crist by soule, herte, bones, and body. For certes, it semeth that ye thynke that the cursede Jewes ne dismembred nat ynough the preciouse persone of Crist, but ye dismembre hym moore . . .' (X, 590ff.). See also G. R. Owst, *Literature and Pulpit in Medieval England* (Oxford, 1966), pp. 414–25.

2. A garment made of skin dressed with the hair.

3. William Sawtre, sometime priest of Lynn, was burnt for Lollardy at Smithfield in 1401.

Chapter 17

1. The Vicar is later named (chapter 43) as Richard of Caister (d. 1420). He has been credited with writing one of the most popular Middle English devotional lyrics, *Jesu, Lorde, that madest me*, although 'he may well have expanded and rearranged an already popular poem' (*Medieval English Lyrics*, ed. R. T. Davies, London, 1963, pp. 146–8, 332). After his death Margery seems to pray to him as to a saint (chapter 60).

2. The *Scale of Perfection* of Walter Hilton, the *Revelations* of St Bridget of Sweden, the *Stimulus Amoris* of the pseudo-Bonaventura, and the *Incendium Amoris* of Richard Rolle. Margery here mentions the same books as those later read to her by the young priest (chapter 58). On Margery's reading, see Introduction, p. 15ff.

3. St Katherine of Alexandria, supposedly a fourth-century virgin martyr, whose cult was very popular in the Middle Ages. A girl of noble birth, and persecuted for her Christianity, she refused marriage with the emperor because she was a bride of Christ; she triumphed over fifty philosophers enlisted to persuade her of the errors of Christianity. She was tortured by being broken on the wheel that became her symbol, and then beheaded.

4. As Richard of Caister is known to have died on 29 March 1420, this would date Margery's appearance before the Bishop's officers to *c.*1413.

Chapter 18

1. The Carmelite William Southfield is reported to have received supernatural visitations, and the Virgin appeared to him.

2. Wisdom i, 4, 5.
3. Psalms li, 17.
4. Isaiah lxvi, 2.
5. i.e. Dame Julian of Norwich (born *c.* 1343), anchoress at St Julian's Church, Norwich. Julian's revisions of the account of her meditations on her own visions, in the two versions of her *Revelations of Divine Love*, suggest her scrupulous and anxious care in the correct interpretation of such experiences.
6. I Corinthians vi, 19.
7. James i, 8.
8. James i, 6–7.
9. Romans viii, 26.
10. Popularly attributed to St Jerome, although no precise equivalent has been found in his writings. The Middle English treatise *Speculum Christiani* has St Jerome say, 'Prayers please God but tears constrain him,' and St Bernard says, 'Tears of a sinner torment the devil more than every kind of torture.'
11. cf. II Corinthians vi, 16; Apocalypse xxi, 3; also Ezekiel xxxvii, 27–8; and the texts from St John echoed in chapter 10 above.
12. Luke vi, 22–3.
13. Luke xxi, 19.
14. This abrupt transition suggests that in the unique MS this material has been wrongly brought forward from the end of the next chapter, which concerns Margery's dealings with several widows.

Chapter 20

1. The model for herself provided by the example of St Bridget of Sweden was evidently much in Margery's thoughts; in this chapter God confirms the connection explicitly.
2. No earthquake in England is subsequently mentioned by Margery, or, apparently, by contemporary English records.
3. St Bridget of Sweden and St Catherine of Siena were the most celebrated examples of medieval women mystics whose visionary life also included a concern for the affairs of the world.

Chapter 21

1. This conversation with God when Margery is pregnant is apparently out of chronological order, and must have preceded the chastity agreement with her husband in chapter 11.
2. Blessed Angela of Foligno heard the Holy Spirit saying to her: 'I love thee more than any woman in the valley of Spoleto.'
3. cf. *The Cloud of Unknowing*: 'For it is not what you are or have been that God looks at with his merciful eyes, but what you would be ... St Augustine is speaking of this holy desire when he says that "the life of a good Christian consists of nothing else but holy desire" ' tr. C. Wolters (Penguin, 1978), chapter 75.
4. According to medieval legend she was an actress and courtesan in fifth-century Alexandria who, after her conversion, lived as a hermit in the Jordanian desert. When her clothes wore out, her hair grew long and took their place.

Chapter 22

1. The cult of this legendary virgin martyr was popular in the later Middle Ages. Shut up in a tower by her father so that no man should see her, she became a Christian; her furious father was killed by lightning after he handed her over to a judge to be condemned. Patron of those in peril of sudden death.

Chapter 24

1. i.e. Pentney Priory, an Augustinian house on the River Nar near Narborough, some seven miles south-east of Lynn; 'founded before 1135. Quite a big house, usually with 15–20 canons. The imposing gatehouse alone remains ...' (Pevsner, *Buildings of England: North-West and South Norfolk*, Penguin, 1962).

Chapter 25

1. Margery is describing the situation in Lynn, with its parish church of St Margaret, and its two chapels-of-ease, St Nicholas and St James. By virtue of his office, the Prior of Lynn was parson and curate of the parish of St Margaret's.

2. The Red Register of Lynn records that an earlier attempt had been made in Margery's childhood, during the second mayoralty of her father, to secure privileges for the administration of the sacraments of baptism, matrimony and purification, for the chapel of St. Nicholas. A papal bull was obtained in October 1378, which granted privileges, provided there was no derogation to St Margaret's. The attempt was opposed by, among others, John Brunham, Margery's father, and one John Kempe, probably her father-in-law. A further attempt is recorded in 1431–2.
3. The Prior at this period was John Derham.
4. William of Alnwick (d. 1449), Bishop of Norwich 1426–36; 'a relentless persecutor of the Lollards in his diocese' (DNB).
5. A noble was worth six shillings and eight pence.

Chapter 26

1. The season would seem to be the autumn of 1413: after her agreement with her husband at Midsummer (chapter 11), Margery visits the Bishop of Lincoln (where she has a three-week wait), and then visits Archbishop Arundel at Lambeth, who receives her in his garden, which suggests the summer months.
2. Probably Master Robert Spryngolde. The offer to settle her debts may well have been underwritten by a legacy following her father's death sometime between December 1412 and October 1413.
3. i.e. Margery offered at the high altar of the Cathedral of the Holy Trinity at Norwich, and perhaps in the Chapel of the Virgin at St Nicholas's, Yarmouth.
4. i.e. since the instruction received in chapter 5.

Chapter 27

1. By contemporary standards, Margery would seem to have set off from Lynn quite well provided with money for her expenses on the journey, but she would have had to think ahead to such necessary outlays as the purchase in Venice of articles for use on the voyage to Jaffa.
2. From the accounts of other late medieval English travellers, it is a reasonable surmise that Margery took between six and eight weeks

to travel from Lynn to Venice. She would thus have arrived in late 1413 or early 1414, and then waited thirteen weeks for one of the pilgrim galleys, which usually left Venice in spring or early summer. The 'Venetian Process' for the canonization of St Catherine of Siena (1411–13) would have been very recent news.

Chapter 28

1. Pilgrims should buy for the voyage in Venice 'a feather bed, a mattress, two pillows, two pairs of sheets and a quilt,' as well as various provisions and utensils, medicines and laxatives, a chest with a good lock, even a cage of hens . . . cf. the fifteenth-century guide by William Wey, *Itineraries to Jerusalem*, 1458 (Roxburghe Club, 1857).
2. The galley's month-long voyage was along the Dalmatian coast, through the Greek islands, to Crete, Rhodes, Cyprus, Jaffa, with frequent stops for provisioning. There was a general cabin for pilgrims in the hold; a berth consisted of a space big enough to lie down on, chalked on the boards, where one spread one's mattress and belongings.
3. The port for Jerusalem was Jaffa, then in ruins, where pilgrims were processed on disembarking by Moslem officials, for pilgrimage was strictly controlled. Pilgrims were accommodated at Jaffa in some noxious caves, before being escorted on donkeys to Jerusalem under guard, with a stop at the town of Ramleh (mentioned by Margery on her return journey, chapter 30).
4. Margery calls this the 'Temple'. She would have seen both the round church containing the Chapel of the Holy Sepulchre, and also another part of the building which enclosed under its roof the mound of Calvary, rising fifteen feet above the floor with another chapel on its summit, the northern part of which rested on the rock itself, while the southern part (revered as the site of the nailing of Christ to the cross) was supported on arches.
5. The door to the Church of the Holy Sepulchre was guarded by Moslem officials, who controlled admission, charged the pilgrims entrance fees, and locked them into the church for the duration of their vigils. Margery's stay seems to have been longer than the usual vigil in her day, which lasted from evening until the following morning.

6. The Franciscans had a convent adjoining the Church of the Holy Sepulchre, and had been granted important rights at various sites in the Holy Land, including the Chapels of the Holy Sepulchre and of the Apparition, in the Church of the Holy Sepulchre.

7. For Margery this experience is the culmination of all her preceding absorption in hearing and practising meditation upon the Passion. St Bridget, in her *Revelations*, had described her visions on the life of Christ and Mary received during her own pilgrimage to the Holy Land.

8. Margery's 'cries' – by which she seems to mean a crying out, a scream – start at this moment, and she was to be subject to them for some ten years. Her *Book* makes a careful distinction in its terminology over this, and Margery does not use the term 'cry' about her fits of weeping before her visit to Jerusalem, or later in life.

9. In the margin of the MS here is a fifteenth-century note that Richard Methley and John Norton, both Mount Grace mystics, also experienced this weakness in association with the Passion.

10. cf. Richard Rolle's *Meditations on the Passion*: 'Sweet Jesu, thy body is like unto a dove-cote. For as a dove-cote is full of holes, so is thy body full of wounds. And as a dove pursued by a hawk, if she may reach a hole of her house, is safe enough, so sweet Jesu, in temptation thy wounds are the best refuge for us' (modernized from Allen, *English Writings*, p. 35). Behind Rolle is the Song of Songs, ii, 14, and St Bernard's *Sermons on the Song of Songs*, 61.

11. cf. Blessed Angela of Foligno: 'Then I reached so much greater a fire of love that, if I heard anybody talking of God, I screamed. And even if somebody had stood over me with an axe to kill me, I would not have been able to stop ...' cf. *Le Livre de la Bienheureuse Angèle de Foligno*, ed. P. Doncoeur (Paris, 1926), p. 15.

Chapter 29

1. i.e. the Franciscans conduct them over the Via Dolorosa.

2. The Franciscan convent on Mount Zion was believed to contain the holy places of the Last Supper, and of the Holy Spirit's descent upon the apostles.

3. The Church of the Tomb of the Virgin, in the valley of Kedron, was also in Franciscan custody.

4. i.e. the Church of St Mary of the Nativity at Bethlehem (similarly in Franciscan custody), beneath which two grottoes were believed to be the sites of Christ's birth and of the manger.
5. i.e. Franciscans.

Chapter 30

1. i.e. the mountain near Jericho upon which it was believed that Christ fasted forty days and was tempted by the devil. (The term 'quarantine' originally meant a period of forty days.)
2. Occupied by the Church of the Franciscan monastery of St John.
3. i.e. the Chapel of the Apparition, in the Church of the Holy Sepulchre. Margery evidently returned to the church after her travels in the Holy Land; pilgrims customarily visited the church more than once.
4. John xx, 14–15.
5. Pilgrims travelled about the Holy Land under Moslem escort.

Chapter 31

1. i.e. 'Jesus is my love'. Beads left by William of Wykeham to Archbishop Arundel bore the same inscription. Although made at a divine command, Margery describes the ring as her marriage ring to Jesus, which could suggest she assumed it with the mantle on making a vow of chastity. While her *Book* leaves the taking of the vow undescribed (chapter 15), it is later assumed (chapter 76).
2. Like some recorded pilgrims, Margery had perhaps brought back a cord or other object on which the measurements of the sepulchre were marked.
3. Margery's attempt to record the woman's Italian.
4. i.e. a Franciscan.
5. Our Lady's veil, kept in the Lower Church of St Francis at Assisi.
6. Blessed Angela of Foligno had screamed and shrieked at the door of St Francis's church in Assisi, and had also received revelations in Assisi on Lammas Day (1 August).
7. Probably Lammas Day 1414. In Chapter 44 Margery is delayed at Bristol by the King's requisitioning of shipping (which must refer to Henry V's expedition to France in 1417), and in Whitsun week she there meets and pays back Richard, whom she says she had left in Rome two years previously.

8. The 'Portiuncula Indulgence', traditionally granted to St Francis himself by Honorius III, gave plenary remission of sins to those who at Lammas visited the Portiuncula Chapel, where St Francis had worshipped.

9. A hospice for English pilgrims in the Via Monserrato, started in 1362, and now the English College in Rome.

Chapter 32

1. i.e. the Church of Santa Caterina in Ruota.

2. By tradition St John acted as confessor for women who lacked access to a mortal confessor.

3. cf. Jeremiah ix, 1: 'Oh that my head were waters, and mine eyes a fountain of tears, that I might weep day and night for the slain of the daughter of my people!'

Chapter 35

1. The Church of the Santi Apostoli, almost completely rebuilt in the eighteenth century.

2. Probably 9 November 1414, the feast of the dedication of St John Lateran.

3. cf. Psalms xc, 11 (A.V. xci, 11).

4. 'Blessed is he that comes in the name of the Lord.'

5. cf. the prologue to Richard Rolle's *Incendium Amoris*: 'I cannot tell you how surprised I was the first time I felt my heart begin to warm. It was real warmth too, not imaginary, and it felt as if it were actually on fire. I was astonished at the way the heat surged up, and how this new sensation brought great and unexpected comfort. I had to keep feeling my breast to make sure there was no physical reason for it! ... It set my soul aglow as if a real fire was burning there ... If we put our finger near a fire we feel the heat; in much the same way a soul on fire with love feels, I say, a genuine warmth ...' (*The Fire of Love*, tr. C. Wolters, Penguin, 1972, p. 45).

Chapter 37

1. Probably Christmas 1414.
2. See chapter 44.

Chapter 38

1 The Church of San Marcello, rebuilt in the sixteenth and seventeenth centuries.
2. i.e. Margery attempts to recall the questions and her own response in broken Italian.
3. Coins current in fifteenth-century Rome.

Chapter 39

1. In 1349 St Bridget had left Sweden for Rome, where she spent most of the rest of her life and died in 1373, i.e. forty years before Margery's visit. Her canonization in 1391 was being considered by the Council of Constance while Margery was in Rome and was confirmed in 1415.
2. St Bridget, who was a great lady of high birth, and her daughter, St Catherine of Sweden, are known to have had three maids with them on their pilgrimage to the Holy Land in 1370.
3. The Church of Santa Brigida in the Piazza Farnese is on the site of St Bridget's home.
4. This revelation occurred five days before St Bridget's death.
5. Probably the feast of St Bridget's canonization (7 October 1414), rather than the feast of her death (23 July) or translation (28 May), since Margery was in Assisi until after 1 August. This visit evidently preceded chronologically the experience in chapter 35, which occurred on 9 November, but Margery has grouped together in this chapter some recollections connected with St Bridget.
6. i.e. the paying of visits, with appropriate prayers, to certain churches of Rome.

Chapter 41

1. The Basilica of Santa Maria Maggiore.
2. Margery may have been confused by a chapel of St Laurence within Santa Maria Maggiore; the saint's remains are buried in the Basilica of San Lorenzo fuori le Mura.
3. For St Jerome on tears, see chapter 18.

Chapter 42

1. Probably Easter 1415.
2. Middelburg, in Zealand.

Chapter 43

1. Probably Saturday, 18 May 1415. After her crossing (probably landing at Yarmouth), Margery proceeds straight to Norwich, where she is in the week before Trinity Sunday (chapter 44), which in 1415 fell on 26 May.
2. Probably one Thomas Brakleye, a Benedictine monk, of whom record survives.
3. Founded before 1248 as a hospital and chapel in open fields south-west of the city, 'in a short space of time, aided by various bene-factions, the foundation became a collegiate church on a noble scale . . .' (*Victoria County History: Norfolk* II, 1906, p. 455).
4. Priests were customarily addressed as 'Sir' or 'Master'. The will of Thomas Brakleye names a 'Sir Edwarde Hunt' among his executors.

Chapter 44

1. The year is probably 1415, when Trinity Sunday fell on 26 May.
2. In the MS margin here is the note: 'so dyd prior Norton in hys excesse', referring to John Norton, Prior of Mount Grace.
3. A mark was worth thirteen shillings and fourpence.
4. This evidently refers to requisitioning of ships for Henry V's second expedition to France in 1417.

Chapter 45

1. Probably 10 June 1417.
2. Possibly Newcastle under Lyme, in Staffordshire, rather than Newcastle upon Tyne, in that Thomas accompanies Margery as far as Leicester and Melton Mowbray (chapter 49), but apparently not on her subsequent travels to Lincoln and York.
3. Thomas Peverel, Bishop of Worcester 1407–19. He came of a Suffolk family, which explains his knowledge of Margery's father. He was responsible for the conviction on a charge of heresy of the Lollard John Badby, who was burned in 1410. The bishops of Worcester had a manor near Bristol at Henbury, Gloucestershire.
4. If Margery waited six weeks from Whitsun, she probably sailed for Santiago in early July. She was evidently away twenty-six days.
5. The Cistercian abbey of Hailes in Gloucestershire boasted a relic of the Holy Blood. 'By the blood of Crist that is in Hayles' is among the oaths Chaucer's Pardoner preaches against in his tale. 'All that remains above ground is the shell of the cloister ... The surviving architectural detail is of very high quality ...' D. Verey, *Buildings of England: Gloucestershire; The Cotswolds*, Penguin, 1970.

Chapter 46

1. According to extant records, the Mayor of Leicester between Michaelmas Day 1416 and Michaelmas Day 1417 was one John Arnesby.

Chapter 48

1. All Saints Church, which still stands in High Cross Street, Leicester.
2. Richard Rothley, who succeeded Philip Repyngdon in the abbacy in 1405, on the latter's appointment as Bishop of Lincoln.
3. Possibly the Dean of either of the two colleges of St Mary the Less or St Mary the Greater.
4. Questions about the sacrament might expose a suspected Lollard, but Margery's answer is orthodox.
5. Genesis xviii, 21.
6. In 1399 Richard II had prohibited the entry into England of 'a new

sect of certain people dressed in white clothes and pretending a great holiness', probably the Flagellant *Albi* or *Bianchi*, who had entered Italy from France in 1399.

Chapter 49

1. A house of Augustinian canons dedicated to St Mary; only the foundations now remain.
2. Leaving Bristol in late July or early August (chapter 45), Margery thus probably left Leicester in late August or early September 1417.

Chapter 50

1. Probably the Eve of the Nativity of the Virgin Mary, 7 September 1417; fasting at such a time would be customary piety.
2. cf. Matthew vii, 15 ('Beware of false prophets, which come to you in sheep's clothing, but inwardly they are ravening wolves').

Chapter 51

1. Genesis i, 22 ('Be fruitful, and multiply . . .'); held by some heretics to justify free love.
2. John Aclom has not been identified.
3. John Kendale was a vicar choral, not a canon, of York Minster at this time; each canon delegated some or all of his duties in the church to his own vicar choral, hence Margery's confusion.
4. Perhaps one of the two chaplains of the Chantry of All Saints, established on the south side of the Lady Chapel in 1413 by Archbishop Bowet, near to the tomb he had built for himself.
5. i.e. the Chapterhouse which still stands.
6. William Fitzherbert, Archbishop of York (d. 1154); miracles were reported at his tomb in the Minster, and he was canonized in 1227; his relics were translated to a new shrine in 1281. There was a strong cult of the saint at York.
7. The palace of Archbishops of York at Cawood, south of York. 'All that remains is the tall Gatehouse . . .' (built later than Margery's visit) (Pevsner, *The Buildings of England: Yorkshire: The West Riding*, Penguin, 1959).

Chapter 52

1. Henry Bowet, Archbishop of York 1407–23; he showed zeal against the Lollards. He is also said to have had a great reputation for hospitality and sumptuous housekeeping.
2. St John of Bridlington (d. 1379), Prior of the Augustinian canons of Bridlington, who combined his official duties with a life of fervent prayer, and had the gift of tears. Miracles were reported at his tomb, and he was canonized in 1401. His confessor, William Sleightholme (referred to by Margery as 'Sleytham' in chapter 53), was himself reported to be a worker of miracles.
3. Luke xi, 27–8.
4. i.e. that like various contemporary Lollard women, Margery has been studying scripture. See C. Cross, ' "Great Reasoners in Scripture": The Activities of Women Lollards 1380–1530', in *Medieval Women*, ed. D. Baker (Oxford, 1978), pp. 359–80.
5. I Corinthians xiv, 34–5.
6. i.e. six shillings and eightpence.

Chapter 53

1. John, Duke of Bedford (1389–1435), third son of Henry IV, and at this time Lieutenant of the kingdom, during Henry V's absence in France.

Chapter 54

1. i.e. the Chapterhouse no longer extant at Beverley Minster.
2. cf. Matthew v, 48.
3. Margery is here accused of being the spiritual daughter of the contemporary arch-Lollard, Sir John Oldcastle, Lord Cobham. Pronounced a heretic by Archbishop Arundel in 1413, Oldcastle escaped from the Tower and was in hiding in his home county of Herefordshire until recaptured late in 1417. He was hanged and burnt as an outlaw, traitor and heretic on 14 December 1417, in the presence of the Duke of Bedford.
4. i.e. because Lollards disapproved of pilgrimages.
5. Joan de Beaufort (d. 1440), Countess of Westmorland, daughter of

John of Gaunt and Katherine Swynford, sister of Cardinal Beaufort and aunt of the Duke of Bedford.

6. Elizabeth, daughter of Joan de Beaufort, who married John de Greystoke.

7. Margery is probably speaking in the autumn of 1417, and left for Jerusalem in 1413.

8. Margery will have remembered that St Bridget 'had a laughing face' (chapter 39).

9. It is noticeable how many events in her life are remembered by Margery as occurring on Fridays, the day of Christ's Passion.

Chapter 55

1. Matthew x, 19–20.

2. West Lynn, on the west bank of the River Ouse, just across the river from Lynn itself.

3. Arundel's successor, Henry Chichele, Archbishop of Canterbury 1414–43.

Chapter 57

1. Referring to the old custom by which all those moving house within the same district did so on the same day.

2. Extant records mention him as an early fifteenth century Prior of Lynn.

3. Archbishop Chichele's letter is more liberal than Arundel's allowance of Sunday communion (chapter 16).

4. At the end of Holy Week the crucifix was customarily wrapped in silk and buried with the Host in the Easter Sepulchre (a special recess with tomb-chest for the purpose, usually in the wall of the chancel), and a vigil was then kept.

5. One Mount Grace annotator comments in the MS margin '*langor amoris*', i.e. the languishing of love.

6. Actually, it has not been written before. Margery has said that her eight years of illness (which evidently started several years after the visit to Jerusalem when her cries began) were followed by increased cryings (chapter 56).

7. The Mount Grace annotator notes in the margin 'petite et accipietis', referring to John xvi, 24 ('ask, and ye shall receive . . .').

Chapter 58

1. Luke xix, 41–4.
2. i.e. the *Revelations* of St Bridget of Sweden, probably Hilton's *Scale of Perfection*, the pseudo-Bonaventuran *Stimulus Amoris*, and Richard Rolle's *Incendium Amoris*. On the books known to Margery, see Introduction, p. 15ff.

Chapter 59

1. cf. the anxiety of Julian of Norwich: 'Another part of our same belief is that many creatures will be damned ... all these shall be condemned to hell everlastingly, as Holy Church teaches me to believe. This being so I thought it quite impossible that everything should turn out well, as our Lord was now showing me' (*Revelations of Divine Love*, tr. C. Wolters, Penguin, 1966, chapter 32).

Chapter 60

1. Richard of Caister died on 29 March 1420. Miracles were reputed to have happened at his tomb, which was a place of pilgrimage.
2. i.e. an image of the Virgin seated with the dead body of Christ in her lap. For evidence that such images were fairly common in fifteenth-century England, see 'The History of the Pietà', in R. Woolf, *The English Religious Lyric in the Middle Ages* (Oxford, 1968), pp. 392–4.
3. This priest – who is never named by Margery – probably thus came to Lynn about 1413.

Chapter 61

1. A marginal note in the MS in chapter 63 (see below), names the friar as 'Melton', perhaps identifying Margery's enemy as the Franciscan preacher William Melton, although the authority of the note remains doubtful.
2. The other chapel-of-ease in the parish of St Margaret's, Lynn.
3. Presumably Master Alan and Master Robert Spryngolde.

Chapter 62

1. 25 July; the year is uncertain.
2. On Mary of Oignies, see Introduction, p. 18ff.
3. Perhaps a Middle English translation of the *Stimulus Amoris*; cf. *The Prickynge of Love*, ed. H. Kane (Salzburg, 1983), chapter 2, p. 20.
4. i.e. Richard Rolle. See *The Fire of Love*, tr. C. Wolters (Penguin, 1972), chapter 34: 'And his shout, excited and bursting out from the core of his longing love, goes up, of course, to his Maker ... I have not the wit to describe this shout or its magnitude ...'
5. St Elizabeth of Hungary (1207–31). Happily married to the Landgrave of Thuringia, after his death on crusade in 1227 she became a Franciscan tertiary, devoting herself to the care of the poor and sick and to a life of austerity. Canonized in 1235, her relics at Marburg were a popular object of pilgrimage.

Chapter 63

1. From the Old French *gesine*, 'childbed'; a chapel in St Margaret's Church devoted to the Nativity.
2. Here an annotator writes '*nota contra Melton*' in the MS margin; see chapter 61, n. 1.
3. Margery perhaps looks forward here to her own sainthood.
4. cf. chapter 8.

Chapter 64

1. Matthew vii, 12.

Chapter 65

1. Margery has not recorded this revelation; St Paul is quoted against her at her examination in chapter 52.

Chapter 67

1. This fire is recorded as having happened on 23 January 1420/1421.
2. Probably Robert Spryngolde.
3. Note Margery's caution in divulging her revelations.

Chapter 68

1. A Dominican, Thomas Constance, is mentioned in contemporary records.
2. Presumably Mary of Oignies; see chapter 62.

Chapter 69

1. i.e. Prior Thomas Hevingham; see chapter 57.
2. John Wakering (d. 1425), consecrated Bishop of Norwich in 1416.
3. i.e. Alan of Lynn and Robert Spryngolde.
4. Thomas Netter (d. 1430), elected Provincial Prior of the English Carmelites in a council held at Yarmouth in 1414, and one of the English representatives at the Council of Constance. He had taken a prominent part in the prosecution of the Lollards and had been present at the examination of Oldcastle before Archbishop Arundel in 1413. He is also recorded as a special patron of women recluses and an encourager of holy women, although disapproving of publicity for them.
5. Neither has been positively identified, although a Thomas Andrew was presented as rector of St Peter Hungate, Norwich, in 1457, and a John Amy was presented as Vicar of Appleton (1417) and Sedgeford (1426), both villages in north-west Norfolk, not far from Lynn.
6. Not identified.

Chapter 70

1. Probably Thomas Netter; see chapter 69, n. 4.

Chapter 71

1. Extant records identify the two Priors in this episode as Thomas Hevingham and his successor, John Derham.
2. Henry V died in France on 31 August 1422.
3. Henry Beaufort (d. 1447), son of John of Gaunt and Katherine Swynford, half-brother of Henry IV; Bishop of Winchester 1405–47; nominated a cardinal in 1426, and later referred to by Margery as a cardinal (Book II, chapter 9), suggesting the present incident preceded his elevation.

Chapter 72

1. Romans viii. 28.

Chapter 73

1. In the MS margin a fifteenth-century note: 'Father M. was wont so to doo', referring to the Mount Grace mystic, Richard Methley.
2. Recalling our Lord's words to Margery on her way from Jerusalem, which may well have taken place on the feast of the Translation of St Nicholas (9 May), although Margery did not specify this in chapter 30.

Chapter 74

1. Margery is in accord with St Bridget's revelations on the date of the Virgin's death; the Blessed Elisabeth of Schönau's revelations put the date a year after the crucifixion.
2. It is appropriate for Margery to identify herself with the tearful Magdalene.
3. After his conversion, St Francis of Assisi similarly wished to kiss lepers, although he had previously found them repellent, and St Catherine of Siena also cared for lepers. Mary of Oignies and her husband turned their home into a hospital for lepers, whom they personally nursed.
4. Margery had herself endured sexual temptations; cf. chapter 59.

Chapter 75

1. This recalls Margery's own troubles in chapter 1.

Chapter 76

1. i.e. to drain the wound.

Chapter 77

1. cf. Song of Songs ii, 16, vi, 3.
2. Matthew v, 44; Luke vi, 27, 35.

Chapter 78

1. This chapter touches on such Palm Sunday observances as the procession into the churchyard, the priest's entering the church with the sacrament while followed by the people, and the pulling away of the Lenten curtain.

Chapter 80

1. In the celebrated late-fourteenth-century retable in Norwich Cathedral the flagellation scene shows Christ with arms tied above his head to a pillar, and torturers with three-branched scourges.
2. The maximum under Mosaic Law (cf. Deuteronomy xxv, 3). Sixteen men each giving forty lashes with an eight-tipped scourge might result in 5,120 wounds to Christ's body. In various late-medieval devotions and revelations the numbering of Christ's wounds varied between 4,732, 5,475, even 6,666.
3. Margery had visited the scene of this incident in Jerusalem (chapter 29).
4. In the Wakefield Mystery Play of the Scourging, Mary offers to carry the cross; see *English Mystery Plays*, ed. P. Happé (Penguin, 1975), p. 519.
5. cf. the York Crucifixion Play: 'It failis a foote and more, / The senous [sinews] are so gone ynne' (Happé, p. 529).
6. The cross is similarly raised and dropped into a mortise in the York Crucifixion Play (Happé, p. 533).
7. Margery had seen this stone for herself in Jerusalem (chapter 29).

Chapter 81

1. cf. *Meditationes Vitae Christi*: 'If you will use your powers, you too will know how to obey, serve, console, and comfort [Our Lady], so that she may eat a little ...' (chapter 83).

2. cf. *Meditationes Vitae Christi*: 'But then there was a knock at the door
... John went to the door, and looking out recognized Peter, and
said, "It is Peter." And Our Lady said, "Let him in." Thereupon
Peter entered shamefacedly, with great sobbing and weeping'
(chapter 84).

3. Perhaps the Chapel of the Apparition, in the Church of the Holy
Sepulchre, which Margery herself had visited (chapter 30). The risen
Christ's appearing first to his mother (in contradiction of Mark xvi,
9, where he appears first to Mary Magdalene) was a widespread
medieval tradition.

4. 'Hail, holy parent.'

Chapter 82

1. i.e. 2 February. Margery's experience here recalls that of Mary of
Oignies, who at Candlemas had a vision of our Lady offering her son
in the Temple and of Simeon receiving him in his arms. cf. the
English *Life* of Mary; ed. by C. Horstmann, 'Prosalegenden: Die
Legenden des MS Douce 114', *Anglia* 8 (1885), p. 173.

Chapter 83

1. Evidently St Michael's Church at Mintlyn, just east of Lynn, now in
ruins.

Chapter 84

1. Denny Abbey, a house of Franciscan nuns, near Waterbeach, north-
east of Cambridge. The mid-fourteenth-century refectory survives;
fragments of the church are incorporated into an eighteenth-century
house.

Chapter 86

1. Probably alluding to Margery's meditations on the infancy of Christ.

Chapter 88

1. See chapter 8.

Book II

Chapter 1

1. Extant records suggest a Margery Kempe became a member of the Trinity Guild at Lynn before Easter 1438.
2. i.e. 28 April 1438.

Chapter 2

1. The Priory of Our Lady at Walsingham, one of the most celebrated places of pilgrimage in medieval England with its image of the Virgin and shrine of the Holy House.
2. Romans viii, 31.

Chapter 3

1. Probably 2 April 1433.
2. In England the Host and the cross were usually raised from the Easter Sepulchre early on Easter morning.

Chapter 4

1. Probably referring to hostilities in 1433 between Poland and the Teutonic Order, to which Danzig belonged.
2. When the church at Wilsnack in Brandenburg was burned down in 1383, three Hosts were reputedly found in the ruins, miraculously unscathed and sprinkled with blood. The site became the object of pilgrimage; see J. Sumption, *Pilgrimage* (London, 1975), pp. 282–4.
3. By 1433 there were serious disagreements over trading privileges and payment of dues between England and the Teutonic Order.
4. Margery's amanuensis spells it 'Strawissownd', i.e. Stralsund in Pomerania, a Hansa town.

Chapter 5

1. Margery's giving of her age here suggests that she was born *c.* 1373.
2. Probably 10 June 1433.

Chapter 6

1. i.e. the period of eight days beginning with the day of the festival; 11–18 June in 1433.
2. i.e. Psalm cxxvi, 5–6: 'They that sow in tears shall reap in joy. He that goeth forth and weepeth, bearing precious seed, shall doubtless come again with rejoicing, bringing his sheaves with him.'
3. They call her an English 'sterte', which means 'tail', referring to a very old jibe on the continent that English people had tails.

Chapter 7

1. St Bridget of Sweden and Blessed Dorothea of Montau were among those who went on pilgrimage to Aachen, a place of pilgrimage for its four great relics: the smock the Virgin wore at Christ's birth, the swaddling clothes of Jesus, the cloth which received St John the Baptist's head, and the loin cloth that Christ wore on the cross. By St Margaret's Day Margery probably means 20 July here.

Chapter 9

1. The only appearance of Margery's surname in her book.
2. i.e. declining a humble fish but eating a better one.
3. i.e. Cardinal Beaufort; see chapter 71.

Chapter 10

1. Allowing for Margery's travels from Aachen, this is perhaps 1 August 1434.
2. Margery here mistakes Sheen for Syon Abbey. Henry V founded a

Carthusian monastery at Sheen, Surrey, and also, on the other side of the Thames from Sheen, a Brigettine house of Mount Syon, which in 1431 was moved further downriver to Isleworth (now the site of the Duke of Northumberland's Syon House). The Carthusians of Sheen and the Brigettines of Syon formed a great centre of contemplative piety in fifteenth-century England. The 'Pardon of Syon' was an indulgence for pilgrims to the abbey; it was available at Lammastide.

Further Reading

Aers, D., *Community, Gender, and Individual Identity: English Writing 1360–1430* (London, 1988), chapter 2.

Arnold, J. and Lewis, K. (eds.), *A Companion to Margery Kempe* (Woodbridge, 2004).

Aston, M., *Lollards and Reformers: Images and Literacy in Late Medieval Religion* (London, 1984).

Atkinson, C. W., *Mystic and Pilgrim: The Book and the World of Margery Kempe* (Cornell, 1983).

Barratt, A. (ed.) *Women's Writing in Middle English* (London, 1992).

Beckwith, S., 'A Very Material Mysticism: The Medieval Mysticism of Margery Kempe', in D. Aers (ed.), *Medieval Literature: Criticism, Ideology and History* (Brighton, 1988) pp. 34–57.

Beckwith, S., 'Problems of Authority in Late Medieval English Mysticism: Agency and Authority in *The Book of Margery Kempe*', *Exemplaria*, 4 (1992), 171–200.

Beckwith, S., *Christ's Body: Identity, Culture and Society in Late Medieval Writings* (London, 1993), chapter 4 ('The uses of Corpus Christi and *The Book of Margery Kempe*').

Beer, F., *Women and Mystical Experience in the Middle Ages* (Woodbridge, 1992).

Bennett, H. S., *Six Medieval Men and Women* (Cambridge, 1955).

Bhattacharji, S., *God is an Earthquake: The Spirituality of Margery Kempe* (London, 1997).

Brundage, J. A., *Sex, Law and Marriage in the Middle Ages* (Aldershot, 1993).

Bynum, Caroline W., *Jesus as Mother: Studies in the Spirituality of the High Middle Ages* (Berkeley, 1982).

Bynum, Caroline W., *Holy Feast and Holy Fast: The Religious Significance of Food to Medieval Women* (Berkeley, 1987).

Cholmeley, K., *Margery Kempe: Genius and Mystic* (London, 1947).

Clay, R. M., *The Hermits and Anchorites of England* (London, 1914).

Cleve, G., 'Margery Kempe: A Scandinavian Influence in Medieval England?', in *The Medieval Mystical Tradition in England*, V, ed. M. Glasscoe (Woodbridge, 1992), pp. 162–78.

Colledge, E., 'Margery Kempe', in *Pre-Reformation English Spirituality*, ed. J. Walsh (London, 1965).

Collis, L., *The Apprentice Saint* (London, 1964).

Delany, S., *Writing Woman: Women Writers and Women in Literature, Medieval to Modern* (New York, 1983), pp. 76–92.

Despres, D., *Ghostly Sights: Visual Meditation in Late-Medieval Literature* (Norman, Okla., 1989).

Dickman, S., 'Margery Kempe and the English Devotional Tradition', in *The Medieval Mystical Tradition in England*, I, ed. M. Glasscoe (Exeter, 1980), pp. 156–72.

Dickman, S., 'Margery Kempe and the Continental Tradition of the Pious Woman', in *The Medieval Mystical Tradition in England*, III, ed. M. Glasscoe (Woodbridge, 1984), pp. 150–68.

Dinshaw, C., 'Margery Kempe', in C. Dinshaw and D. Wallace (eds.), *The Cambridge Companion to Medieval Women's Writing* (Cambridge, 2003), pp. 222–39.

Duffy, E., *The Stripping of the Altars: Traditional Religion in England, c.1400–c.1580* (New Haven and London, 1992).

Dyas, D., *Pilgrimage in Medieval English Literature, 700–1500* (Cambridge, 2001).

Ellis, R., 'Margery Kempe's Scribe and the Miraculous Books', in H. Phillips (ed.), *Langland, the Mystics and the Medieval English Religious Tradition* (Cambridge, 1990), pp. 161–75.

Erler, M. C., *Women, Reading and Piety in Late Medieval England* (Cambridge, 2002).

Evans, R. and Johnson, L. (eds.), *Feminist Readings in Middle English Literature* (London, 1994).

Fries, M., 'Margery Kempe', in P. E. Szarmach (ed.), *An Introduction to the Medieval Mystics of Europe* (Albany, 1984), pp. 217–35.

Gallyon, M., *Margery Kempe of Lynn and Medieval England* (Norwich, 1995).

Gibson, G. M., *The Theater of Devotion: East Anglian Drama and Society in the Late Middle Ages* (Chicago, 1989), chapter 3.

Glasscoe, M., *English Medieval Mystics: Games of Faith* (London, 1993), chapter 6.

Glück, R., *Margery Kempe* (London, 1994).

Goodman, A., *Margery Kempe and her World* (Harlow, 2002).

Harding, W., 'Body into Text: *The Book of Margery Kempe*', in

L. Lomperis and S. Stanbury (eds.), *Feminist Approaches to the Body in Medieval Literature* (Philadelphia, 1993), 168–87.

Heffernan, T. J., *Sacred Biography: Saints and their Biographers in the Middle Ages* (New York, 1988).

Hirsh, J. C., 'Author and Scribe in *The Book of Margery Kempe*', *Medium Aevum*, 44 (1975), 145–50.

Hirsh, J. C., 'Margery Kempe', in A. S. G. Edwards (ed.), *Middle English Prose: A Critical Guide to Major Authors and Genres* (New Brunswick, 1984), pp. 109–19.

Hirsh, J. C., *The Revelations of Margery Kempe: Paramystical Practices in Late Medieval England* (Leiden, 1989).

Holbrook, S. E., 'Margery Kempe and Wynkyn de Worde', in *The Medieval Mystical Tradition in England*, IV, ed. M. Glasscoe (Woodbridge, 1987), 27–46.

Howes, L. L., 'On the Birth of Margery Kempe's Last Child', *Modern Philology*, 90 (1992), 220–25.

Hudson, A., *The Premature Reformation: Wycliffite Texts and Lollard History* (Oxford, 1988).

Hussey, S. S., 'The Audience for the Medieval Mystics', in M. G. Sargent (ed.), *De Cella in Seculum: Religious and Secular Life and Devotion in Late Medieval England* (Cambridge, 1989), pp. 109–22.

Kieckhefer, R., *Unquiet Souls: Fourteenth-Century Saints and their Religious Milieu* (Chicago, 1984).

Knowles, D., *The English Mystical Tradition* (London, 1961).

Knowles, D., *The Religious Orders in England*, vol. 2 (Cambridge, 1957).

Kurtz, P. D., 'Mary of Oignies, Christine the Marvellous, and Medieval Heresy', *Mystics Quarterly*, 14 (1988), 186–96.

Lachance, P., *The Spiritual Journey of Angela of Foligno* (London, 1985).

Lachance, P. (trans.), *Angela of Foligno: Complete Works* (Mahwah, 1993).

Lawes, R., 'The Madness of Margery Kempe,' in *The Medieval Mystical Tradition in England*, VI, ed. M. Glasscoe (Woodbridge, 1999), pp. 147–67.

Lewis, K., *The Cult of St Katherine of Alexandria in Late Medieval England* (Woodbridge, 2000).

Leyser, H., *Medieval Women: A Social History of Women in England, 450–1500* (London, 1995).

Lochrie, K., 'The Book of Margery Kempe: The Marginal Woman's Quest for Literary Authority', Journal of Medieval and Renaissance Studies, 16 (1986), 33–55.

Lochrie, K., Margery Kempe and Translations of the Flesh (Philadelphia, 1991).

Maisonneuve, R., 'Margery Kempe and the Eastern and Western Tradition of the "Perfect Fool"', in The Medieval Mystical Tradition in England, II, ed. M. Glasscoe (Exeter, 1982), pp. 1–17.

Margherita, G., The Romance of Origins: Language and Sexual Difference in Middle English Literature (Philadelphia, 1994), chapter 1.

McEntire, S. J. (ed.), Margery Kempe: A Book of Essays (New York, 1992).

McNamer, S. (ed.), The Two Middle English Translations of the Revelations of St Elizabeth of Hungary (Heidelberg, 1996).

Meale, C. M. (ed.), Women and Literature in Britain, 1150–1500 (Cambridge, 1993).

Medcalf, S., The Later Middle Ages (London, 1981), chapter 3.

Meech, S. B. and Allen, H. E. (eds.), The Book of Margery Kempe, Early English Text Society, original series, 212 (London, 1940).

Mooney, C. M. (ed.), Gendered Voices: Medieval Saints and their Interpreters (Philadelphia, 1999).

Morrison, S. S., Women Pilgrims in Late Medieval England (London, 2000).

Owen, D., The Making of King's Lynn: A Documentary Survey (Oxford, 1984).

Partner, N., 'Reading The Book of Margery Kempe', Exemplaria, 3 (1991), 29–66.

Petroff, E. A. (ed.), Medieval Women's Visionary Literature (New York, 1986).

Power, Eileen, Medieval Women, ed. M. M. Postan (Cambridge, 1975).

Raguin, V. and Stanbury, S., Mapping Margery Kempe: A Guide to Late Medieval Material and Spiritual Life, http://sterling.holy cross.edu/departments/visarts/projects/kempe.

Riehle, W., The Middle English Mystics (London, 1981).

Ross, R. C., 'Oral Life, Written Text: The Genesis of The Book of Margery Kempe', Yearbook of English Studies, 22 (1992), 226–37.